400 YEARS
IN AMERICA

(Hadley, Ford, Collett, Smead)

James E Hadley

Paperback ISBN: 979-8-90235-080-4

Hardcover ISBN: 979-8-90235-081-1

eBook ISBN: 979-8-90235-079-8

LCCN: 2026904153

Published by Kinetic Digital Publishers

www.kineticdigitalpublishers.com

For permissions, inquiries, or other correspondence, please visit our website.

TABLE OF CONTENTS

REFERENCE MAPS

Colonial America 1771

United States 1818

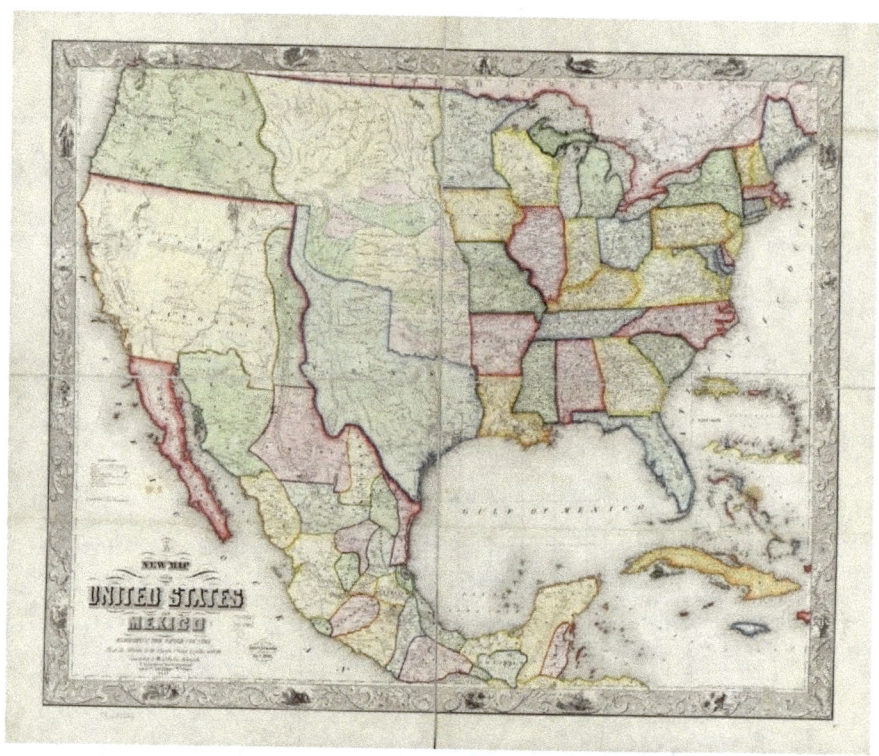

United States 1847

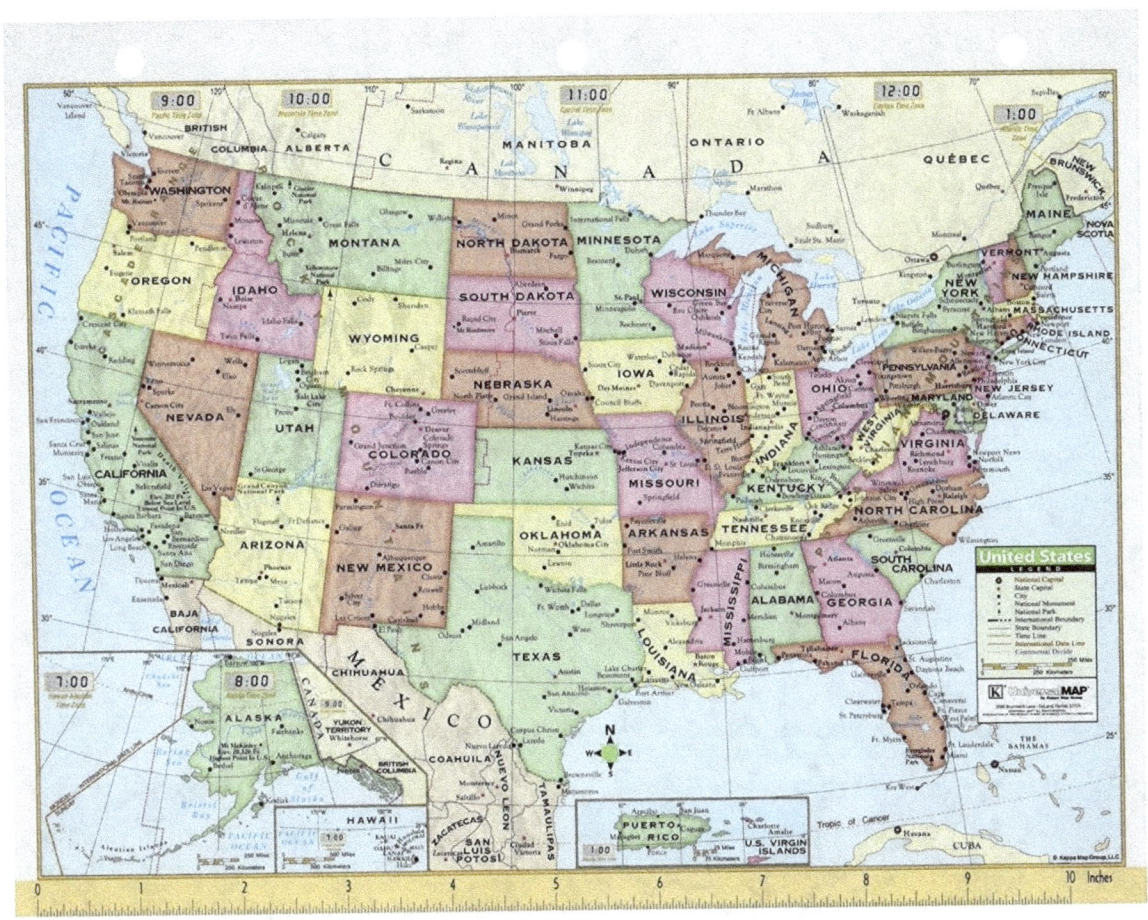

Continental United States as of 1912

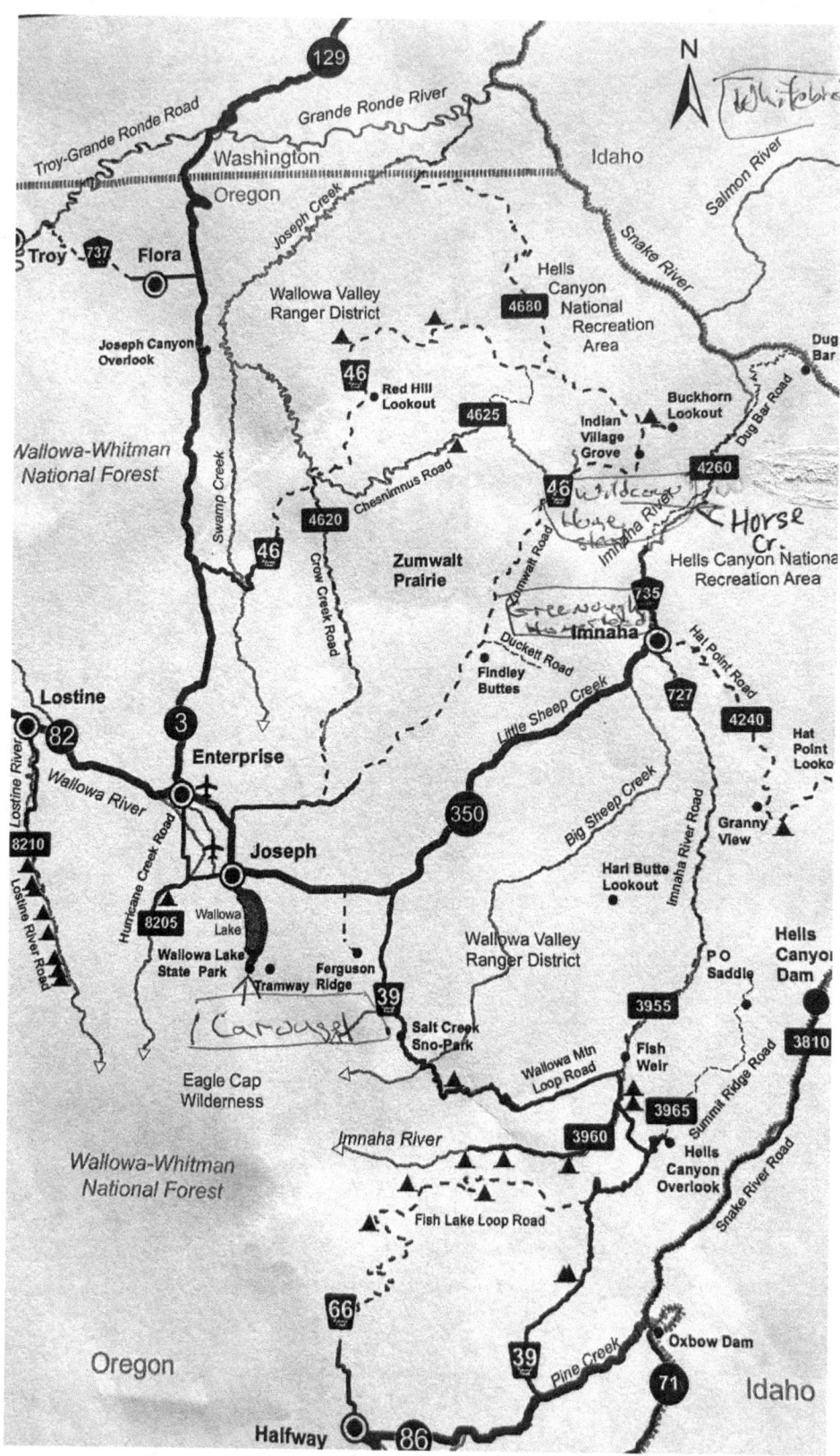

Wild Cow Homestead

PROLOGUE

This effort started with the goal of honoring my parents' desire that their memories be passed on to future generations. My father, Howard Hadley, dictated tapes of his early life. On my mother's passing I received materials she had accumulated over her lifetime regarding family history matters. In the midst of the Covid pandemic with the benefit of the internet and my sleuthing skills learned as a lawyer, slowly an amazing story revealed itself creeping out of the shadows of time. A deeply humbling undertaking, foraging through reams of information unearthing the lives of generations of forbearers.

The journey included moments of seeming greatness having been knighted and Oxford educated, to selling portions of their lives as indentured servants to pay for passage to America. A genealogist specializing in the Hadley line and conducting DNA studies once told me our Hadley line likely descended from William the Conqueror who was King of England from 1066 until his death in 1087. Further research could likely take one there or even further back to the Dukes of Normandy in the early 900s A.D.

I learned early on that this type of effort has no beginning and no end and at best catches snippets of information.

After arriving from the British Isles, ancestors traveled on foot, by horse and sometimes wagon from New England and Virginia, some along the east coast and then all participated in the Westward expansion often among the first to settle in a wilderness area. Some joined wagon trains moving as a group from place to place with intermarriages along the way. The Fords came to Virginia and then southeast and into Ohio, before heading west, while the Hadley's took a more northerly route after leaving New Jersey through Michigan.

The first settlements in America outside of the native Indians were in what is now Puerto Rico and St. Augustine, Florida by the Spanish in the 1500s. The first immigrants from England arrived somewhat later in Jamestown, Virginia, mostly to work in the tobacco and cotton trade. The Mayflower in 1621 was reputed to be sailing to Virginia, but due to adverse weather conditions, it reached land at Cape Cod, forming a small community in what is now Massachusetts at an abandoned Indian settlement.

Our Hadley, Collett and Smead lines appear to all be among the earliest immigrants to New England arriving after the Mayflower and most likely prior to 1644 after which civil war was underway in England. The Ford line starts in Virginia at about the same time. Our ancestors were Pilgrims, Puritans and Quakers.

Before the use of steamships in the late 1800's roughly one in seven died during the voyage to America in sailing ships. It appears Ford and Smead ancestors may have come as indentured servants paying for their passage with the promise to work for a period of time, often seven years, during which they received room and board but no wages. Given that period of history 80% were farmers and the promise of having one's own land was a huge draw.

Some family members served (and died in) the Indian wars of early America, the Revolutionary War, the War of 1812, the Civil War and others. During the Revolutionary War given their location in the northeast of what is now the United States there were family members involved in and impacted by the war that resulted in the formation of the United States. One great uncle was conscripted into the British Navy running away twice in the period leading up to the War of 1812. Family members and relatives served on both sides of the Civil War, some as enlisted men and others as officers. Beyond the ancestors described below my cousin Tom Prien found a General serving during the war of 1812 and a relative who ran for the Virginia Legislature against John Adams (who later became the fifth president of the United States). Minor Hall which once housed the law school at the University of Virginia is named after John Minor who is reputedly related.

It appears that some family members were granted land prior to or after immigrating to the colonies (e.g., Collette's). The US government made available lands ever further westward after the Revolutionary War and the Civil War, sometimes in return for military service. Many of our ancestors were also "homesteaders", i.e., people able to own significant parcels of land by grant or by working a parcel "claimed".

Tracing family roots prior to the formation of the United States is difficult as people were constantly on the move and there was no consistent overall record keeping. In 1790 when George Washington was the first US president, his secretary of state Thomas Jefferson conducted the first census of US citizens

Families were large resulting in the need/desire of some siblings to set off on their own to acquire their own places. Many times, several families would move as a group (often by wagon train if needed for safety), which explains how many of the family names found over generations are related.

The family included a number of firsts with Richard Headley, Jr. born about 1691, the first child born in Mamaroneck, New York. One hundred and seventy years later Warren Smead was the third white (non-Indian) child born in Boulder County, Colorado. There were at least two "moonshiners" which was not an unusual source of additional income during troubled times. "The Longest Rope" by my grandmother Lillie Collett's cousin, Bill Walker, provides a description of the Old West and many of the characters we see in films. It describes his witnessing events during the Johnson County cattle wars between cattlemen and sheepmen.

During this period, there were people like Eber Osborn who at age 14 ran away from his guardian (both parents having passed) and grew up with the Indians. There was my grandmother, Lillie Lenora Smead Collett, who kept a loaded double barreled shotgun next to her back door, having dealt with cougars and rustlers in her younger days.

Our ancestors were not only farmers, pioneers and explorers but tried their hands at creating new towns including the William Pell villages Eastchester and Mamaroneck, New York in the late 17th century, Headleyville which was renamed Union, New Jersey; and during the westward expansion: Eldred, Illinois; Collett, Indiana; and White Bird, Idaho. Another, laid out the streets of Ellensburg, Washington where members of the Hadley, Ford, Osborn, Collett and Smead lines lived in the 1940's and thereafter.

Following the lineage of those forbearers out in all directions is beyond my energy and focus. My initial sources were: "The Forbearers and Descendants of Henry and Abigail Barringer" (1978) by Ross Milo Curry; "Ford" by Lester V. Ford and Clara N. Ford of Dixon, Iowa circa 2000; and "Collett and Osborn Families 1775-1995" by James R. Vrooman (1994), Whirlwind Press, Albany, Ore. The Barringer book in particular traces one family line through the various kings of England back to the 9th century and Viking Lords. Late in the process I stumbled onto "A Genealogical Record of the Descendants of Leonard Headley of Elizabethtown, N.J." by Rev. A.J. Fretz published 1905 by Joseph W. Headley, Printer, Milton New Jersey. I have borrowed extensively from their work and copied some sections of their publications without accreditation, changing and supplementing content without their guidance. My hat is off to these relatives who spent years researching and preparing their tomes. I have been able to supplement their work through general internet search, searching Ancestry.com and through Google Earth finding the places where they lived. Family stories were also revealed in newspaper clippings, letters and my parents' notes. I was fortunate to interview my grandmother, Lillie Smead, while she was still living forty years ago.

My father was Howard Hadley and my mother was Mary Collett Hadley. Names were often spelled phonetically so early records saw Hedly become Headlee become Headley and eventually standardized as Hadley. My grandparent's surnames were respectively Hadley and Ford on my father's side, and Collett and Smead on my mother's. This document reflects my attempt to follow those four lines back in time from their English roots through their 400 years traversing America. On occasion I have drifted from that theme to include close relatives who were influential in their lives. In some cases, I have also included others who were possibilities during my search and whose lives aid in depicting the experiences of our forbearers. As a separate effort not included here is my own autobiography.

A huge thanks and acknowledgment to my wife Beth Taylor for her patience and diligence in formatting this book, inserting family crests and photos and for her support, guidance and effort in making this quest a reality.

HADLEY

Hadley is an English locational surname of Anglo-Saxon origin. It derives from the Olde English pre 7th Century "heath", heather land, heather, and "leah", wood, clearing. It could also derive from the Olde English personal name "Hadda", a short form of a personal name beginning with "heard", hardy, brave, strong with "leath" as before. The first recorded spelling of the family name is shown to be that of Matikda de Hadlegha dated 1194 in the "Pipe Rolls of Suffolk" during the reign of Richard 1, known as "The Lionheart", 1189-1199. The coat of arms associated with the name is a red shield with two chevronels between three silver falcon beaked, legged and belled gold, holding in the mouth a gold buckle. Spellings include Hadley, Hadleigh, Headley, Hedley, Haddeleye, Hadlege, Hadlai, etc. It appears the common spelling of our family name was changed from Hedley to Headley in the late 1500's and then from Headley to Hadley in the late 1600s. One source confirms Hedley was both a Scottish and English surname.

<u>A Genealogical Record of the Descendants of Leonard Headley of Elizabethtown, N.J.</u> by Rev. A.J. Fretz printed 1905 contains this information:

The Headley family is undoubtedly of English origin, though one tradition says they came from Scotland. The name in the 12th century was "De-Haddeleigh," and in the Latin form "de Hadleins," the significance of the name being "Out of the woods." The name has in later years undergone several changes and is now variously written; as, Heaeley, Hedley, Hedly and Hadley. There is a tradition that two brothers, tanners and curriers by occupation, came from Manchester, England, about 1665. [It is possible that Mr. Fretz had mistaken Manchester for Monkchester located in Northumbria.] John Hedley, one of the brothers, settled himself in Newport, R.I., at the first settling of that place about 1665. The name of the other brother and where he is located is not positively known, but may have been Leonard Headley, pioneer of the New Jersey Headleys, who located at first, perhaps, somewhere in Connecticut, and later in Elizabethtown, N.J., whither on the 19th day of February 1665, he took the Oath of Allegiance and fidelity to King Charles II. and to be true and faithful to the Lord Proprietors."

As noted below our Headley descendants appear to come from the Newcastle upon Tyne (present day Newcastle), Northumberland area of England which is on the border with Scotland. I once surmised a connection to Manchester to what I was told was Hadley Castle, only to find that it was a windmill. I was contacted by a family genealogist Jim Hadley from New York, on my father Howard Hadley's passing who was in search of a line of the family his ancestors had lost contact with. In any event, the earliest "Hadleys" that I was able to locate lived in a place called "Hedley on Hill" near Newcastle, which could possibly have been the source of their "Hedley/Headley" name, as people were often named after the place they were from.

Newcastle upon Tyne, Gateshead

St. Nicholas Church, Newcastle upon Tyne

Newcastle Upon Tyne (now also known as Newcastle) is located on the northeast coast of England where the Tyne River enters the North Sea. Inland and west the Tyne River courses near Hedley on Hill where Richard Headlee was born. To the south in the countryside is Shipton north of Yorkshire. These locations would be consistent with Thomas working as a farmer, and moves would be consistent with his working on farms of others, and not owning his own property.

During the civil war in England during the 1600s, a gun was mounted on the tower of St Andrews. The church suffered severe damage during the siege and subsequent storming of the city in 1644.

One can imagine the impact of the Civil war on the young Headley family. The siege of Newcastle and probable movement of vessels in the Newcastle harbor likely provided the motivation and opportunity for the family to escape to America.

St. Andrews Church, Newcastle Upon Tyne (Church where Cutbart Hedley married about 1600 in whose graveyard early family members from the 1500s and quite possibly before are buried)

Records for this period frequently reflect phonetic spellings. Cutbart's first name was variously spelled Cutbart, Cuthbart and Cuthbert. Cutbart's wife, Ann Bag Enderby passed away October 9, 1654 in Leeds, Yorkshire, England,

Throughout the Middle Ages, Newcastle was England's northern fortress. In 1400 Newcastle was separated from Northumberland and made a county of itself by Henry IV. Newcastle was given the title of the county of the town of Newcastle upon Tyne. The city was given a new charter granted by Elizabeth in 1589. A 25-foot-high stone wall was built around the town in the 13th century to defend it during the border war against Scotland. The Scots king William the Lion was imprisoned in Newcastle in 1174, and Edward 1 brought the Stone of Scone and William Wallace south through the town. Newcastle was successfully defended against the Scots three times during the 14th century.

During the English Civil War, the North declared for the King. In a bid to gain Newcastle and the Tyne, Cromwell's allies the Scotts, captured the town of Newburn. In 1645, the Scots then captured the reinforced fortification of the Lawe in South Shields following a siege and the town was besieged for many months. It was eventually stormed and sacked by Cromwell's allies. Charles 1 was imprisoned in Newcastle by the Scots in 1646-47.

In the 14th century the city grew as an important center for the wool trade and later became a major coal mining area. The port developed in the 16th century, along with the shipyards lower down the River Tyne and was amongst the world's largest ship-building and ship repairing centers.

My DNA study revealed 44% to be Scottish and 32% English. Given the dates and locations of Thomas Hedley/Headley (1550) and son Cutbart (1560-1655), they clearly lived very close to the Scots, the River Tyne, and Hadrian's wall.

Newcastle upon Tyne is the closest major city in this area. It was developed around the Roman settlement Pons Aelius (Hadrian's bridge). The Roman fort and bridge over the River Tyne were given the family name of the Roman Emperor Hadrian, who founded it in the 2nd century AD. This rare honor suggests that Hadrian may have visited the site and instituted the bridge on his tour of Britain.

The population of Pons Aelius during the second century is estimated as 2000. Fragments of Hadrian's Wall are visible in parts of Newcastle, particularly along the West Road. The course of the Roman Wall can be traced eastwards to the Segedunum Roman Fort in Wallsend, the "wall's end", and to the supply fort Arbeia in South Shields. The extent of Hadrian's Wall was 73 miles spanning the width of Britain; the Wall incorporated the Vallum, a large rearward ditch with parallel mounds, and was built primarily for defense, to prevent the unwanted immigration and the incursion of Pictish tribes from the north, not as a fighting line for a major invasion.

After the Roman departure from Britain was completed in 410, Newcastle became part of the powerful Anglo-Saxon kingdom of Northumbria, and was known through this period as Munucceaster (sometimes modernized as Monkchester).

Conflicts with the Danes in 876 left the settlements along the River Tyne in ruins. After the conflicts with the Danes and following the 1088 rebellion against the Normans, Monkchester was all but destroyed by Odo of Bayeux. Because of its strategic position, Robert Curthose, son of William the Conqueror, erected a wooden castle at the site of Pons Aelius in the year 1080. The town was henceforth known as Novum Castellum or New Castle. (William the Conqueror is thought to be in the Headley line although that is yet to be confirmed.) The wooden structure was replaced by a stone castle in 1087, and rebuilt again in 1172 during the reign of Henry II. Much of the keep which can be seen in the city today dates from this period.

The good news is that Hedley on Hill, which is a tiny, tiny place, and Newcastle Upon Tyne are common to conflicting trees in roughly parallel timelines. The online records of St Andrews Parish in Newcastle upon Tyne, where marriages, Christenings, and burials were common to the Headleys, have online records dating back to 1538. I have not inquired but it is possible they have other records as the church dates from the 12th century.

My present belief is the correct line using birthdates is Thomas Hedly (1550); Cutbart Headley (1550-1655); Leonard Thomas Headley (1623-1682), Richard Headley (1642-1701); Thomas Headley (1664), Richard Headley (1690), and so on. This is consistent with a note in our family Bible. There is some confusion in various family trees, particularly relating to the six sons of Richard Headley (1642-1701) who had offspring with similar names and close birthdates. There were likely other Headley's from Hedley on Hill as a Thomas Hedley (1570) and his offspring were noted in my search.

The founders of Hadley, Massachusetts, were from Hadleigh, Surrey, England, near Ipswich (east of London near the coast), i.e., close but a different part of England. Samuel Hadley, killed in the first battle of the Revolutionary War at Lexington, was from this line, as was a Hadley burned in the Salem witch trials.

THOMAS HEDLEY (1550) Hedley on Hill Origins

Born: 1550 (Northumberland, England)

Married: Ayles Hollingsbirth (1560)

Died: unknown

Children: Cutbart Headley (1580-1655)

Hedley/Headley christenings, marriages and burials took place at St Andrews church on Newgate Street, Newcastle Upon Tyne. The church was originally built in the twelfth century, but was extensively altered several times thereafter. It appears that Thomas's family were farmers living in the countryside between Newcastle and Yorkshire, likely Hedley on Hill, although the only record I located was an unverified reference in a family tree.

There are references to a Sir Thomas Hedley (1570-1655) and Sir Thomas Hedley (1658-1790), both born in Hedley on Hill, neither of whom appears to be in our direct line. "Sir" was at one time used as a title before the given name of a knight or baronet.

There remains a strong Hedley presence in Newcastle including Headley Hall, a manor house located on Headley Lane, Newcastle and business' bearing the Thomas Hedley name. These include Thomas Hedley and Sons, a roofing and general contractor, Thomas Hedley Co. founded in 1837 manufacturing soap and candles and Hedley Transport providing haulage services.

CUTBART HEDLY (1580-1655)

Born: September 15, 1611 (St. Andrews, Newcastle, Tyne, Northumberland)

Married: June 3, 1638 (to Margratt Anderson (1612-1700) at Saint John, Newcastle Upon Tyne, Northumberland); February 8, 1654 (to Anne Mordie at St. Andrews, Newcastle Upon Tyne, Northumberland)

Died: 1702 (Hedley on Hill, Northumberland)

Parents: Thomas Hedly (1550) and Ayles Hollinworth (1560)

Children: Leonard Thomas Headley (1623-1682)

Son Leonard Headley (1645-1683) is shown as being born at Elizabethport, Union, New Jersey

THOMAS LEONARD HEADLEY (1613-1683) Migration to America

<u>Born</u>: 1612/1613 (Shifton [Shipton], Yorkshire, England)

<u>Married</u>: Mary Ward (1619-1679)

<u>Died</u>: February 1, 1683 (New Jersey)

<u>Parents</u>: Cutbart Headley/Hedley (1580-1655) and Ann Bag Enderby (1580-1654), passed in Yorkshire, England.

<u>Children</u>: Richard Headley Sr (1642-1709)

Leonard Thomas Headley aka Thomas Leonard Headley was baptised July 11, 16'13 at Newcastle Upon Tyne (likely at St Andrews Church), Northumberland, England. Son Richard was born 1642 at Hedley on the Hill, Northumberland, England.

Wife Mary Ward passed away on February 2, 1979, in Farmington, Hartford, Connecticut.

Sometime after their son Richard's birth in 1642 and certainly before 1650 the family migrated to America as both Thomas and his wife Mary Ward are recorded as dying in the colonies. Given the war in England after about 1644, it is probable their move would have occurred in the 1643–1644 time frame. As described under Richard 1642 below, it is likely the family was Puritan and may have had some relationship through their religious belief to Puritans already in or migrating to the colonies.

RICHARD HEADLEY, SR. (1642-1709) Thomas Pell Puritan Settlements

<u>Born</u>:1642 (Hedley, Northumberland, England)

<u>Married</u>: 1670 (Fairfield Conn. Hannah Drake (1665-1688); about 1690 second wife Mary)

<u>Died</u>: 1709 Mamaroneck, Westchester, New York

<u>Parents</u>: Richard was the only child of Leonard Thomas Headley (1612-1683) and Mary Ward 1619.

<u>Children</u>: He had eight children including three with Hannah born in Eastchester: 1. Robert (1670); 2. Samuel (1680); 3. Thomas (1688); and then from Mary born in Mamaroneck: 4. Richard (1690-1750); 5. Robert (1688 [?]); 6. Elizabeth (1692); 7. Joseph (1694), and 8. John (1696). Mary also had a son, Sylvanus, prior to marrying Richard.

According to a reference connected with the Stephen Owen Hadley family Bible and Barringer by Curry, Stephen Owen's great-grandfather is Robert Headley, born in Witcham, Cambridgeshire, England, and died in Connecticut. On searching, there is a Robert Headley 1688, 1693 born in Witcham, Cambridgeshire, England, in 1688 and died in Connecticut. His parents were Richard Hadley (1642-1690) and Hannah Drake (1651-1710).

Richard Headley's name was spelled in records as Headley, Hedley, Hadly, Hoadly and Healy. He married about 1669-70 to Hannah Drake (1643-1688), daughter of Samuel Drake and Anne (Barlow) Drake. On Hannah's death in Mamaroneck, Westchester, New York, he remarried to Mary in about 1690.

Richard was granted a property in 1665 in Eastchester, New York, a new village established by Thomas Pell. After Hannah's death, the home was deeded to his son, Samuel Hadley, in 1677/1678. Presumably he then moved to Mamaroneck (also founded by Thomas Pell - about six miles away) with his new wife Mary.

Although the name of the ship used and the actual arrival date are unknown, it was too long after the Mayflower left Plymouth, a port in southern England, taking 66 days to cross the Atlantic. It departed September 6, 1620 and arrived November 9, 1620 carrying 102 passengers. That vessel was only ninety feet long with a 25-foot beam. The Mayflower originally set out for territory granted in Virginia, but due to rough seas landed on Cape Cod at what is now Provincetown, Massachusetts. Hopefully Richard and Mary's trip was earlier in the year, when weather conditions in New England were better.

Between 1629 and 1643, approximately 21,000 Puritans immigrated to New England as part of the "Great Migration" beginning in 1629 with the founding of the Massachusetts Bay Colony, and ending in 1642 with the start of the English Civil War when King Charles 1 effectively shut off emigration to the colonies. Emigration was officially restricted to conforming churchmen by the King's Privy Council. The Headley's were most certainly Puritans as confirmed by Richard Headley's grant of land by Thomas Pell as one of the original founders of the new Puritan settlement called Eastchester.

From the foregoing, it is quite likely Thomas Leonard Headley, his wife Mary Ward, and their infant son Richard arrived in the 1642–1643 time frame, certainly prior to 1650.

The Great Migration of Puritans to New England was primarily an exodus of families. Between 1630 and 1640 over 13,000 men, women and children sailed to Massachusetts. The wave of Puritan ships was "laden" with ordinary people, old and young, families as well as individuals. Just a quarter of the emigrants were in their twenties when they boarded ships in the 1630s, making young adults a minority in New England Settlements. John Winthrop, governor of the Massachusetts Bay Colony led the Great Migration.

In the 16th and 17th centuries, there was a Protestant movement by people who believed that the Church of England was insufficiently reformed, retaining too much of its Roman Catholic doctrinal practices and teachings. They opposed the royal ecclesiastical policy under Elizabeth 1, James 1 and Charles 1 of England. For the most part they were tolerated within the established church, but Calvinist in their theology. Major points of controversy were liturgical ceremonies such as wearing clergical vestments, kneeling to receive Holy Communion and making the sign of the cross during baptism. Under Charles 1 the bishops became less tolerant of Puritan views and more willing to enforce controversial ceremonies. Controls were placed on Puritan preaching, and some ministers were suspended and removed, leading to unrest and a belief among these parishioners that they needed to emigrate if they were to escape persecution and worship freely, creating a religious refuge. In March of 1629 they received a royal charter from King Charles establishing the Massachusetts Bay Colony, and in 1630 the first ships of the Great Puritan Migration sailed to the New World, led by John Winthrop. The English Civil War, which started in 1641, was won on the Puritan side, making English life more congenial to Puritan viewpoints, reducing the need to emigrate to "escape prosecution" in England.

Thomas Leonard, Mary, and their son Richard were located in Fairfield, Connecticut by 1650. Fairfield is about 140 miles southwest of Boston on Long Island Sound. In 1635, Puritans and Congregationalists in the Massachusetts Bay Colony were dissatisfied with the rate of Anglican reform and sought to establish an ecclesiastical society subject to their own rules and regulations. The Massachusetts General Court granted them permission to settle in an area now known as Connecticut. On January 14, 1639 administrative regulations were adopted establishing Connecticut as a self-ruling entity. Roger Ludlowe, one of the founders of Connecticut purchased the land presently called Fairfield. Sometime after their arrival in Boston about 1640 Richard and Mary moved to join the Puritans in Fairfield. Richard was a carpenter.

In 1664, an English fleet captured New Amsterdam from the Dutch, which then became the colony of New York. Eastchester began settlement in 1664 when ten families migrated from Fairfield, Connecticut. Thomas Pell granted a deed to the group to "settle down in Hutchinson". Another 26 families joined the original ten shortly thereafter. Records show that Richard Headley was from Fairfield and granted a home in Eastchester in 1665 so part of these original residents. In 1665 laws for the region were established under an agreement called the "Eastchester Covenant" which was a rare document for this time including 26 provisions including education of children, disposition and upkeep of property, support of a minister, etc. The 1664 patent was confirmed in 1666 by Governor Richard Nichols. Eastchester was a farming community at the outbreak of the Revolutionary War. Over a hundred Hessians fighting on the side of the crown are buried in its cemetery. When President John Adams left Philadelphia in 1797 due to the yellow fever epidemic the temporary White House was located in the home of his daughter who lived a short distance from St. Paul's church. Researching the town's history reveals a vital connection to the "freedom of the press" and is sometimes referred to as the "Home of the Bill of Rights."

Mamaroneck is another William Pell village formed about the same time as Eastchester and a few miles distant. This is where both Hannah Drake (in 1688) and Richard Headley died.

SAMUEL HEADLEY (1688-1755) Settlement in Headleytown, NJ / Revolutionary War Notes

There were multiple listings for Samuel found in my search. They notably have the same location and date of death and could be cousins. The places of birth given are almost the same as Elizabeth, New Jersey, which is just outside the present borders of Essex County, where Newark is now located, and may have been part of what was known as Essex County at that time. After struggling with these inconsistencies, I have included the information I believe to be accurate. Information on Richard Headlee, Samuel's brother, is included in this section as he was at one time believed to be in our line instead of Samuel, and had heirs named Samuel. Note that the Samuel Hadley killed in the first battle of the Revolutionary War is not in our line.

Born: 1690 Essex, New Jersey [from the description of Richard Hadley, Sr. above it would follow that the place of birth should have been a few miles distant in either Eastchester or Mamaroneck New York which are on the opposite sides of East Bay separating New Jersey and New York; Another site has the birthplace as Unionville, Burlington New Jersey. We now know that Unionville was formerly known as Hadleytown and is likely the correct location.]

Married: 1712 or 1716 (Newark, Essex County, New Jersey Colony to Mary H (Foster) Headley (1694-1788)

Died: 1755 (Essex, New Jersey)

Parents: Thomas Headley (1664-1739) and Mary Parker Headley (1668-1692) [Some sites state Richard Headley and Hannah Drake].

Children: Mary Headley (1720-1784); **Robert H Headley** (1720-1806); Isaac Headley (17161784); Joseph Headley (1718-1785); Samuel Headley Jr (1723-1787); Sarah Headley (1724-1756); Rachel Headley (1727-); and

Phebe. [I have included only those shown in Samuels will dated May 30, 1745 as it appears in the Descendants book.]

Most children were born in New Jersey, including Monmouth, Newark, Essex, etc. However, daughter Sarah (1724-1756) is shown as being born in Lancaster, Lancaster County, Virginia.

Samuel's family lived in Headleytown (now Unionville). The property accumulated by Samuel Headley consisted of large tracts of land in the vicinity. They were members of the Presbyterian church [as are current family members in the 21st century] at "Connecticut Farms" and were buried there, but there is nothing to identify their graves. "Connecticut Farms" are in the northern part of the township, four miles northwest of Elizabethtown and six miles southwest of Newark. Prior to 1749, a number of families from Connecticut purchased a large tract of land there and gave it the name "Connecticut Farms." The Presbyterian church there, established sometime prior to 1749, is still known as the Conn. Farms Presbyterian Church, however the village has been renamed Union.

The first Presbyterian church was a wooden structure and burned along with the village by the Hessians under Hessian general Wilhelm von Knyphausen during the Revolutionary War. During the fighting Hannah Caldwell, the wife of Continental Army chaplain James Caldwell, was shot dead through a wall or window as she sat on her bed with her children. The parsonage today serves as a local history museum. Samuel Headley is buried at the cemetery there. At the close of the Revolutionary war the church was rebuilt by the parishioners using stone from their own quarries, brick from their own kilns and timber from their own woodlands. The church is still standing.

During the war of the Revolution, the battles of Connecticut Farms and Springfield were fought, partly on Headley property, in which John Thompson Headley, Cary Headley, and others in the family fought against the foe. Robert's son, (Captain) Samuel Headley (1768-1820) was an American Revolutionary War Veteran, quite possibly serving with Colonel Jacob Ford appearing under Ford in this text. Francis Headley served as a major in the Revolutionary War along with other Headleys.

On the sixth of June 1780, General Mathews was sent with 5000 men from Staten Island with orders to penetrate New Jersey and attack Washington at Morristown. The next day the British took possession of Elizabethtown and began their march toward Springfield intending to defeat the Continentals there and proceed on to Morristown. The route taken was along the Galloping Hill Road, which led through Connecticut Farms (now the village of Union). Here, the militia offered resistance, the enemy opened fire, defeated the handful of men, torched the few buildings of the village, and continued on their way to Springfield. Warning of the enemy's approach was given and at Springfield the British met a detachment of men from Washington's camp at Morristown (possibly led by Colonel Ford described elsewhere in this book). A sharp skirmish ensued in which the British were driven back along the coast.

For two weeks after their repulse at Springfield, the enemy hovered around the vicinity of Elizabethtown, afraid to attack the Continentals with the force at their command. On June 22, Clinton came up from the south with additional troops and another move against Washington was planned. It was decided to draw the Americans into a general engagement and capture the stores at Morristown. Feigning an expedition to the Hudson Highlands, Clinton deceived Washington who marched away in that direction with a considerable body of men. General Green was left to guard Springfield and the country west and north of the village.

When Washington was well on his way, Knyphausen marched along the Galloping Hill Road with 5000 infantry, twenty pieces of artillery, and 800 cavalry. On the 23rd they attacked General Green at Springfield. The battle waged all day. At one time it seemed as though the British would win. They succeeded in forcing a passage across the bridge spanning the Rathway River there, but at last the Continentals repulsed them and sent them scurrying back along the road up which they had marched so confidently that morning. So great was their confusion that they ran until they reached the coast. The British lost 300 men, while the American loss was less than 100. The British had 6000 men, while the Americans had 1000. During the Revolutionary War battles were fought on the Connecticut Farms and Springfield partly on Headley property during which.

A full copy of Samuel's will is contained in the Descendants book. Among other things, it provides that his plantation of 100 acres was to be divided equally among his sons, Joseph, Robert, and Samuel, with Samuel's portion to include the dwelling house and orchard. Also, to be divided amongst these three sons was his salt meadow. A salt meadow is a meadow subject to flooding by saltwater. His personal property was divided among his daughters.

RICHARD HADLEY, JR. (1690 to 1750) British Navy Conscription During Revolutionary War

Born: 1690 (Middletown, Monmouth, NJ)

Married: Rachel Cox (1690-1747)

Died: 1750 (New Jersey)

Parents: Richard Headley (1642) and Mary (second marriage)

Children: Mary Headley (1722-1750). Mary was born in Upper Freehold, New Jersey when her father Richard Headley was 38 and her mother Rachel Cox Headley was 32. She died as a young mother in Upper Freehold, New Jersey, at age 28. Her mother Rachel passed away in 1747 in Upper Freehold, New Jersey at age 57.

A post July 4, 2018 by Larry Hawk included the following:

"Richard Headley, Junior was the first child born in Mamaroneck, New York and was born out of the second marriage of Richard and Mary Headley. He was born about 1691. Nothing is known about his wife. By 1716, he seems to have moved, like most of his brothers, to New Jersey. He settled in Hunterdon County, New Jersey. Hunterdon was one of the Counties split out of the old East Jersey Colony. Morris County was cut out of Hunterdon County. We will see that the family next appears in Morris County, but that is only before Morris was established. The family probably always lived in the same area. Family tradition indicates that Richard was conscripted into the British Navy, escaped from the ship, and took refuge in central New Jersey. He was later caught by the English and returned to sea. At any rate the family was located in New Jersey through the Revolutionary War. Richard probably died there in the 1770s. Richard Headley Junior had at least three sons and most likely daughters as well, but I have no records on them. The children were Francis Headley. Francis Headley was born in Northern New Jersey in about 1731 and died in Randolf County, Virginia in 1805. He married Huldah Cary, a daughter of John Cary. Their children were: John Cary who married Mary Hathaway. Samuel Cary who married Abigail Trace. Susannah Cary had three other daughters. He was in Hardiston Township of Sussex County, New Jersey in 1774 and served as a MAJOR in Sussex Company A during the War, [my emphasis, probably knew Jacob Ford under the Ford section]. After the Revolution, they moved to Washington County, Pennsylvania. By 1796 they had moved to Randolph County, Virginia. John Headlee. John Headlee, born in 1735, is in our line. Joseph

Headlee was born on February 3, 1746, and died in 1840. He married Abigail Morris, and they had: Thomas Headlee, John Headlee, and Joseph Headlee, who married Sarah Blair. Phebe Headlee who married John Clutter. Samuel Headlee who married Rachel James. Elias Headlee who married Catherine Dickson. Eunice Headee who married Benjamin Rowley. Morris Headlee Hannah Headless who married William Weir. Nancy Headlee Amos Headlee who married Experience Lindsey and then Christine Clutter. It is said he had served in the Revolution, but there is no record. After the War, he also moved to Washington County, Pennsylvania and then to Trumbull County, Ohio in 1828. He died there on February 22, 1840."

Takeaways from Larry Hawks' work include: 1. Richard was likely impressed into service with the British Royal Navy; 2. Richard's son Francis served as a Major during the Revolutionary War along with son Elias; 3. Headley was changed to Headlee by 1735; 4. there was a grandson named Samuel; and 5. in 1828 son Elias moved to Trumbull, County Ohio.

ROBERT H HEADLEY (1720-1806) Escape from Wyoming Valley, PA Massacre

Born: 1720 (Connecticut Farms, Union County, New Jersey Colony)

Married: ca. 1744 to Susannah (Cary) Headley (1725-1770); abt 1758 to Phoebe Ann Baldwin (Garner) Headley/Hadley (1736-1786)

Died: April 28, 1806 (Milton, Morris County, New Jersey)

Parents: Samuel Headley (1690-1755) and Mary H (Foster) Headley (1694-1788)

Children by Susannah Cary: (1725-1770): Moses Headley (1746-); **Robert Headley** (1748-1789); Lois Headley (1750-1821); and Mary Headley.

Children by Phoebe Baldwin Gardner: (1736-1727): Issac Headley (1735-1802); Mary Headley (17521821); Joseph Headley (1758-1842); Samuel Headley (1759-1831); Samuel Headley (17651841); William Headley (1769-1856); and Phebe Headley (1778-1857).

[Although the names of wives and children are generally consistent with the Descendants book, there are probable errors in this information as a date of death given for wife Phoebe in one place is provided as being before the birth of her children, and there are overlaps in birthdates for children from the two wives. The important thing is there is little doubt that Robert (1720-1806) is the father of Robert (1748-1789) in our line below.]

Residences are shown in 1783 as Springfield, Essex County New Jersey and on December 13, 1791 as Stafford, Monmouth County, New Jersey. He made his will in 1758 while residing in Essex County.

The Descendants book provides that at some time after 1758 he moved to Wyoming Valley, Pennsylvania and was one of the few who escaped from the terrible massacre that followed. Robert was very friendly with the Indians, one Indian in particular was a great friend to Robert and just before the massacre warned him to leave as the town would be burned that night. Robert said to the Indian, "You wouldn't hurt me would you?" The Indians say, "In time of war, the Indian knows no friend." Robert got an old high top Pennsylvania wagon and put all the goods he could and at 4 o'clock that afternoon of July 2, 1778, started with his wife, sons Joseph, Samuel, William and daughter Phebe for New Jersey. The Battle of Wyoming also known as the Wyoming Massacre was an encounter during the American Revolutionary War between American Patriots and Loyalists accompanied by Iroquois raiders which took place in the Wyoming Valley of Pennsylvania on July 3, 1778, in Exeter and Wyoming, Pennsylvania. More than 300 Patriots were killed in the battle.

After east going through the wilds of Pennsylvania and New Jersey, he finally reached the Hopewell mountains in Sussex County, New Jersey in the beginning of the winter of 1778, where he built a cabin and passed the winter. Early in the spring of 1779, he located at Milton, Morris County where he built a log house which was still standing in 1905 when the Descendants book was written, as part of the Headley Homestead and continued in the Headley name, in 1905 owned by great grandson Frank J. Headley. The original lands owned by Robert Headley consisted of about six hundred acres. Sussex County is west and a little northerly of present-day New York City.

There is a copy of his will in the Descendants book. Milton, Morris County, New Jersey where he is recorded as dying is just south of the family homestead in Sussex.

Note there is also a Samuel Headley, a grandson or nephew born about 1836 in Westfield, Union County, New Jersey, about 1842 in New Jersey, drafted in the Civil War as shown on draft registration records, and shown in residence in New Jersey on July 1, 1863. passing away on November 5, 1856, in Westfield, Union, New Jersey (possibly during the Civil War).

ROBERT LYMANN HEADLEY (1748-1789)

Born: 1748 (Monmouth, New Jersey)

Married: Susanna Cary Headley (1725-1770); Phoebe Ann Baldwin (Gardner) Headley (1736-1786)

Died: 1789 (Wayne, PA)

Parents: Robert H Hadley (1720-1806) and Mary H (Foster) Headley [another listing has Susanna Cary-the, the second wife under the listing above which is likely correct]

Children: **Stephen Headley** (1785-1868)

Monmouth, New Jersey, is Robert Headley's recorded birthplace, where his grandfather was born in 1690, a little east of the Connecticut Farms/Elizabethtown area, where the Headleys had fairly extensive land holdings. Robert H Headley's residence was shown as 1781 Hardyston, Sussex, New Jersey. Sussex County, New Jersey was the location of the Headley Homestead where his parents lived.

STEPHEN HEADLEY (HADLEY) (1785-1868) Move from NJ to MI

Born: April 22, 1785 (NJ)

Married: July 18, 1808 (Elizabeth "Betsey" Owen Hadley 1788-1832)

Died: December 23, 1868 (Lyndon, Washtenaw, MI)

Parents: Robert Lyman Headley (1748-1789) and either Susanna Cary Headley (1725-1770) or Phoebe Ann Baldwin (Garner) Headley (1736-1786)

A brother Samuel was a Captain presumably during the War of 1812.

They had a daughter Joanna Hadley (1819-1910 who married her first cousin Hiram Morrison (1816-1897) of Warren County, PN.

Children: Their eleven children were: Sylvia Hadley (1809-1879); Elsie Hadley (1810-1883); Lydia Ami Hadley (1812-1895); Orange Emmons Hadley (1815-1903); Sarah Hadley (1817-   ); Lewis Hadley (1818-   ); Joanna Hadley (1819-1907); **Stephen Owen Hadley** (1821-1901); Jane Priscilla Hadley (1823-1894); Laura Hadley (1826-1848); and Phoebe Rosella Hadley (1829-1853).

It is interesting to note that during Samuel's life "e" was dropped in the spelling of Headley so that it became commonly known as Hadley.

One site suggests two or more of their children accompanied Stephen Hadley to Michigan in the late 1830s after Elizabeth Owen's death.

Elizabeth Owen's father, John Owen II, was a veteran of the Revolutionary War and was 107 years 10 months and 23 days old when he died. He was 6'7" tall. Her Owen ancestors were: John II, Aaron, Joseph, and John I. John Owen I of Windsor was born in 1622 in Wales. He is first listed in New England records in 1642. He married Rebecca Wade of Hartford in 1650. Her father Robert Wade was one of the original 127 settlers of Hartford in 1639. See Ralph Dornfield Owen, "Descendants of John Owen of Windsor, CT" (1941).

STEPHEN OWEN HADLEY (1821-1901) Marriage to Calista Barringer in MI

Born: December 6, 1821 (Carroll, Chautaugua NY)

Married: March 23, 1845 (Washtenaw, MI - Calista Abigail Barringer (1830-1893). After Calista's death married Mrs. Benamin Boyce, a widow.

Stephen Owen Hadley

Died: July 18, 1901 (Unadilla, near Gregory, Washtenaw County, MI).

Records also show Stephen Owen Hadley born December 6, 1821 in Rhinebeck, Dutchess County, NY and passed away July 18, 1901 buried in North Lake Cemetery, Chelsea, Washtenaw County, MI.

Children: Stephen Owen Hadley and Calista Abigail Barringer had thirteen children as follows: Lyman Kinney Hadley (1846-1937); **Charles Henry Hadley** (1848-1930); Laura Roselva Hadley (1849-1930); Lewis Stephen Hadley (1850-1894); Emma Jane Hadley (1853-1834); Harrison Daniel Hadley (1850-1934); Angeline Elizabeth Hadley (1856-1946); Lydia Anna Hadley (1859-1938); Della M. Hadley (1860-1906); Sylvia Abigail Hadley (1862-1935); Justin J. Hadley (1868-1938); Minnie Hadley (1870-1870); and Lavinia Hadley (1870-1870).

Rhinebeck, New York is eighty-eight miles north of Eastchester, New York (now part of the Bronx-see Richard Hadley 1642). Carroll, New York is located in the western corner of what is now the state of New York. It was settled in around 1809 with the town established in 1825 from part of the town of Ellicott. In 1853 part of Carroll was used to form the town of Kiantone. Warren County, Pennsylvania is immediately to the south.

Stephen Owen Hadley's wife and the mother of Charles was Calista Barringer Hadley (1829-1893), daughter of Henry and Abigail Barringer. The Barringer's were of German heritage. They married on March 23 1845 in Washtenaw, Michigan. She was 15. She was born in Williamstown, New York October 30, 1830. She moved with her parents to Dexter Township, Michigan in 1844 where she met and married Stephen Owen. Her parents soon moved to Illinois and Wisconsin. It is believed she never saw her mother again and her father only once. The county seat for Washtenaw County is present day Ann Arbor, Michigan.

Stephen Owen Hadley came to Lyndon Township, Washtenaw County Michigan from Carroll. New York in 1839 and became a prosperous farmer in a good agricultural area. The history of Washtenaw County, Michigan, lists him as a prominent citizen and says "of the many fine and attractive places none is more conspicuous than that belonging to (Stephen and Calista Hadley) . . . on section 11, Lyndon Township." Stephen O. Hadley was a democrat in politics and he and Calista were active members of the Methodist Episcopal Church of North Lake for more than 40 years. They were also active in many other community affairs.

After Calista's death on March 11, 1893 Stephen Owen married Mrs. Benjamin Boyce, a widow and mother of Andrew Boyce, who married Stephen and Calista's daughter, Sylvia. Stephen Owen Hadley died July 18, 1901.

Calista and Stephen Owen are buried in North Lake Cemetery which is three or four miles from where they lived in Unadilla near Gregory, Michigan. Hadley Road is the main street leading into Unadilla from the south towards Chelsea where the North Lake Cemetery is located. Chelsea is a small farming community SE of Lansing and west of Detroit. It was first called Kedron, but became Chelsea in 1850 when Elisha Congdon renamed it for his old home in Connecticut. It was also in 1850 when the Michigan Central Railroad built a new depot there.

The following is presumptively from a newspaper article.

Stephen O. Hadley; Washtenaw County is an Eden of farms and agricultural tracts. There are comparatively few very small tracks, and each farmer tries to outdo neighbors in the cultivation and improvement of the land. Of the many fine, attractive places, none is more conspicuous than that belonging to our subject and located on section 11, Lyndon Township. He has here two hundred and fifty acres of land, upon which he has lived since April. 1855.

Mr. Stephen O. Hadley made his advent into the State in 1839 and lived in Lenawee County for two years hence removing into this county and settling in the township of Dexter, where he cleared off a farm and resided for fourteen years, hence removing to this place. Since coming here, he has erected all the buildings which now distinguish it as being one of the best-improved places of the locality. He has made of it a finely productive farm, having paid a great deal of attention to the raising of fine fruits of all varieties.

Stephen O. Hadley is a native of Carroll Township, Chautauqua County, N. Y., and was born December 6, 1831. He is the son of Stephen Hadley and Betsey E. (Owen) Hadley. natives of the Empire State. Until coming West in 1839, the original of our sketch was engaged in the lumber business and was quite successful. His mother having died in 1832. Stephen O. Hadley's father, Stephen Hadley, made his home with him, of whom we write, until his death, which occurred in 1869. On coming to Michigan, the father and son drove through from New York with a horse team. They were on the road for two weeks, and the journey was a memorable one for the young man.

Stephen Hadley, Sr., was born in 1781. He was the father of a family of ten children, six of whom are now living. They are Lydia, who is now Mrs. Letts; Orange E.; Sarah, who is Mrs. Pulsifer; Johanna, who is a Mrs. Morrison; and our subject and lane, who is Mrs. Wilsey. Those dead are Laura, Phoebe R., Sylva and Elsie. They were all married but Laura; Sylva was Mrs. Harrison Daniels; Elsie was Mrs. Peter Evans; Phoebe R. was Mrs. Calvin Goodspeed. The elder Mr. Hadley was in his younger days a Democrat and later in life a Republican. He served as a soldier in the War of 1812. In church preference he was a Methodist.

Stephen O. Hadley received his education in New York and was brought up with a more intimate knowledge of the lumber trade than of anything else. This he followed until he came West and he assures us that he never saw a spear of wheat growing until he came to Michigan. Since coming here, he has been engaged in farming, and his efforts in the agricultural line have been very successful. His marriage took place on March 23, 1845, at which time he was united to Miss Calista Barringer of New York. The lady was born in Williamstown, Oswego County, in 1829 and was a daughter of Henry and Abigail (Hough) Barringer, natives of the Empire State. The former was a farmer and came to Michigan at an early day. Later he removed to Illinois, thence to Wisconsin, where both he and his wife died. They were members of the Methodist Episcopal Church and the father was a soldier in the War of 1812. having been all his life an ardent Democrat. He was the father of ten children, eight of whom are now living.

The children of whom Mrs. Hadley is one are William, Susan, Peter E., Truman, Mrs. Hadley, and Ann. Elizabeth and George. Our subject is the father of eleven children. They are Lyman K., Charles H., Laura R., Lewis S., Emma, Augehne E., and Harrison. Delia, Sylva, Lydia A. and Justin J. The eldest son married Sarah Bull and has three children—Polina, Cora and Emmet. **Charles married Nettie Clark**; they have five children—Bert, Rosa, and Orral. Ina and Bee. Laura is Mrs. Rutland and is the mother of two daughters—Agnes and Minnie. Lewis S. married Delia Ward and is the father of seven children—Stephen, Josephine, Jay, and Fred. Harrison. Calista and Sylva. Emma is now Mrs. Kennie and is the mother of two daughters—Grace and Mabel; Angeline is Mrs. Backus and has two children—Mary and Seward; Harrison married Flora Goodwin and is the father of two children—Roy and Ray; Delia is Mrs. Blakely and has one son, Ira; Sylva is Mrs. Boice and has two children—Wirt R. and Myrtie; Lydia A. is Mrs. Boice and has two children—Calista and Floyd S.; Justine J. is still at home.

In his political predilections our subject is a Democrat and his first vote was cast for James K. Polk and he has been true to his party ever since. For fifteen years he has been Highway Commissioner of the township. Mrs. Hadley is a member of the Methodist Episcopal Church. Our subject has ever taken an active part in all matters pertaining to the welfare of the locality and State, and is an enterprising businessman of broad and intelligent views.

CHARLES HENRY HADLEY (1847-1930) Move to SD

Charles Henry Hadley and Nettie Clark Hadley

Born: November 5, 1847

Married: February 13, 1873 (O'Brien County, Iowa-Francella Annette (Nettie) Clark)

Died: November 16, 1930 (Mound City, SD)

Claude's father was Charles Henry Hadley 1848-1930 and mother was Francella Annette (Nettie) Clark (1852-1909). Charles Henry Hadley was second to the eldest of 13 children.

Children: Charles Henry and Nettie's children were: Lewis Birton Hadley (IA); Roselva Pearl Hadley (IA); Oril May Hadley (born in Palo Alto County, IA); Henry Lee Hadley (Livingston, MI); Nina Grace Hadley (Livingston, MI); George Hadley (Livingston, MI); Harvey Lyle Hadley (born in Livingston, MI); Joseph Hadley (died young in IA); and **Claude Clark Hadley** (Livingston, MI).

James E Hadley

Son, Claude Clark Hadley

Nettie Clark and Brother Lee

The <u>Barringer</u> family history by Curry contains a detailed listing of decedents from the above children, including those through Oril May Hadley who married George Shepherd, had a daughter Zina, who married George Ver Hoven, who with his wife Dorothy Groen had children Alvina, Marilyn, Merlin and William. They lived on a farm near Lynden Washington, which I visited while in my teens, getting a workout bucking bales.

CLAUDE CLARK HADLEY (1892-1967) Move from SD to WA, / Whiskey Still

<u>Born</u>: January 18, 1894 (Unadilla, Livingston, Co., MI)

<u>Married</u>: June 26, 1913 (Blanche May Penrod Ford Hadley – August 22, 1893-September 16, 1985)

<u>Died</u>: September 16, 1967 (Ellensburg, WA)

Claude Clark Hadley and Blanche May Hadley Wedding Photo

NOTE: Claude appears on Claude Clark Hadley's birth certificate as his middle name, however Claude (with an "e") appears on his death certificate and other records.

Children: Their eleven children, all born at Selby, Walworth County, SD were: Ernest Hadley; Mildred Hadley; Howard Claude Hadley; Wesley Hadley; Gerald Hadley; Irene Hadley; Helen Hadley; Hazel Hadley; Dale Hadley; Lois Hadley; and Joyce Hadley.

Like many of the Hadley's Claude was a farmer in his early years, although he worked some as a carpenter with his sons after the family's move to Washington state. While in South Dakota, he appears to have sharecropped on properties belonging to others, living in homes without indoor plumbing or electricity. With a failed potato crop during the dust bowl of the 1930's, he operated a whisky still to support the family and was investigated by federal agents. The family times in South Dakota and their move to Ellensburg, Washington are described in their second son Howard's description of his early life.

Particulars of family members are provided in more detail below.

HOWARD CLAUDE HADLEY (1919-2011) Riding the Rails

<u>Born</u>: Jan. 10, 1919 (SD)

<u>Married</u>: May 2, 1942 (Mary Collett Hadley-Seattle, King County, WA), Nov. 13, 1993 (Rebecca Sowell Hadley-Seattle, King County, WA)

<u>Died</u>: November 4, 2011 (Yakima, WA, buried in Ellensburg, WA)

<u>Children</u>: James Eldon Hadley (July 27, 1946); George Howard Hadley (May 22, 1948); and Kirk Jackson Hadley (August 19, 1949).

Howard was born on January 10, 1919 on a farm near Selby, South SD. The family doctor, Dr. George, came on horse and buggy through the snow for the delivery. The old farmhouse had no insulation, electricity, telephone or running water. Howard was the third of eleven children, five boys and six girls. He told many stories of working on the farm at an age as young as eight to ten years with his older brother, Ernest, using teams of horses for work and a horse and buggy for transportation. He attended a one room country school for all eight grades during his elementary education. By his high school years his family had moved to town and he took great pride in playing on the Java High School basketball team. They even managed to caravan through snow to neighboring towns for contests. On Sunday mornings he rang the church bell and stoked the furnace.

Following graduation in 1937 times were tough. There was no work to be had, they had sold off their livestock, and his father had lost what money he had when the banks closed. Always one to look for a solution and a bent for adventure, Howard called a family meeting and said they had to get out of South Dakota. He hatched a plan and with his father and younger brother, Wesley, got a ride to Mobridge where they hopped a fast freight and rode the rails to Washington State as far as the Kittitas Valley. They sent money home earned from picking thistles, and the rest of the family drove out in a 1936 Dodge that his mother somehow managed to buy.

Howard was drafted into the Army in 1941 and served in the South Pacific, in New Guinea and the Philippines as a truck mechanic and truck driver with the 198th Engineers 1 16th Quartermaster Corp building roads for future US bases. After discharge in 1945 he returned to Ellensburg and became a journeyman carpenter, by passing an apprenticeship by watching others and using his natural talent. He started his family with his wife, Mary, and built their first home from scratch in Kittitas. They had three sons, James (Jay), George, and Kirk. He held a private pilot's license and flew several small planes, including an open cockpit.

He eventually settled in Auburn where he owned acreage and raised livestock, continued as a carpenter, and became a small business owner of a floor covering store and a real estate broker. Howard was an elder in the White River Presbyterian Church, chaired the Christian Education Department, and volunteered in the building of the current church structure. Seeking warmer climes, he moved to Arizona where he lived throughout the seventies and eighties. He returned to the Northwest in 1991, met and married Becky Bowton. They settled in West Seattle and in 2006 moved to Yakima seeking sunshine. Becky has three sons, Eric, Dan, and Brett. Between them they have 20 grandchildren and Howard has an additional seven great-grandchildren.

He loved traveling in the US, Mexico, and Europe. His last big trip was in January 2011 when accompanied by two of his three sons he enjoyed a father-son reunion with his third son who lived in Samoa.

Howard lived by the values he learned from the hard lessons of his youth in South Dakota. He also credits his Sunday School teachers for having a positive influence on his life. He loved well and was well-loved.

Anecdotes from the Life of Howard Claude Hadley

[The following was dictated by Howard prior to his death on November 4, 2011, and is in his words with some minor editing. His immediate family was composed of: Claude Clark Hadley (1892-1967) (father), Blanche May Ford Hadley (1893-1985 (mother), and their eleven children Ernest (1915), Mildred (1917), Howard (1919), Wesley (1921), Gerald (1922), Irene (1924), Helen (1926), Hazel (1928), Dale (1929), Lois (1932) and Joyce (1935).]

Introduction

Everything that follows is true to the best of my memory. Although some of this may seem funny, none of it is made up. These were different times, the times when horse drawn wagons were displaced by cars, before the days of running water, central heat and electricity, at least on the farms I grew up on.

My First Home

I was born on a farm a few miles south of Selby, South Dakota. The farm was owned by the owners of the only bank in Java, South Dakota, Hicks and Helm. The Hicks and Helm farm was around 200 acres. Helm owned several other farms as well.

Our family doctor, Doctor George from Selby, came by the farmhouse with a horse and buggy for my delivery. It was January and there was too much snow to get the car out of the barn. It was 1919. Dad was making decent money raising cattle and grain and wheat but also oats and corn) and selling cream and milk on this farm, but never owned it. We primarily used the farm for raising beef, cattle and grain. The cattle were beef and dairy - beef mostly. We had milk cows but just for the family. Our cows were the source of our cream milk, butter, cheese as well as raw milk for the new calves, for the dogs and the cats.

The old farmhouse wasn't much, post on beam construction, no insulation, electricity, telephone or even running water. Heat was always a problem as there is little firewood in this part of the country. I remember my dad going along the railroad tracks picking up coal that had fallen off the tender. When we could we would buy coal in bulk which we would haul from town out to the farm in our wagon. Everything was done with the wagon with our team of horses.

One winter shelled corn was worth $10 dollars a bushel. That was the price but we had to husk the corn and then take the dry corn kernels off the cobb. It took a lot of corn to make up a bushel. We burnt the cob intact with corn (the whole thing) that winter for heat. We would feed the corn stalks to the horses and to the cows.

My current wife, Becky and I visited Selby, South Dakota in 1999 and were able to see some of Doctor George's equipment in a private museum. The owner of the museum was in his 90s and collected things and put them on display in his private barn/shed "museum".

My first childhood memory is of falling into the cistern. I may have been four years old. Our water was so hard that we would collect rainwater off the roof, which would be collected in a cistern. The cistern was at the end of the porch. We would use this water for doing our laundry and other household chores. I fell through the small opening we would use to pull out the water. Boy, was I scared - it was dark and wet down there. Got pulled out safe and sound.

Hicks and Hill Farm photo

31

In the spring of 1924 when I was a little over five years old, our family awoke one night to a ruckus in the chicken house. I recall it was spring because I remember there were piles of straw left over from the prior fall. Dad would leave the straw piles out for the cattle to lie on. At that time our family was composed of us kids Ernest, Mildred, me, Wesley and Gerald (in that order by age) plus my father Claude Clark Hadley and my mother Blanche May Hadley. We were raising chickens to sell. It was popular at that time to fry a young chicken at parties and such. Our family was raising fryers [type of chicken - brown] for income. We had around two hundred chickens. We would take eggs from under the chickens and examine them to see which ones were fertile. The fertile ones we placed in incubators [what kept the incubators warm?] The eggs had to be rotated manually once a day or once a week (I'm not sure). We had several roosters to fertilize the eggs. These chickens made good plump fryers but weren't good egg layers!

At daybreak my father went out to see what had happened. There were dead baby chicks all over the place. Dad said he knew it wasn't a weasel as weasels would go after the blood from the chickens and wouldn't mess with the chicks. Dad determined that it had to be a badger that came in and helped himself. Dad got a 50-gallon wooden barrel, a bucket and a badger trap and put them in our wagon. The badger trap was like a steel gopher trap but much larger and stronger. Dad, my brother Ernest (five years older than me), and I went hunting for a badger hole. Two horses pulled the wagon, and Ernest sat in the back. I sat next to my dad driving the horses. The metal rims rolled over the dirt road in the farm field. Eventually we found the badger hole, with fresh evidence (tracks and fresh dirt) that he was still in there.

Dad decided the best way to get the badger out was to pour the water in the hole and pour it in fast, as badgers were known to be able to dig fast and block the hole. Dad set the trap upside down over the hole so that whatever came out would have to go into the trap. Ernest filled the bucket from the barrel and handed it to Dad. Dad would pour it on the side of the trap into the hole. This had to be done fast. I was just a spectator - no job for me. I was all excited as I had never seen a badger up close - they were big scary animals - the size of a dog. Sure enough, this idea worked profitably as the badger ignored the trap and wanted to exit the hole, so they caught him in the badger trap. And was ever the badger mad, being caught in the trap and fighting him!! Dad hit the badger on its head with a farm tool and that was that. No more badger, no more killing of the chickens, that is until the weasels arrived . . . another story!

Horses

My first experience riding a horse was riding on the back of the saddle with my brother Ernest (on the flaps behind the saddle seat hanging onto Ernest). It was a special day for me. I was about five.

We had a mare with this same SADDLE HORSE, Bird. She was a foal and had quite the personality. My dad sent Ernest out to check on the cattle. The horse turned sharper than Ernest anticipated and he fell from the horse breaking his arm near his right elbow. Dr. George set Ernest's arm but it had a crook in it when it healed. That was what kept Ernest from passing the physical for the service during World War ll. (Never bothered him as he worked all his life with it.) All the rest of us boys served in World War ll.

We always had horses around as they were our primary source of transportation and necessary to work the farm. We didn't have tractors or any motorized equipment. We had a team of horses to pull the wagon and buggy, saddle horses and a number of work horses, maybe 30 in all. It would take a team of six horses to plow. We would use horses for thrashing, for cutting hay, disking, plowing, harrowing, seeding, and harvesting - all with horses. We also had horses for trading. There were times when they were all necessary.

My dad would trade horses. It was something most farmers would do. One time he traded for a team of horses. I got them out into the field, and they would balk. I didn't know what to do. They refused to move. My dad wasn't around. I thought to myself who is the boss here - is it these horses or me. I got a pitchfork and poked them in the butt. I had to draw blood before they would move but they did. My dad would probably not have approved. They balked again with me later. I got the pitchfork but didn't need to use it. They had learned their lesson.

One time, my dad traded with a neighbor for a horse that would run when it heard the sound of a car's horn. After it was delivered, we learned it was blind. My dad laughed and said he got me this time! On some equipment we used three horses. We put the blind horse in the middle and she worked just fine.

At one time we had a black thoroughbred, Lady, that could run like the wind. We rode her too. Ernest and Mildred at one time rode Bird and Lady to high school, after the Model T gave out on us. We had a team (the grey) that we used all the time. You could drop the reins on the ground and they would stay there. One-time Helen, my younger sister (about age 4 or 5) decided she would make them go. She said "giddee up" - they didn't flinch a muscle. She also tried clicking noises telling them to move. The horses ignored her.

When I was about 10-12, I would ride Bird. When I fell off or got off, she would wait for me. When it was cold, she didn't want to leave the barn. I went in and asked Mom what to do. Mom said to back the horse out. It worked for a while then she caught on. Bird was good at rounding up cattle. If one of the herd strayed or got behind, she would bite it in the behind to keep it moving. I was too small to mount Bird from the ground, and had to find a rock or fence to climb onto to get on board. Bird wouldn't socialize with the other horses in the field. I would ride Bird bareback when moving the cattle, and sometimes leave her with the cattle overnight when we were moving fields. The horse field was L-shaped, so it wasn't far to get back to the house. Bird wasn't as fast as some of the other horses, but she would put all the horses in the barn without my assistance. I just sat on her back, hanging on for dear life. She would run and make sharp turns.

We ultimately traded Bird to my mom's niece, Zina Verhoven. Bird bucked their oldest son, Wilbur, off. He was Ernest age. To my knowledge, Bird wasn't ridden again after that. Wilbur later decided to come west. He got as far as Spokane and came back home. He said there wasn't work in Washington. Zina's grandchildren ultimately moved to Lyndon, Washington. We saw them from time to time decades later.

We had a barn dog, a mongrel who had a special trick. When one of our horses would balk our dog would bite one back heal then dodge the resulting kick and then bite the other heal. Back and forth. Finally, the horse would give up and move forward.

At the Valley

Our buggy had one seat with a box in the back for putting groceries or carrying supplies. It was a place where we could ride if more than three wanted to go. In the winter the trick was to wrap our cat in the blanket and put it at our feet to keep our feet warm. Two horses would pull the buggy.

The Revenuers

When I was around five, during the prohibition period, a report had been made that Dad was making whiskey on the farm. Whiskey was usually made out of wheat but could be made from potatoes. We grew wheat at that time on the Hicks and Helm farm. I remember that strangers came to the farm searching for whiskey. Mom was very upset. They looked everywhere in the house for a still, for bottles - any whiskey making evidence they could find. They looked in the kitchen cupboards, closets, in the root cellar, and through all our personal belongings. They looked all through the upstairs, downstairs and searched the barn and under the straw piles, everything they could think of. In the barnyard there was the main barn with stalls for the horses, a covered area for the cow, a separate chicken house and a separate small shed with an attic. I was just a kid all "bug eyed" at strangers going through everything on the farm. They found nothing. Dad's whiskey making equipment was up in the attic in the little shed. I didn't say a peep. The equipment was not in use at that time. Dad could have gone to jail if the equipment (the cooker, coils, etc.) had been found - certainly if it were in use. Mom was really scared.

A couple of years later, at the Spring Lake Farm, Dad did make whiskey. This would have been in the late 1920s when the Midwest suffered a terrible drought. Our crops failed. We did have some potatoes left, which Dad made into whiskey and sold. It was a way of supporting our family in those tough times.

A few years later when the family moved west, Ernest sold the whiskey making equipment.

The Spring Lake Farm

When I was six, we moved from the Hicks and Hill farm to a smaller farm near Spring Lake in the vicinity of Java, South Dakota. We used the farm for raising wheat, rye and some corn. There was very little pasture ground. This was before the big drought and the depression.

One winter, we had a terrible snowstorm. The wind blew with the snow. Our porch faced into the wind. It was so cold that occasionally a pheasant would freeze in the air and blow through the screen door. My family would salvage the pheasant for dinner.

Another time in the afternoon a big storm was brewing. Dad, knowing what could happen moved the family to the root cellar, taking kerosene lanterns for light and blankets for heat. We did have security by being in the root cellar and sure enough a tornado hit our farm. Not much damage except the garage that was attached to the barn was spread out into the field although the car that was in the garage didn't seem to be damaged at all. After several hours we felt a sudden calm. Dad said it was all over and we could go back into the house. It was night then.

A cute thing that brought us a lot of laughs was when my father harvested duck eggs and put them under a sitting hen. The resulting ducklings played in the puddles when it rained and the hen would scold the ducklings for being in the water, not aware that this was natural for them.

The bull calf that dad had purchased (because he couldn't afford a bull) only did his poopy job in one corner of his stall. How about that?

When spring came and dried out the cow chips and the folks had me gather them for fire for the stove.

On the property near Spring Lake I found what I believed to be an Indian grave, with a mound and decorated in the Indian style. I lived with the thought of digging it up to see if it was true that Indians were buried with their hatchet and other personal belongings. Probably for the best this was something I never had the opportunity to do.

One evening the folks left for some social engagement and they left Ernest, Mildred and myself at home alone. And we are supposed to be old enough to take care of ourselves. And we were playing a game at the table or we were playing anyway at the table and accidentally

Tough times at Spring Lake Farm

tipped the kerosene lamp over and of course the kerosene spilled and we were so afraid of setting the house on fire. We knew what we had done and didn't know what to do but somehow, we got the fire out and no damage was done. Now comes the crucial time. What shall we tell the folks when they come home? Well, it was decided amongst the three of us that having cleaned up all the evidence they wouldn't know and why should they know. None of us was going to tell, period. Nothing was ever said. No one ever knew.

The spring lake house like the other homes I lived in wasn't much of a house. No bathrooms, no running water, no electricity. For drinking we had a bucket of water with a dipper in it. Mom would heat water in a warming oven which was next to the baking oven - a place to put water and the baking would heat the water. Our water came from hand dug well with a hand pump or when there was wind, the windmill would bring it up. We had a tank for the cattle, but that was it. We bathed in a washtub on the floor about once a month in the winter.

We wore long underwear all winter. It had drop seats with buttons across the back we could drop to go to the bathroom. When we bathed once a month, we would change our long underwear. We four boys slept on straw ticks. Once a year, Mother washed the cover, and we would put in new straw. Mother made her own soap with lye and lard. Cooked it up and we called it Fels Naphtha because that's what we bought when we went to the store. Ernest and I slept together upstairs where there were holes in the roof. There were times when in the morning we awoke to fresh snow on the bed. The ridge boards were off and the snow was so cold and hard that it blew through the openings. Also, upstairs were Gerald and Wesley. The upstairs wasn't separate rooms, just an open attic with a floor in it.

School Days

I was six years old when I started school. The one room school house was two miles from the Spring Lake farm. There were eight grades with one teacher and no janitor. Slate boards were passed out to all the students (a piece of slate with a wood frame around it). We were also furnished with chalk. (This was in lieu of pencil and paper.) Each pupil had his own desk. The teacher followed an order of instructions for each class. This was true for the school near the Valley Farm I attended for the end of the second grade.

My first problem with going to school was getting notes from the girls my age. Somehow the older boys would intercept the notes and I got teased which I detested. To get to school we walked and carried our lunch. The only days we didn't walk were when the snow was so deep that it was necessary for my father to take us in a two-horse sleigh with blankets to keep us warm. I was the youngest going to school then, with Ernest (five years older) and Mildred (three years older).

When we lived in the Valley farm toward the end of what would have been second grade for me, the school was located about a third of a mile away. It was also a one room, one teacher, no janitor school through the eighth grade. The teacher didn't have a student in the second grade. The teacher tried to put me in the third grade. I couldn't cut the mustard at that level so I became a second grade of one.

The most convenient place to stay for our teacher, given my family's proximity to the school, was our house. Arrangements were made and the teacher, Myrtle Green would sleep with Mildred, my older sister. To my disappointment the fact that the teacher stayed at our house didn't result in any extra privileges to me at school. Myrtle Green was maybe 22-24 years old. She was young, teaching for maybe two years. Myrtle had great professionalism and was a very nice person, fitting herself into our family. Contrary to regulations for one room school marms, which were "no boyfriends", she had many. The manual said: [quote from school manual I have] Her boyfriends met her after school and she often came home late.

She was never reported by our family or anyone else to my knowledge. We liked her and she was a good teacher. My brother Ernest has told me she had a crush on him. I know nothing about this.

The high school was in Java. When Mildred and Ernest went to high school, they drove a Model T we had then, although they rode Lady and Bird to school after the Model T gave out on us. The Model T's used to have a flywheel with magnetos to generate a spark in lieu of a generator. One of the magnetos had come loose and made a hole in the casing. Dad thought that if he could get the engine running, it could run without it. Not so. We didn't know much about engines at that time as they were new to us. I was more mechanically minded than Ernest or Dad, always trying to figure these things out. I remember Mildred teaching me some of her French - "Ferme le buch" (shut your mouth) and "parlevous Frances" are some of the phrases I remember.

I had the seventh and eighth grades in Java, and then went to high school. I played on the varsity team as the sixth man (first in after the starters).

Valley Farm

When I was eight, we moved around twenty miles north to another farm. This farm had both room for cattle and grain. We milked cows for cream to feed the family. We also sold the cream. We lived on the cream check and had to take the cream to the train station in eight-gallon cans to be shipped. We received a check for every shipment.

The Valley farm had fences but didn't have lots of pasture land. There was open ground between the farm and the railroad tracks to the north (which ran east west) and also out west toward the section line which was around 100 feet wide. There was also some open land on the other side of the railroad near our Spring Lake farm, so the horses had some idea where they were. We would let the horses out each winter while at the Valley Farm to fend for themselves. I recall my father asking me to go find and bring back the horses toward the end of March, the first of April. I went out but didn't find them, got tired and came back in the afternoon. He told me to turn the horse around and bring it back. I learned my lesson and came back as it was turning dark. When the horses were out loose like that they would stay together as a herd and the other farmers wouldn't bother them.

On my lower left leg, I have a scar. It was when Ernest was tossing hay up to the hayloft. I was in the hayloft stacking the hay. We had an accident and he stuck me a good one - I had to reach down and pull the pitchfork out. We put Lysol on it which made it all pussy.

Moving to Java

Times were hard and money was slow. It was now 1932 in the heart of the depression. The dustbowl the Midwest had become due to the terrible drought enveloped the Valley Farm along with everything else. The dust was so heavy that it would pile up on the tumble weeds against the fences on the side of the road. We could then walk over the fences. I also remember the roads covered with grasshoppers, so many that the roads were slippery and driving conditions were dangerous.

We had borrowed money from Helm, the primary owner of the Hicks and Helm bank. He would loan money to people. We weren't able to pay the loan. Dad settled the loan by giving Helm our livestock, everything we had except for one team of horses, a hayrack (a wagon that could be used for hauling hay) and two milk cows which we took with us to Java. We had to give up farming. We moved to Java across from the Gieses. During the summer time we would stake the cows out. There was no water where they were staked out. It was my job to move the cows, water then and then milk the cows. I did this for two years straight. I was also playing basketball, practice and pretty busy. Ernest, Gerald and Wesley then took over this chore.

I finished the seventh grade and graduated from eighth grade in the little town of Java. I had secured a privileged job at the local newspaper with the owner offering to tutor me in the newspaper business as it was then. I learned to set type, to set bills, linotype, and everything for learning how to make paper. That job was terminated because the owner of the paper became a state senator which consumed so much time. Someone else then ran the paper.

We also had a movie theater in Java. Eugene Perman was one of my friends. His folks owned the movie theatre. He asked me to help with the janitorial work in the theater. In return I got to see all the picture shows. We used to get posters to put in the window, maybe 12 X 18 and also put in the paper what the show was going to be. Bing Crosby and Fred Astaire were movie actors and dancers of that era and in the shows.

The Feekner Place

When I was about 14, the family moved back out to another farm because Dad was asked to take care of some cattle. We were just there for a short time. It was here that Bird kicked my front tooth out. I laid out there on the ground for a while. They saw me and the blood lying out on the ground. I remember my Mother asked, what's the matter Howard? I said, nothing, but she could see that something was wrong. She put me in her bed which was next to the kitchen on the main floor - the best room in the house. That was in the wintertime. There was a question about getting me to the doctor and of course that would be Dr. George. Because the road was blocked with snow the mailman was late coming. We had to rely on him to take the message to Dr. George who was six miles away in Selby. Some people had phones, but we didn't. Since I was doing okay, I never went to the hospital. I laid there a couple of weeks. Mother fed me alphabet soup. My lip lay pretty open for quite a while until the scar tissue sealed it shut. I was missing my left front tooth. That's why to this day I cut the corn off the cob with a knife.

Another time for some reason, Mother sent me to the neighbor's home to make an urgent call. The woman refused to make the call because my mother told me to do it. In those days if your mother told you to do something, you did it!

Move Back to Java

We gave up farming for good then. In Java while I worked at the movie theater, I also had a big dog, owned by a farmer. The dog used to bite the hogs' ears and shred them with his eye teeth. They had his eye teeth cut in half. It didn't stop the dog from chewing on the hog's I

Mount Rushmore

One summer day in 1936 (l was 17 and going to be a senior in high school) Eugene Perman and I decided we would like to go to the Black Hills. We had heard that Mount Rushmore was under construction. I got my parents' permission to go with Eugene. We had about twenty dollars each. There was no conversation as to how we were going to get there or come back. We decided to hitchhike. We had very little success hitchhiking. We got as far as Pierre, the capital of South Dakota, by the evening of the first day. Having no money Eugene and I slept down by the railroad tracks in a pile of warm sand. Eugene told me that at two thirty in the morning a passenger train would be coming through. Being from Java we had seen guys riding on the train. We got on the tender (the coal car behind the steam locomotive). It was dark so no one saw us. There was another party on the train that had gotten on at Aberdeen and had been kicked off at a water stop. (Steam engines had to stop for water every so often - it stopped in Pierre for water). He advised us that when the train stopped for water to be sure to get off and stand in the dark and get back on after the boiler on the engine was filled. By daylight we had passed a freight train on a siding. I suggested to Eugene that we get out, as we surely were going to get caught, as it was daylight. We agreed to wait for the freight train. We got on the freight train in an open box car and rode that into Rapid City, South Dakota. We left the railroad yard as quickly as we could so the railroad "Bulls" would not write us up for riding on the train.

We walked up town, got a hotel for the night for two dollars and a meal for fifty cents. The meal at the hotel was family style (all sitting at the same table).

The next day we got on the highway that would take us to Mount Rushmore. No luck with hitchhiking, however, a car went by us traveling too fast, slipped on a curve on the fresh asphalt, and came to a stop. It was about 8 A.M. By that time, I was getting pretty desperate for a ride. I went over and asked the gentleman if it would be all right for Eugene and I to ride with him. His response was "where are you going?" I told you we were hoping to go to Mount Rushmore. His response was that that was where he was going. Eugene recognized the man as being the sculpturer of the faces of Mount Rushmore, Gulzon Borglum. He gave us a ride in his coupe - no seat belts. On the way to the mountain, he drove very fast and Eugene got car sick. We got there in the middle of the day deciding to stay on the mountain overnight.

There were cables from the ground to the mountain to take the workers up. We built a fire. A ranger came over and said boys it's all right for you to have a fire, but showed us how to build a fire in the mountain. He showed us how to clear a spot, put rocks around and how to put it out. We spent three or four days their walking around. We didn't stay at any hotels, and ate the groceries we brought with us from home - canned pork and beans and some bread. In our walking we wound up on a road that would take us back to Mobridge. A truck driver picked us up and said he was going to Isabel (a little town just short of Mobridge) - so we had a ride almost the whole way back to Mobridge. From there we had no problem getting back to Java- hitch hiking was more favorable to us then.

When we took our family trip in 1953, we visited Mount Rushmore, and I have been back three other times. Each time I remember this adventure I had when I was in high school.

Trip West

I graduated from high school in May 1937. Ernest and Mildred graduated three years earlier. Ernest had been held back so that he would be in the same class with Mildred and could take her to school. There were no jobs or a future for any of us at that time in Java. What littler money my dad had was lost when the local bank closed. He showed up one day and the doors were locked -just like that. Ernest was not employed (he played cards), and Dad was doing pick and shovel work, putting in a water line for the WPA. Shortly after I found out I didn't have the job at the paper anymore it became clear to me that I had to leave Java. I asked for a family meeting. My father, mother, Ernest and I met. They asked me what I had in mind. I said I was thinking about going to Washington, and if we didn't get a job there, go to Oregon, and if no jobs there go to California. We had heard that a lot of people from South Dakota had gone to the Sacramento Valley to work. There was no work in South Dakota. My idea was not to go where everyone else had gone. I wasn't taking charge; I just had an idea and knew we had to do something.

We decided that Dad and I would make a trip west to see what was possible.

There was a question as to how we were going to get to Mobridge to catch the fast freight train. Giese, our friend (and mailman) took us.

Mom asked me if I would take Wesley as she didn't want to deal with Wesley and Gerald both at home while we were gone. I said, Yes, we could take Wesley. Although only 16, he was as big and strong as I was. Dad, Wesley, one of Dad's friends, and I set out for the trip west.

[JEH comments: Dad told me that in the 1930's a loose network of "hobos" was riding the rails, some in search of work and others as a way of life. He was careful to distinguish between "hobos" and "bums" who were not really interested in working. Blanche May packed meals for the trip. Other "hobos" told them which box cars to ride in that would be empty and dry for the trip, of good places to catch a meal, including a woman in Boise who could bake a wonderful apple pie. Growing up on the plains it was their first look at mountains, and they asked to be awoken as they crossed the continental divide in the middle of the night. They were also coached on when and where to get off the freight train to avoid the "bulls" and on freight schedules.]

We were planning to get off in Ellensburg and look around. It was my dad's idea to get off in Kittitas and visit his friend. When we met with him, he said to be up at the pool hall at 7 in the morning and the farmers would come in and pick up day labor. We were there the evening before when Shortie told us he had hired all of us.

He didn't have much, but he offered us the dirt floor in his garage temporarily. We had our bed rolls and made do. There was no place to wash or clean up. Dad would go buy some pork and beans in cans which we would eat as we had no stove either. Within a few days, Dad found us a little house we could stay in. It was small. When the rest of the family eventually came out, we boys all spent the winter in a tent we pitched in the yard.

Work in Kittitas

Within a day after arriving in Kittitas we met a fellow called "Shorty". Shorty told us that if we wanted a job, we needed to show up the following morning and get into a pickup truck that would take us out to a farm. We did this. The farmer asked us what we were doing there when we arrived, as Shorty was funning with us and had no authority to hire us. The job was pulling Canadian thistles in the wheat fields. They were very sharp. He could see we had no gloves. Since we were there, the farmer, Aiken, decided to put us to work on his farm out in Badger Pocket. He found some old gloves in the pickup. We did a good enough job that he said we could come back the next day. He had nice new gloves for us then. We stayed on with this farmer well into the winter. In the end it was Dad, me and Harley McFarland. Wesley, Shorty and all the other hands had been let go. The farmer had water rights up Park Creek which came out of the hills between Wenatchee and Ellensburg. Aiken had me drive his pickup truck all the time I worked for him. Harley McFarland who is my friend to this day, was riding in the back of the pickup truck, an early 30s Chevrolet or Dodge with three on the floor. We cleared out the portions of the creek and did a number of odd jobs on the farm till there was nothing we could do in the cold of winter. Mrs. Aiken was a rough and tumble gal and would watch us working in her binoculars. Some of the guys knew and would tease her by pulling their pants down. They didn't have electricity at their house but did have a generator. One time I was eating in their paint shed. I reached out and hit a light switch which turned on the generator and scared the daylights out of me. I didn't know about such things.

I remember mom sending me a letter asking me if she should buy a Model A with the money we had been sending home. I wrote back no, as it didn't have the power to climb the mountains going west or to pull a trailer with the family's belongings. I said we needed a bigger car with a stronger motor. She wrote back that there was a 1936 Dodge [1935 Plymouth?] she could buy. The car was only a year old. I wondered how she could ever buy it as Ernest didn't have a regular job and we were just making pennies in Kittitas. She said that the car mortgage company would finance it. She bought it. We had an old Buick. Ernest made a trailer to tie onto the car. Ernest would drive with Mom, Mildred, Gerald, Helen, Hazel, Dale, Lois and Joyce (my brothers and sisters remaining in Java) all as passengers. They brought a little furniture, but not much. There were no expressways at that time, just one- and two-lane roads. The mountain passes were slow and steep, not like the railroad grades Dad, Wesley, and I had gone over a few months prior.

Friend Harley McFarland and Howard pulling thistles in Kittitas

Car Ernest drove west with family in 1937

During the winter I had nothing to do. I was offered a job at the high school. I don't remember if I was paid or not. I became friends with the wood shop teacher and also with the principal. I would make handles for broken tools and things like that. It was the principal, {name} who coached me about going into the service. He told me to tell them that I was a "teamster". I wasn't sure what that meant as the only teamster I knew ran teams of horses. Nonetheless, I did so and wound up in the quartermaster corps driving a truck. Most of those going into the Army from Kittitas wound up in the infantry with the [unit] and fought at Guadalcanal.

Military Service

I served as a T-5 with the 116th Quarter Masters-198 Engineers out of Fort Lewis, Washington from March 4, 1941 to September 30, 1945 during World War II.

I served in the South Pacific for two and one-half years and at Fort Lewis for two years. I received the Asiatic-Pacific Service Medal, Philippine Liberation Medal, and Bronze Star, Good Conduct Medal.

I recall sailing to Australia on a President ship with 3000 servicemen. Memorable highlights of the trip are the sighting of a Japanese submarine, sailing through a bad storm (water spout) and experiencing a "glassy sea."

[JEH comment: The following was not dictated or written by Howard but reflects my memory of his stories.]

Howard in New Guinea

During the war while in New Guinea Howard became friends with local villagers. He has several pictures from this period. At one point he asked some village women if he could take their picture. They responded that he should wait. They ran back to their homes and changed into fresh leaf skirts (which is all they wore). Some of the village men told him they knew where there was gold in the hills but he did not have an opportunity to pursue it. Years later a large gold find was mined there.

New Guinea women dressed up for photo

Howard got very sick (typhus or typhoid fever) and was removed to Australia for his recovery. He then "hitch hiked" his way back to his unit which by then had moved on. He was on a ship as part of McArthur's invasion of the Philippines. He recalled kamikaze pilots diving into ships around him, some of which were sinking (quite possibly the invasion of Leyte Gulf). The landing craft he was on was hit by a bomb shortly after he left for shore. He drove a deuce and a half truck involved in road building and other construction activities. He told of driving back and forth over an anaconda that stretched across the roadway and on his return run saw that it had survived and moved on.

Howard was a car buff and pretty savvy with all things mechanical. My grandfather had a car all apart in his garage in Ellensburg (a Chevrolet from the early1930s). Howard managed to determine why it didn't work, found or made parts for it, and got it running. He often told stories about the 1934 Pontiac straight eight coupe with a rumble seat that he owned when stationed at Fort Lewis. He would use it to make trips to visit family in Ellensburg. As gas was rationed, he adjusted it to run on kerosene. I looked for one several times when I could afford it as a possible gift or just something to have, but they are pretty rare and I had no luck locating one at the time. In 1953, he purchased a new Chrysler, and in 1961, a Chrysler with a 413 cubic inch engine (we hit 120 mph with light snow drifting across a two-lane highway with the family aboard in Nevada). He tried an Audi and even bought a Renault Dolphine and a Ford Cortina, which George and Kirk learned to drive. I recall going to Doxon Motors in Auburn to admire a Mercedes Gullwing and 300 SL convertible on sale (worth millions today).

Howard Hadley wearing school letterman sweater in front of his 1934 Pontiac straight-8

During the war Howard had applied for flight school but wasn't accepted until the war was coming to a close. Once back in Ellensburg he took flight lessons. He learned on a WW2 Fairchild P-19 trainer from a crop duster who had been a fighter pilot. He had many stories to tell, particularly as he practiced aerobatics. A favorite was one of doing triple loops and having the plane stall at the top of the third loop, pumping the fuel pump feverishly as he lost elevation, to have it restart just as he was preparing to bail out. Another way of a trick he played on his friend Harley McFarland. Approaching as if to land he inverted the plane and flew over the runway upside down. Much to his chagrin, when he looked at the back cockpit with a big smile on his face, Harley was nowhere to be seen. After circling and looking at the ground Harley crawled back into his seat from the floor of the plane where he had slipped and held on for dear life. There are others taking off in the cleared snow in the taxiway with the runway closed, landing on one wheel. He also flew a Piper and a Cessna 180 which weren't as much fun. He was working on a commercial license when there was a change of priorities with my arrival, and not long after my brothers. He never lost his love of flying. When I was in my 60, I arranged a ride in a glider, which he thoroughly enjoyed.

The Claude Charles Hadley and Blanche May Ford Hadley Family (Howard's brothers and sisters)

HOWARD HADLEY SIBLINGS

Ernest Leon Hadley (1915-2011)

Born: January 30, 1915 (in South Dakota)

Married: June 11, 1944 (Hellen (Nell) Donald Fuller (February 25, 1901- 2002) Helen died at age 101 1/2)

Died: February 10, 2011 (Kittitas Valley Community Hospital after a short illness)

Children: Ruth Ann Fuller Epperson (November 19, 1924-stepdaughter); Earl Donald Fuller (November 21, 1927-stepson: Donna Duncan Hadley (July 1, 1944)

In 1937 Ernest came to Washington from South Dakota, bringing his mother and eight of his siblings to join his father and two brothers. He was the tallest of the Hadley boys, about 6' 2". One of his greatest pleasures was ushering at the Ellensburg Rodeo, which he did for a great many years. He became a member of the IOOF lodge and he and his wife were also members of the Good Sam's Club and enjoyed their outings. Ernie spent many relaxing hours playing cards with the friends he met throughout the years.

He was preceded in death by his wife, Helen (Nell) Hadley, three sisters and two brothers. Survivors include his daughter Donna Duncan of Ellensburg; stepdaughter Ruth Anne Epperson of Tracy, Calif.; stepson Don Fuller of Ellensburg; six grandchildren; seven great grandchildren and one great-great-granddaughter. He is also survived by three sisters; Irene Hadley Miller of the Dalles, Ore., Lois Hadley Sims of Modesto, Calif., Joyce Hadley Frederickson of Ellensburg and two brothers; Howard Hadley of Yakima and Gerald (Jerry) Hadley of Kennewick.

JEH comments: [Ernest and Nell's home on Sampson Street in Ellensburg had a creek running through one corner, with a bridge across it. On the other side there was a house where Nell's parents lived and also a garage where Ernest had his upholstery shop. Their house had originally been two stories but with my father's help (and presumably that of other family members) the top floor was removed and a thorough remodel done with the addition of a bath and kitchen on the side facing the stream. There was always a small vegetable garden and a good crop of ripe raspberries when we visited. Nell was a wonderful, vivacious person. She was petite (most probably less than five feet) and always kept her hair dark. She was Scottish and had bagpipes playing at her 100th birthday party and at her funeral service at the cemetery.

Ernest bought several inexpensive houses in Ellensburg that he maintained as rentals, many for college students. He was handy at keeping them fixed up himself, which came to provide a good income. At one time he was able to purchase a greyhound sized motorhome that was quite luxurious. He and Nell were among the relatives who didn't smoke cigarettes (most Hadley's did). He was tall and bald in later years with the prominent "Hadley" nose.]

Mildred Ellen Clement Moore Hadley (1917-2007)

Born: May 2, 1916 (Java, SD)

Married: 1936 (Carl Clement); Jan. 31, 1977 (Fred Moore)

Died: January 18, 2007

Children: Leilani Freya Clement (Nov. 29, 1937)

Mildred was born in Java, SD, on May 3, 1916 to Claude and Blanche Hadley, the second of 11 children. In 1936 she married Carl Clement and they moved to Honolulu where Carl went to work for Pearl harbor. In 1937 their daughter, Leilani was born. After Pearl Harbor was bombed in 1941, Mildred and Leilani were shipped back to the mainland where they lived with Mildred's parents in Washington. When Carl was offered a job in the San Francisco Shipyards, the family moved to San Francisco. In 1948 they moved to Millbrae California. She recalled watching the Japanese bombing Pearl Harbor from her home. Mildred lived in Millbrae until 2000, when she moved to Citrus Heights, CA.

Mildred was very active in many facets of the San Bruno United Methodist churches, including mentoring youth as they studied to join the church. In Citrus Heights she joined the Pathway Fellowship Church.

As an active member of the Order of the Eastern Star chapter in San Bruno, Mildred was Deputy Grand Matron in 1968.

Always busy with something, Mildred was known for her flowers and gardening.

Mildred is survived by three brothers and sisters, her daughter, Leilani Marshall, grandchildren Michael Marshall and Teresa Martin, and great-grandchildren Madison Martin, Justin, Stephanie, and Melanie Marshall.

Wesley Clinton Hadley (1921-2003)

Born: March 25, 1921 (Java, South Dakota)

Married: March 1, 1946 (Georgia Benson Lacy); Teresa

Died: September 26, 2003 (Okanogan, Washington)

Children: Claudeia Hadley (March 21, 1947); Susan Hadley (Sept. 23, 1948); Charlene Hadley (Feb. 4, 1953); and Sharon Hadley (Jan. 19, 1955)

Wesley Clinton Hadley

Wesley "Wes" Clinton Hadley 82, died Sept. 26, 2003; at his home in Okanogan. He was born March 25, 1921, in Java, S.D.; the son of Claude and Blanche Hadley. A retired cowboy and carpenter, Wes was a veteran of World War having served in the U.S. Army and Air Force from 1942 to 1945. He served as an airplane mechanic and was recognized for his ability to tune aircraft engines. Wes grew up in Java, SD, and later moved to South King County and to the Okanogan area. He was a member of the Eagles Lodge, enjoyed playing pool and loved horses. He was the founder of the K-M Saddle Club in 1990 and was inducted into the Appaloosa Hall of Fame in 1990.

Wes was preceded in death by his parents; sister, Helen Prien of Ellensburg; and brother, Dale Hadley of Gresham, Ore: He is survived' bf his wife, Teresa Hadley of Okanogan; children: Claudeia Newell of Cap Coral, FL Sue Walt of Chehalis, Charlene Schaaf of Kent and Sharon Duncan of Battle Ground; brothers, Ernest Hadely of Ellensburg, Howard Hadley of Seattle and Gerald Hadley of Ellensburg; sisters, Mildred Moore of Milbrae, CA,

Irene Miller of Ellensburg, Hazel Roadhouse of Auburn, Lois Sims of Santa Cruz, CA, and Joyce Frederickson of Ellensburg; special friend, Fred Prien of Ellensburg; 15 grandchildren; 12 great-grandchildren; and many longtime friends.

Gerald (Jerry) Earl Hadley (1922-2011) Cowboy and Rancher

<u>Born</u>: September 7, 1922 (Java, SD)

<u>Married</u>: before 1945 (Chloe Nunnelly); Louise

<u>Died</u>: June 21, 2011

<u>Children</u>: Geraldine Hadley (March 26, 1949); Glenn Hadley (July 24, 1951).

Wesley and Jerry

The good Lord opened heavens gates and welcomed a great cowboy home on June 21, 2011. Jerry Hadley, who was born on Sept. 7, 1922, is in that beautiful arena above watching over his family and friends that l' he so dearly loved.

Now he can ride and V rope all day long and enjoy his family who preceded him in passing. Hadley was such a good-natured cowboy and a very skilled horseman. One of the friendliest guys you could ever meet and one of the toughest to beat.

Jerry, with his parents and 10 siblings, immigrated to the Kittitas Valley in 1937 from Glenham, SD, when he was a young boy. Jerry and horses were a good fit. Early in life he was breaking and riding wild horses for Bill Heaverlo, who would sell them to the U.S. Army. This love for horses became his lifetime work. On the way along his life's journey, Jerry became a World War Il veteran. He joined the Navy in 1943 and saw duty in the South Pacific and Alaska as a gunner on a destroyer. He was honorably discharged in 1946.

Jerry did a lot of different things during his life. He shod horses, ranched, worked on ranches in the Kittitas Valley, bought and sold several ranches, managed a feedlot near Quincy for a while, ran wild horses, and broke lots of horses for folks so they could ride those horses. Jerry liked problem horses and made good horses out of them. $1 would get a good horse broke so someone else could handle him and then sell him and start another. He rodeoed when he was Younger with guys like Jim Gurke, George Gates, Keith Weeks, Howard Sachs, Buck and Mike Biram, Larry Wyatt, Buck Minor, Frank Wallace, and Chet Morrison. He entered the cowboy horse races, steer wrestling, wild bronc riding, roping events, and the wild horse race which he won a go-round at the Ellensburg Rodeo when he was in his early 50s.

Jerry had a couple of horses that he was proud of— one named Wide Country and the. other Tradewinds. These were horses Jerry rode and used, but they wouldn't quit bucking. Both of these horses became RCA bucking horses, and Tradewinds was the bucking horse of the year five years in a row. Jerry was always proud because he could ride those horses. As a young man, Jerry would get to the various smokers (boxing matches) that were in his area. Throughout his life he liked to attend dances and more often than not he would dance every dance with most, if not all, of the girls there. When he went out on the town, you would always see him dressed in a fine white shirt with a cowboy hat. Don Harmon and Jerry Hadley made and sewed beautiful Western shirts in the Mill's Saddle and Togs building. Their talent was in such demand and is still missed today.

Jerry caught the thoroughbred racehorse bug and that led him and his wife, Louise, on an adventure racing horses across the U.S. from Washington to Florida. Their loving children, Shelly and Levin, accompanied them throughout this journey. Once again Jerry had the opportunity to use his horse skills by buying horses he could fix and get to the point someone would claim (buy) them. He was also licensed to shoe on the track and several times corrected a horse that couldn't win until he was shod right. Jerry was a renowned farrier from the time he was a young man and definitely helped pay the bills with his trade. Jerry and a 14-year-old kid met back in the middle 50s when Jerry was shoeing his horse. They seemed to fit each other and get along and as that kid grew up, he would help Jerry on his ranch and Jerry would help him when he finally got a ranch. For more than 50 years Jerry Hadley and Paul Weaver would remain close friends. Their bond was so very special.

Wonderful sidekicks of Hadley's were Ed Tucker and Roy Doak. Together these fellows shared many stories, enjoyed good times, and truly loved one another. They were definitely the three amigos. Jerry spent many years cowboying with Buck Minor for ranchers in the valley and will never be forgotten for his hard work and dedication to being a true cowboy. He was so tough and had no fear of any bull or bronc. The bigger the challenge, the better for Hadley. For many years, Jerry helped Buck Minor and Frank Wallace run the cattle through for the Ellensburg Rodeo. They would be up before dawn sorting, penning, and making sure that the performance would go on without a hitch. In later years, Hadley was happy being a member of the KCRC. The competition between friends was Jerry's favorite reason as well as the beautiful buckles he won and treasured. He entered the breakaway roping and team roping and loved going to the jackpots with Shelly and his buddies.

Everyone at the roping's so enjoyed his company. Hadley always had a smile and a twinkle in his eye whether he won money or got to donate to the other ropers. Until he could no longer ride, Jerry roped at the Luke Mezich Memorial Roping held each Father's Day weekend to benefit children in medical crisis. Hadley's heart was golden for others as well as his own grandkids, whom he lovingly called rug rats. Jerry was a generous man and material things didn't mean a lot to him. He would loan you anything he had, sell or trade it to you, or maybe just give it to you. He was a great craftsman with leather, wood, nylon rope, or metal and had the ability to fix most things. Baskets, reins, and leather things were his specialty. As Jerry grew older his pride and joy were his wares. He loved peddling them to friends and strangers alike. Because Jerry was so well thought of, many fine animals acquired Hadley's namesake. Jerry is survived by Louise, his wife of 35 years; and his children; Geraldine and her daughter, Andrea, Glen (Geri) Hadley; Shelly (Earl) Voshall; and Devin (Kelly) DeKoning. Proud grandchildren include Sarah and Brayton DeKoning, Justin and Jake Voshall, and Leonie Hadley. Numerous nieces and nephews so loved him, too! His dear niece, Donna Duncan, was with him until the end. As Jerry was an icon in the valley, there are hundreds of friends who will cherish his memory. Now that your earthly walk is over, Hadley, may you always rest in fields of clover. May you never bust a cinch, may you never sell your saddle, may your new boots never pinch, and may you always enjoy chasing horses and cattle. Adios Hadley, you will be missed dearly. Thanks for the great memories and for being a wonderful friend to young and old alike. You taught us many lessons in life. Now ride, cowboy, ride!!!

Irene May Hadley Miller (1924-2018)

Born: December 26, 1924 (Java, SD)

Married: February 15, 1942 (Verdon Miller)

Died: January 9, 2018

Children: Kenneth Verdon Miller (April 6, 1943); David Lee Miller (May 22, 1944); Rebecca Irene Miller (November 24, 1950).

She was a fun-loving lady. She and her husband, Verdan Miller sold their farm in Culver, OR and followed both of his sons and son-in-law in studying to become a chiropractor. He ended up being a Naturalpath in Caldwell, ID, where Irene was his X-ray technician.

Helen Marie Hadley Prien (1926-2002)

<u>Born</u>: April 16, 1926 (Java, SD)

<u>Married</u>: Fred Prien

<u>Died</u>: July 20, 2002 (Ellensburg, Washington)

<u>Children</u>: Judith Prien (January 30, 1948); Thomas Prien (July 27, 1949); and Debra Prien (December 10, 1954).

Helen Marie (Hadley) Prien, 76, died July 20, 2002, in her home of 45 years in Ellensburg.

She was born April 16, 1926, in Java, SD, to Blanche Mae and Claude Clark Hadley, the seventh of Il's children. In 1937, at the age of 10, Helen, her mother, and six of her brothers and sisters came to Washington to follow their father and three brothers who had come west to find work. They were reunited in Kittitas, where they lived for seven years, and then moved to Ellensburg. Helen completed her senior year at Ellensburg High School and graduated in 1944.

She married Fred W. Prien on June 26, 1945 whom she had met when her brother, Wesley, brought Fred home on leave to meet his sisters. Living in Ellensburg all their married life, Fred and Helen raised three children and celebrated 57 years of marriage.

Helen dedicated her life to staying home doing what she loved, which was taking care of her children, husband and home. Living in the same town with her parents, there was always a lot of family around either visiting or moving in and out of town. Helen was a favorite aunt to many of her nieces and nephews and kept close to them as adults.

Helen worked at Sigmand Grocery for a short time and was active in the Carpenters Auxiliary and Degree of Honor and had attended church at Kittitas Community Church and First Baptist Church in Ellensburg.

Helen was preceded in death by her father in 1967, her mother in 1985 and a niece, Peggy Alberts, in 1980.

She is survived by her three children, Judy Prien Calvert of Ellensburg, passed away October 5, 2020; Tom (Susan) Prien of King George, VA and Debbie (Prien) Brown from Roseburg, OR; five grandchildren, Brian (Liza) Calvert of Mount Vernon, Travis (Jessica) Prien and Angela (Declan) Hickey of Virginia, and Kiel and Lindsay Brown of Roseburg, OR. She had two great-grandchildren and two more on the way. She is also survived by her 10 brothers and sisters: Ernest (Nell) Hadley of Ellensburg, Mildred Moore of Citrus Heights, CA, Howard (Becky) Hadley of Seattle, WA, Wesley (Teresa) Hadley of Omak, Gerald (Louise) Hadley of Ellensburg, Irene Miller of Ellensburg, Hazel Burwell of Auburn, Dale (Jackie) Hadley of Gresham, OR, Lois (Vern) Sims of Modesto, CA and Joyce Frederickson of Ellensburg; as well as 27 nieces and nephews.

<u>Children</u>: Jerry Lee Burwell (April 19, 1945); Peggy Ann Burwell (January 24, 1947); Dan Burwell (November 4, 1947).

Hazel L. Burwell-Roadhouse of Auburn died at the age of 78 on June 2, 2006 in Seattle. Hazel was born on January 18, 1928 in Java, South Dakota. She moved to Kittitas County in 1937 where she married Robert Burwell on November 3, 1941. She moved to Auburn in 1953 where she raised her 3 children and later helped run a ceramic shop for many years with her husband. Hazel was preceded in death by her daughter, Peggy, and her husband

Robert. She remarried on September 7, 2002, to Max Roadhouse, Auburn, with whom she spent the last years of her life.

Hazel was also a member of the Auburn Chapter of TOPS. Hazel is survived by her husband, Max Roadhouses sons,' Jerry Burwell of Whittier, CA, and Dan Burwell of Tacoma, WA, seven of her ten siblings, three brothers and four sisters, eight grandchildren, and eight great-grandchildren.

Dale Berton Hadley (1929-2002)

Born: November 6, 1929 (Java, SD)

Married: January 1957 (Jackie Fleming)

Died: October 21, 2002

Children: Shannon Belle Hadley (September 4, 1957); and Dalene May Hadley (May 15, 1963).

Lois Ann Hadley Sims (1932-20)

Born: July 4, 1932 (Java SD)

Married: May 18, 1949 (Vern Sims)

Died:

Children: Linda Sims (September 26, 1949); Richard Sims (June 1951); Eddie Sims (1956);

Ronnie Sims (October 26, 1958); Phillip Sims (December 21, 1962); and Kathy Sims (April 17, 1954 [1964?]).

Joyce Faye Hadley Frederickson (1935-2023)

Born: February 20, 1935

Married: October 2, 1954 (Larry Frederickson)

Died: February 5, 2023

Children: Steven Lee Frederickson (March 29, 1955); Rick Alan Frederickson (June 10,

1956); Scot Dale Frederickson (March 17, 1958); and Laurie Jean Frederickson (November 20, 1960).

Joyce worked as an office manager and bookkeeper for Malmo's Nursery and R. David Adams Landscape. She loved crafts, gardening and scrapbooks. She was the keeper of many Hadley family history matters.

Grandchildren of Claude and Blanche May Hadley

FORD

The surname Ford is of Anglo-Saxon origins and is one of the earliest topographical surnames in existence. It derives from the Olde English pre 7th Century "ford", a shallow place in a river where men and animals could wade across. It was used as a topographic name for someone who lived near a ford.

In their book "Ford" by Lester Ford and Clara N. Ford of Dixon, Ohio they acknowledge that no independent research was done with respect to lineage prior to John Jacob Ford (1850-1933), although they state that his father's name was Henry, that he had a brother named Henry and that they were English. It also states that Jacob (1850) was illiterate and provides no documentation on his ancestors. I had originally thought that the father was Henry Ford (1812-) but in searching for lineage for this Henry ran largely into dead ends. Subsequently, I was able to locate the McDonald (Macdessi) family tree among others, which listed the father of Jacob 1850 as being Henry Ford (1630-1920), included a brother Henry, and although in all probability being "from England", revealed roots back to 1661 in America. I have relied on those databases to create the following information.

JOHN FORD (1661-1714) Virginia Company Roots – Son of Indentured Servant?

<u>Born</u>: 1661 (York River Valley, Lancaster, Virginia Colony)

<u>Married</u>: 1681 (Elizabeth Newton (1663-1718) in Lancaster, Virginia

<u>Died</u>: 1714 (Richmond, Wise, Virginia Colony)

<u>Parents</u>: unknown

<u>Children</u>: **John William Ford** (1683-1756); and Samuel Ford

Given that all of Ford roots discovered thus far are in the Virginia area as early as 1661 I believe the parents of John Ford came to Virginia in the 1630-1640 timeframe (or possibly earlier) to serve as indentured servants for the Virginia Company. There was also a family member on the Smead line who came to Massachusetts as an indentured servant in about the same time frame.

Virginia Company refers collectively to two joint-stock companies chartered under James 1 on April 16, 1606, with the goal of establishing settlements on the coast of North America (one for what is now New England and the second further south in Virginia. The original settlement in New England was abandoned but the one in Virginia at Jamestown established some hard-fought roots.

Virginia was the first part of the country permanently settled by the English, who established Jamestown on the banks of the James River in 1607. The colony then incorporated an area which includes parts of the current states of West Virginia, Tennessee, Kentucky, the Carolinas in addition to Virginia. Virginia also claimed until 1784 a large wilderness area including present-day Michigan, Wisconsin, Illinois, Indiana, and Ohio.

The Virginia Company failed in 1624, but the right to self-government in its charter was not taken away from the colony. The Generall Historie is a book written by Captain John Smith, first published in 1624. The Generall Historie states that in May 1607 the colonists reached Virginia and founded the Jamestown Colony at the mouth of the James River. From late 1609 to May 10, over 80% of the colonists perished, largely due to famine during the harsh winter of 1609 when they were forced to eat leather from their clothes and boots, and in some cases, resort to cannibalism. There was an Indian Massacre in 1622 killing hundreds of settlers. The colony nearly failed until tobacco emerged as a profitable export. It was chiefly grown on plantations using primarily indentured servants for the intensive hand labor involved. After 12 years of peace following the Indian Wars of 1622-1632 another Anglo-Powhatan War began on March 18, 1664 during which 500 colonists were killed. During this time Forts were established inland permitting settlers to establish homes in the York River Valley near the York River where John Ford (1661-1714) was born. After 1662, the colony turned to black slavery, which by 1750 was the primary cultivator of the cash tobacco crop.

Most immigrants were indentured servants, artisans and some merchants. The indentured servants included both men and women who signed a contract by which they agreed to work for a certain number of years in exchange for transportation to Virginia and once they arrived, food clothing and shelter. Adults usually serve for four to seven years, and children sometimes for much longer. Most worked in the colony's tobacco fields. With a long history in England, indentured servitude became, during most of the seventeenth century, the primary means by which Virginia planters filled their nearly inexhaustible need for labor. At first the Virginia Company of London paid to transport servants across the Atlantic, but with the institution of the headright system in 1618, the company enticed planters and merchants to incur the cost with the promise of land. As a result, servants flooded the colony, where they were greeted by deadly diseases and often harsh conditions and left the rest to the mercy of sometimes cruel masters. The General Assembly passed laws regulating contract terms as well as the behavior and treatment of servants. By the end of the seventeenth century, the number of new servants dwindled with the colony's labor needs met largely by enclaved Americans.

Servitude had a long history in England, dating back to medieval serfdom. The Ordinance of Labourers, passed in 1349, declared that all men and women who did not practice a craft must serve anyone requiring their labor. An updated version in 1563, the Statute of Artificers, was still in effect when the English founded Jamestown. Between 1520 and 1630, England's population more than doubled. The updated Statute of Artificers was intended to banish idleness to deal with the near overwhelming number of poor and unemployed persons. In fact, the founding of Virginia was partially in response to this problem. It was argued in 1584 by Richard Hakluyt (the younger) to Queen Elizabeth that the American colonies could energize England's "decaying trades" and provide work for the country's "multitudes of loyteres and idle vagabonds."

Indentured servitude temporarily transformed free men and women into chattel, or property to be bought and sold.

Servants received nothing in addition to food, clothing and shelter and were almost entirely at the mercy of their masters. The Great Charter of 1618 awarded 100 acres of land to planters who had been in the colony since May 1616, and 50 acres each to anyone who covered the cost of transporting a new immigrant to Virginia.

Approximately 50,000 indentured servants, or three quarters of new arrivals, immigrated to the Chesapeake Bay colonies between 1630 and 1680. As indentured servants poured into Virginia, they came to account for fully half of Virginia's population.

Most white settlers would raise their families on subsistence farms. This was likely the case for John Ford born and married in Lancaster, to the north of the York River. He seems to have moved in 1682-83 to Northern Neck to the southeast of Lancaster where his son John Ford (1683-1746) was born. He died at age 53 in Richmond, on the other side of the York River to the east.

The Virginia Colony became the wealthiest and most populous British Colony in North America. The colony was dominated by rich planters who had a major role in gaining independence and in the development of Democratic-Republican ideals of the United States, but there were many poor former indentured servants trying to scratch out a living.

JOHN WILLIAM FORD (1683-1756)

Born: 1683 (North Neck, Rappahannock, Virginia Colony)

Married: 1702 (Elizabeth Thornton (1682-1740) in Richmond, Rapahannock, Virginia with alternates given as King George County Virginia and St Paul's Parish, Stafford, Virginia); and June 27, 1745 (Thankful Rowlandson in Middletown, Connecticut)

Died: March 8, 1756 (Richmond, Wise, Virginia)

Parents: John Ford (1661-1714) and Elizabeth Newton Ford (1663-1718)

<u>Children</u>: **Thomas Ford** (1704-1776); William Ford (1704-1783); Patience Ford (1717-1780); Jane Ford (1728-1804); Mary Ford (1731-1804); and John Ford (1735-)

Northern Neck lies across the York River to the North of historic Williamsburg, Virginia, which in turn is a short distance north of Jamestown. Both Jamestown and Williamsburg lie between the York and James Rivers. Upstream and a little to the south lies Richmond, Virginia.

Living nearby in Christ Church Parish, Middlesex, Virginia and later Spotsylvania, Spotsylvania, Virginia (near Fredericksburg, Virginia) was Henry Goodloe (1675-1748). Although outside the scope of this endeavor additional research could show that a member of the Ford family and the Goodloe family line were related. Henry Goodloe was a property owner and the Goodloe Plantation home is still standing in Spotsylvania County. There was also a Robert Goodloe Harper (1765-1825) born near Fredericksburg, Spotsylvania County who appears through his birthplace and middle name to be related to the Goodloe line. Robert Harper was in Congress, a Major General during the War of 1812 and ran for Vice President of the United States. Louisa County borders Spotsylvania County. It was there that John Barbie Minor (1813-1895) was born. He was also a plantation owner, a lawyer and then an esteemed professor of law for fifty years at the University of Virginia in Charlottesville. The building housing the law school was named after him. I believe these are the parties my cousin Tom Prien was alluding to in an email. Unfortunately, he is suffering from Parkinson's and is unable to assist further with this effort.

Please note that John Ford is noted as last living in Wise, Virginia, which was on the frontier at that time near present day Kentucky subject to Indian hostilities and not secure.

THOMAS FORD (1704-1776)

<u>Born</u>: 1704 (Cople Parish, Westmoreland County, Virginia)

<u>Married</u>: 1724 (Jane Ford (1705-1776) in Charles, Maryland)

<u>Died</u>: December 16, 1776 (Popes Creek, Fairfax, Virginia)

<u>Parents</u>: John William Ford (1683-1756) and Elizabeth Thornton (1682-1740)

<u>Children</u>: Jane Ford (1722-1804); Elizabeth Ford (1723-1776); Sarah Ford (1727-1776); **John A Ford** (1728-1803); Ann Ford (1729-1776); Catherine Ford (1732-1768); Ann Ford (1735-1803); Edward Ford (1738-1814); Priscilla Ford (1740-1805); and Esther Ford (17551816)

Cople Parish, Westmoreland, is on the Virginia side of the Potomac, on North Neck in the general vicinity of where Thomas Ford (1704-1776) and his father, John Ford (1684-1756), had lived.

At age 66 Thomas Ford (1704-1776) in 1770 Rent Rolls shows residence at Fairfax County, Virginia. Note that Thomas Ford (1704-1776), along with his daughters Ann, Sarah, and Elizabeth, all died in 1776. Although the Revolutionary War was underway then there were only a few skirmishes in Fairfax County.

Note that Fairfax County was formed in 1742 from the northern part of Prince William County. It was named after Thomas Fairfax, 6th Lord Fairfax of Cameron (1693-1781), proprietor of the Northern Neck, where Thomas Ford had moved from. The community was formed primarily from farmers moving from the North Neck area as Thomas Ford did, and by others moving from Maryland.

In 1649, the future English King Charles II was driven into exile in Europe by the English Civil War and beheaded by his father, Charles I. While in exile, he granted to seven of his loyal supporters all the land between the Potomac and the Rappahannock Rivers in Virginia as a proprietary. By 1690 this land had come under the control of the Fairfax family. Thomas, sixth Lord Fairfax came to Virginia in 1737, installed his cousin William Fairfax as his land agent and returned to England to defend his right to the land by proprietary. By 1745, the English Privy Council had confirmed to Lord Fairfax the full extent of his proprietary, some 5,282,000 acres.

It was William Fairfax who built the great Belvoir mansion (on the land that is now the U.S. Army's Fort Belvoir where I attended Engineering Officer Candidate school) in 1741. The following year William arranged to have Fairfax County created from the norther part of what are now Loudoun and Arlington counties, and the cities of Alexandria, Falls Church and Fairfax. Note that James Collett (1788-1864) in our Collett line lived in Leesburg, Loudoun County.

Eighteenth century Fairfax was an agricultural society based on the labor of black slaves which had grown from 28 percent of the population in 1741 to 41 percent in 1782.

In 1748 George Washington, then only sixteen years old, came to live with his half-brother Lawrence at Mount Vernon on the Potomac River. After his brother's death in 1752, George rented and later acquired the estate, which by the time of his death in 1799 increased to 8000 acres and held 300 slaves. Nearby lived George Mason who also owned much land and many slaves. Mason was a delegate to the Constitutional Convention and worked with James Madison to add amendments which became the Bill of Rights.

By 1790 the population of Fairfax was over 12,000 about 42 percent of which were slaves. The following year the Virginia General Assembly ceded a portion of Fairfax County to the federal government in order to create the District of Columbia. Originally laid out as a perfect square ten miles to a side, the capital developed almost entirely on the Maryland side of the river, with the land on the south side returned to Virginia in 1847, which became Arlington County and a part of the City of Alexandria.

Northern Quakers (which would have included Colletts) purchased over two thousand acres near Mount Vernon, cutting the white oak forest on the land for lumber to sell to northern ship builders, and worked to show farms could be operated profitably with free white labor, rather than black slave labor.

JOHN A. FORD (1728-1803) Among first Settlers in Fairfax County-home of George Washington

Born: 1728 (Fairfax, Virginia)

Married: 1745 (Rachel Spenser (1725-1770) at Fairfax, Virginia); 1758 (Eleanor Percy (1740-1786) Fairfax, Fairfax County, Virginia); 1771 (Ann Ford (1752-1826); 1766? (Catherine Elizabeth Cheatham (1750-1803)

Died: April 13, 1803 (Newberry, Newberry, South Carolina

Parents: Thomas Ford (1704-1776) and Jane Ford (1705-1776)

Children: Simeon Ford (1742-1833); (1745-1834); Rachel B Spenser (1745-1800); **John Ford** (1745-1834); Jennie "Linney" Ford (1750-1825); Phillip Ford (1750-1785); William Ford (1753-1835); Elizabeth Ford (1755-

1831); Elisha Ford (1757-1833); Spencer Ford (1759-1850); Samuel Ford (1761-1832); Jesse Spencer Ford (1770-1843); Jane Ford (1770-1817); Margaret Verlinda Ford (1778-1821); and Nathaniel Ford.

[The names of children and their birthdates vary among the third-party family trees, although the total number of children appears to be fourteen, with eleven born by Rachel Spencer, two by Eleanor Perry, and one by Ann Ford.]

Children were born primarily in Virginia between 1704 and 1770 (Hanover, Goochland; Fairfax; and Spotsylvania, Wilkes) however son Phillip was born in Craven, South, Carolina in 1750 and then in 1759 son Spensor in South Carolina, and in 1761 son Samuel in Newberry, South Carolina. In 1770 daughter Jane Ford was born in Spartanburg, South Carolina along with daughter Margaret Verlinda in 1778. From the foregoing it appears the family may have moved from Virginia to South Carolina in about 1770, although maintaining visits with extended family members including John Ford's siblings and parents who remained in Virginia. One explanation of the diverse birth places for some of their children during this time frame could be to have family assistance with births.

After 1800, the soil in Fairfax County was exhausted and unfertile from overplanting with tobacco, with many planters and families leaving for new land in the south or west. This may have been a contributing factor to the move of John A Ford (1728-1803) from Fairfax to South Carolina.

It appears that at least one son served in the Revolutionary War.

JOHN FORD JR. (1745-1834) Moves from Fairfax County Virginia, to SC to KY

Born: 1745 (Fairfax, Virginia)

Married: 1775 or abt 1785 (Mary Connell (1745-1839) in Newberry, South Carolina; [likely others given number and birthdates of children]

Died: December 26, 1834 (Shelby Creek, Pike, KY)

Parents: John A Ford (1728-1803) and Rachel Spencer (1725-1790)

Children: Mary Rebecca Ford (1771-1838); John Ford III (1773-1860); Samuel Ford (1812 Casualty); Nancy Ford 1776-1850); James B Ford (1778-1854); Minor Ford (1778-1830); Mary Ford (1779-); Elisha Ford (1780-1812); Charlotte Ford (1786-1864); John Ford (1787-1871); Charlotte Ford (1788-1864); William Ford M.D. (1793-1860); Mary Ford (1793-1851); Richard Spencer Ford (1795-1859); **John Covington Ford** (1800-1849); Sarah Elender Ford (1800-1876); Matilda Ford (1809-); and Arena Sarena Ford (1813-1893).

Eighteen children were born when Mary Connell (1745-1839) was 68, which seems improbable.

Folklore has John Ford, Jr. or one of his relatives accompanying Daniel Boone (1734-1820) in his blazing "Boone's Trace" later known as the Wilderness Road through the Cumberland Gap and into Kentucky in May of 1769. Daniel Boone along with Davy Crockett were perhaps the most famous frontiersmen of that time. Kentucky was wilderness on the western edge of the Virginia Colony, an Indian hunting ground with the Appalachian Mountains serving as a barrier to settlement in that region. By the end of the 18th century, more than 200,000 people had entered Kentucky by the route marked by Boone. Although we don't know precisely when John Ford, Jr. and his family moved to Kentucky it was likely sometime in 1793 when his daughter Mary Ford was born there and subsequently additional of his children. This would have made the family among the earliest settlers in Kentucky.

One of John Ford's (1745-1834) sons, Samuel Ford (1775-1812), was a casualty of the War of 1812. His sister Elisha Ford (1780-1812) died that same year. Although the war is sometimes referred to as a minor theater of the Napoleonic Wars by historians in the United Kingdom, it was a significant war for America as among other things it resulted in damage to the United States capital, the burning of Washington, an estimated15,000 dying on the US side as a result of the war and 10,000 on the British Empire side, and hundreds of vessels on each side captured.

From the American perspective, the major cause of the war was the kidnapping of American citizens to man the Royal Navy, a practice known as impressment. Richard Headley, as described in the Hadley section of this text, may have been so impressed. Between 1793 and 1812, the British abducted more than 15,000 American citizens and forced them to help fight their ongoing wars (with Napoleon) on the European continent. Additionally, the Royal Navy enforced a naval blockade to choke off neutral trade to France, which the United States contested as illegal under international law. Also, the United Kingdom supplied arms to Native Americans, who raided European American settlers on the American frontier, hindering the expansion of the United States and provoking resentment.

With most of its army in Europe fighting Napoleon, the United Kingdom adopted a national siege strategy, focusing on blockading ports and containing the US at its borders. There were significant battles in Canada including the burning of Toronto and failed attempts to capture Montreal. In 1814 the British burned Washington including the White House and the Capital but British attempts to invade New York and Maryland were repulsed. The war ended in 1815 after a peace treaty was signed, but before this news reached the Americas, United States forces heavily defeated the British Army near New Orleans, Louisiana. The war catapulted General Andrew Jackson to national celebrity, culminating in his election as President in 1828.

Son William Ford (1793-1851) became a medical doctor, the only one noted in the family.

Note that brother John Ford (1750-1782) was living in Shelby Creek, Pike, Kentucky, where John Ford Jr (1745-1834) passed.

JOHN COVINGTON FORD (1800-1849)

Born: 1800 (Hart, Shelby County, Kentucky)

Married: Polly Corlett (1790-1848)

Died: 1849 (Salem, Livingston, Kentucky)

Parents: John Ford (1745-1834) and Mary Connell (1745-1839)

Children: Birth of son **Henry Ford** (1830-1920) occurred on June 30, 1830 in TN. John Covington Ford's sister Mary Rebecca Ford (1771-1838) died in Chillicothe, Ross County, OH.

HENRY FORD (1830-1920)

Born: June 20, 1830 (Tennessee)

Married: November 28/29, 1853 (Sarah E. "Sally" Jackson (1834-1907) in Williamson, TN)

Died: March 29, 1920 (Williamson, TN)

Parents: John Covington Ford (1800-1849) and Polly Corlett (1790-1848)

Children: **John Jacob Ford** (1850-1933); Martha Emma Ford (1855-1907); Rebecca Ford (1856-1928); Mary E Foard/Ford (1859-1865); Henry Buell Ford (1862-1933); John P Ford (1865-1949); James Jullies Ford (1867-1931); Amanda (Mandy) Ford (1869-1952); Samuel Marshall Ford (1870-1949); Robert Ford (1873-1875); William Gillin Ford Sr. (1874-1964); William W Ford (1877-); Jesse Munro Ford (1877-1913); James "Bailey" Ford (1896-1970); Willie Wade Ford (1899-); James Henry Ford (1902-); Denny Fulton Ford (1904-1925); and Kate Pauline Ford (1909-)

Eighteen children were born when Polly Corlett (1834-1907) would have been 56. Note that daughter Kate Pauline's listed birthdate is 1909, two years before the date of death given for her mother.

Although son John Jacob Ford's birthplace is given as Ashtabula County, Ohio on August 20, 1850, this was two years prior to Henry Ford (1830-1920) and Sarah H Jackson (1834-1907) being married in November 1853 in Williamson, Tennessee. The other Ford children are shown as being born in Tennessee.

Before locating a family tree on Ancestry, I had assumed based on the assertion in the Ford book that Henry was born in England that he was born about 1812 (Bentley, Hampshire, England (from 1871 England Census; another source provides Lincolnshire, England); married Sarah Eliza MNU Ford "Sally" (1827-1900) died USA with children daughter name unknown (born Lincolnshire, England, died 1847, buried at sea crossing to America); Henry Ford (born Lincolnshire, England, died Ashtabula County, OH); and John Ford (born, August 20, 1850, Ashtabula County, OH, died March 29, 1933, Harried SD). Given the number of ancestry resources cited in the family tree I believe what I presented above is the more accurate of the two approaches. In reaching this conclusion I did note however that immigration to the United States had ceased during the Revolutionary War, and before it could resume the Napoleonic Wars effectively prevented travel across the Atlantic. Some immigration occurred during the so-called "Era of Good Feelings which coincided with the administration of James Monroe, but did not become significant until the 1830s. Suddenly in the mid-1840's immigration changed dramatically due in substantial part to the potato blight in Ireland. The period from 1845 to 1849 held the highest immigration since prior to the Revolutionary War.

There was work to be had on the railroads and canals being constructed in the United States at that time.

The connection to other Ford's in Tennessee and Kentucky at the time seemed an aberration, however I was later to learn that Ohio, which was originally part of the western territory claimed by the Virginia Colony. It was not far from the westward reaches of the original Virginia colony which included eastern portions of what is now Kentucky and Tennessee. I also learned that Henry Ford's aunt Mary Rebecca Ford (1771-1838) was living in Ohio, as her death was recorded in Chillicothe, Ross, Ohio.

JOHN JACOB FORD (1850-1933) OH to SD Farming

<u>Born</u>: August 20, 1850 (Ashtabula County, OH)

<u>Married</u>: February 2, 1871 (Abbie Ann Coon Ford (1854-1889); and December 8, 1889 Cora Penrod Ford (1876-1899) at E Elkport, Clayton, OH)

<u>Died</u>: March 26, 1933 (Herreid, SD)

<u>Parents</u>: Henry Ford (1850-1920), Sara E. "Sally" Jackson (1834-1907)

<u>Children</u>: of John Jacob Ford and Abbie Ann Coon Ford

Lillie Perkins Anderson Ford (Aug. 30, 1872 - Feb. 4, 1971; born Ashtabula, OH); Jacob Ford (February 23, 1876-July 4, 1949; born Clayton County, Iowa); and

Eugene James Ford (Feb. 23, 1883-Sept. 27, 1963; born Clayton County, OH).

<u>Children</u>: of John Jacob Ford and Cora Penrod Ford: Peter William Ford (September 27, 1890-January 24, 1977; born Herreid, SD); **May Blanche Ford** (August 22, 1893-born Howard, SD); and Ellen Almira Vandermartin Ford (Apr 29, 1898-Nov 4, 1938; born Minor County SD).

John Jacob Ford

One website shows John Ford's (1850) father being Henry Ford born in Lincolnshire, England, married to his mother Eliza in Lincolnshire, having children: 1. a daughter-name unknown (born Lincolnshire, England died 1847, buried at sea during crossing to America); 2. Henry Ford (born Lincolnshire England, died Ashtubula County, Ohio?); and (3) John Ford (August 20, 1850 Ashtabula County, Ohio- March 29, 1933 Herried, South

Dakota). Arrived in America in 1847 and in Ohio by John's birth on August 20, 1850. Family records confirm the above, i.e. John was born in Ashtabula County, Ohio. His parents, (Henry and Eliza Ford), a brother, Henry, and an older sister who died in route and was buried at sea came to the United States in 1847 from Lincolnshire, England.

Little is known of John's early life; however, schooling was limited as John grew to adulthood without learning to read and write. This was not unusual at that time.

John Ford and Abbie Coon married in Ashtabula, Ohio February 2, 1871 in Ashtabula, Ohio. Abbie was born on 14 August 1954 in Ashtabula, Ohio, the fourth child of Jacob and Juliette (Gardner) Coon. After their daughter Lillie's birth on August 30, 1872, in 1873, they moved to Clayton County, Iowa, to join John's brother Henry and his wife Ellen. There their sons Jacob and Eugene were born. The family then moved to Howard, Dakota Territory in 1883 and subsequently to Herried, SD.

Jacob Ford

(Son of John Jacob Ford and brother of May Blanche Ford who raised Blanche)

John and Abbie homesteaded the Southeast quarter, Section 8, Township 108, North of Range 56, West of the 5th P.M. on 160 acres. John's sister-in-law Ellen had to feed the Indians before feeding her own children while they lived in South Dakota. This was Ellen's way of keeping the Indians friendly. John did not feed the Indians but ran them off his place. Soon after this, John's barn was burned to the ground and it was thought this was the Indians reprisal against John. Abbie died September 18, 1889.

John returned to Clayton County, Iowa and on 8 December 1889 married Cora Penrod, daughter of George and Julia (Darrow) Penrod. Julia Penrod was the sister of Ellen Ford, Henry's wife. From The Elkader Register,

December 12, 1889. "Cora Penrod was married Sunday to a gentleman by the name of Ford, who hails from the state of Dakota. Miss Cora is but 13 years of age, but is one of our most respected young ladies. Her many friends here wish her a joyous voyage through life. Judge Buck performed the ceremony."

Cora and John returned to Howard, Minor County, South Dakota (about 51 miles northwest of Sioux Falls, South Dakota) along with Cora's mother, Julia Penrod and Cora's sister Amy. Cora and John had three children: Peter William, May Blanche and Ellen Almira. Cora died sometime before 1900. John moved his family to Herreid, Campbell County, South Dakota sometime thereafter. Jacob and Amy Ford moved to Herreid at the same time and they took care of John's young children. Herreid was founded as a village on August 26, 1901 so the Ford family would have been among the earliest settlers there. It is located east of the Missouri River near the border with North Dakota, not far from Mobridge, and north of Selby and Java, where the Hadley's were located at that time.

During the winter, John, Jacob, and Eugene cut ice from the spring creek to keep food through the summer months. They filled a large building called an ice house with straw. The straw kept the ice from melting through the summer months. They had a few animals; cows, pigs, horses those first years.

John and Eugene made moonshine and stored it in a 50-gallon drum in a pit, under the well house floor. Wood planks covered the pit and the planks were covered with dirt to make it look like a dirt floor. A rug and a rocking chair finished the cover. When found out, Eugene served the sentence because John was thought to be too old to survive the time in jail. The mash that was brewing in the barn was fed to the pigs! And that afternoon the pigs were drunk and stumbling around and feeling quite happy.

John lived with Eugene's family until his death on 29 March 1933. He is buried in the Herreid cemetery.

BLANCHE MAY FORD (1893-1985) SD to WA

Born: August 22, 1893 Howard, SD

Married: June 29, 1913 (SD, Claude Charles Hadley 1892-1967)

Died: September 16, 1985 Ellensburg, WA

Parents: John Jacob Ford (1858-1933), Cora Penrod Ford

Children: Claude and Blanche May Ford Hadley's eleven children are listed under Claude Hadley (Blanche's was the fourth child of John Jacob Ford (born August 20, 1850 in Ashtubula, Ohio) and the second child of his second wife, Cora Ford (nee Penrod) (born 1876 in Clayton County, Iowa).

Blanche had seven siblings: Peter William Ford (Sep. 29, 1890-Jan. 24, 1977); Ellen Almira Vander Martin Ford (Apr. 29. 1898-Nov. 4, 1938); and from a prior marriage of John Ford to Abbie Ann Ford (nee Coon) (born in Ohio in 1854 who passed away Sep. 18, 1889 at age 35 in South Dakota); Lillie Perkins Anderson Ford (Aug. 30-1873-Feb 4, 1971); Jacob (aka Jake) Ford (Feb 23, 1876-July 3, 1939); Amy Pearl Penrod Ford (May 31, 1881-April 12, 1960); Eugene James Ford (Feb. 23, 1883-Sep.27, 1963); and Emma Rosina Rische Ford (Jan. 23, 1893- Sep. 19, 1957) [Eugene and Emma were noted as twins so one of the given birthdates is wrong. Note also that Amy Pearl Penrod may have been her sister-in-law married to Jacob Ford.]

Blanche, Mother Pearl Penrod Ford and brother Peter

At about age five, due to the death of her mother, Blanche went to live with and was raised by her older sister [sister-in-law] Amy Pearl Penrod Ford and her brother Jacob.

Her life after marriage to Claude Hadley in 1913 is described in part under Howard Hadley (1919). Her brother, Peter Ford (or uncle Pete) had lost an eye. We visited him in West Virginia during a summer family trip in 1953.

Much of Blanche's early married life was consumed by caring for her eleven children and keeping them fed and clothed, not an easy thing.

Her daughter Joyce recalls that Blanche did not like killing chickens by cutting their heads off; instead, she would wring their necks until the head separated from the body. It was a foul smelly process, gutting the bird, boiling it in water to remove the feathers and ultimately canning the meat. Canning was a constant process as canned meats and vegetables fed the family through the winter.

During and after World War II the Hadley household was often a busy place with Howard (army), Wesley (air force), Gerald (navy), Dale (navy) returning home to Ellensburg when possible, bringing along their friends. Ernest was the only son not serving during the war, and then only due to the fact that he had broken an arm that had not healed straight and was rejected for medical reasons. There was always an extra setting and a place for all. This delighted the Hadley girls, with Hazel meeting Bob Burwell and Helen meeting Fred Prien through these visits.

COLLETT

The surname "Collett" is of early medieval sounding guided spelling in essentially preliterate Middle Ages so variations were common, even among literate people. Variations include Collett, Colett, Colet, Collette, Collet, Coullet, Caullet, Cowlett, Cowllett, Colleyt, Coulett, Caulett, Caullett, Collette, Colette, Coll ete and more. It is a diminutive of Col, itself a 13th Century pet form of Nicolaos, from Greek "Nikolaos", a compound of "nikan" (to conquer) and "laos" (people). This name was a favorite among Christians throughout Europe during the Middle Ages, partly due to the fame of the 4th century St. Nicholas. The name was found in England before the conquest of 1066, usually borne by a monk. The form "Collett" contains the diminutive suffix "et(t)" and is recorded (without surname) in the 1202 Assize Court Rolls of Northumberland.

Although we start with Sir John Collett (1432) below research by others leads to speculation taking the family back to Kimble or Wendover to the south of Aylesbury in Buckinghamshire. There was a Henry Colet born circa 1360 the brother of Thomas Colet who was the rector of Little Kimble up to 1408. Sir John Collette inherited a large sum from his father who was reported to be twice Lord Mayor of London. Family lore has our Colletts coming to America and establishing a colony, which may be an overstatement, but it appears to be true in part as one follows the timeline below.

SIR HENRY COLETT

In John Colett's (1442-) background information (some at St. Paul's School) his father is listed as being a wealthy property owner, likely in Slaughter in the Cotswolds, region of central England. He is also listed as twice the mayor of London.

SIR JOHN COLETT (1432-) Renaissance Scholar and Founder of St. Paul's School

Source: Webster's Biographical Dictionary 1960, Springfield, MA

Born: 1432 (Ireland)

Married: abt 1432 (to Lady Elizabeth Maguire (1432-1492) at St James, Duke's Place, London; or Little Gidding, Cambridgeshire, England)

Died: (England, buried Upper Slaughter, Gloucester, England) (one source states interred in St Paul's Cathedral, London)

Parents: Sir Henry Collet (twice Lord Mayor of London)

Children: **Sir William Collett** (1454-1509), born at Over Slaughter, Gloucester, England

English classical scholar and theologian; one of the leaders of the Renaissance in England. M.A. Oxon (cl 1490); studied canon and civil law, patristics [Of, or pertaining to the Fathers of the Christian Church, or their writings. Started in Italy in 14th Century-gradually spread to other countries. Period: 14th through 16th Centuries.] and Greek and Italy (1493-96); met Bude and Erasmus [(1466-1536); Dutch theologian, classical scholar, and humanist. Original name: Geert Geerts or Gerhard Gerhards,]; influenced by the teachings of Savonarola [1452-1498: Italian Dominican Monk; political and religious reformer; burned as a heretic]. Lectured in Oxford (1496-1504) on New Testament, opposing interpretations of scholastic theologians; Dean of St. Paul's (1504-19); preached against sale of bishoprics, custom of pluralities [the holding at the same time of more than one office, or in the Anglican Church, of more than one living], church lawyers; devoted large fortune inherited from his father to founding and endowing (1509-1512) St. Paul's School, first example of non-clerical education; accused of heresy for liberal opinions but protected by Archbishop William Warham; made Cantebury pilgrimage with Erasmus (1514), preached at Wolsey's installation as Cardinal (1515).

Saint Paul's School, London is a selective independent school for boy's aged 13-18, located on a 43 acre sit by the River Thames, in Barnes, London. Established in 1509, ranked (2001) as the leading boy's school in England academically, with one of the highest Oxford and Cambridge acceptance rates of any secondary school or college. Its School Boat Club) has won the Princess Elizabeth Challenge Cup at Henley Royal Regatta six times.

"Sir" is a formal honorific address for men, derived from Sire in the High Middle Ages. Traditionally, as governed by law and custom, Sir is used for men titled knights, i.e., of orders of chivalry, and later for baronets, and other offices. Note that the title of "Sir" is given to anyone awarded knighthood by the Queen or a member of the royal family acting in her stead. Knighthood can be awarded for military service or to anyone deemed a significant contributor to national life.

SIR WILLIAM COLLETT (1454-1509) Over Slaughter, Gloucestershire

Born: 1454 (Over Slaughter, Gloucestershire, England)

Married: abt 1475 (to Lady Sadie O'Malley (1454-1523) Little Gidding, Cambridgeshire, England; Upper Slaughter, Gloucestershire, England)

Died: 1509 (Over Slaughter, Gloucestershire; buried Upper Slaughter, Gloucestershire, England)

Parents: Sir John Collett (1432-) and Lady Elizabeth Maquire (1432-1492)

Children: **Thomas Collett** (1480-1556); Robert Collett (1485-1544)

Born in the village of Over near St. Ives in Cambridgeshire. It is assumed that the family continued to have ties to Ireland as it was Sadie O'Malley from Ireland whom he married. Their son Thomas was born in Over, where William died on 15 9.

THOMAS COLLETT (1480-1556) Manor of Naughton

Born: 1480 (either Over Slaughter, Gloucestershire or Upper Slaughter, Gloucestershire, England)

Married: 1517 (to Alice Thomas (1485-1557) in Gloucestershire, England)

Died: abt 1556 (Over Slaughter or Upper Slaughter, Gloucestershire, England)

Parents: Sir William Collett (1454-1509) and Lady Sadie O'Malley (1454-1523)

Children: William Collett (1518-1587); Sir **Henry (John) Collett** (1520-1592); Elizabeth Collett (1591-); Alice Collett (1522-); Joan Collett (1534-); and Agnes Collett (1527-)

The Manor of Upper Slaughter

The Manor of Naughton

The Collett Saga by Margaret Chadd provides that Thomas Collett (1480-1556) was Joint Lord of the Manor of Over Slaughter with Mr. Venfield and that he was godfather to ten children. The Manor of Upper Slaughter was in the hands of the Slaughter family from the 1200's to the mid -1700s while the Manor of Lower Slaughter was held by Syon Abbey for centuries until the dissolution of the monasteries, when it passed to the Crown which held it until 1611, when it was granted to Sir William Whitmore. It is therefore assumed that

Thomas Collett and Mr. Venfield have been confused with John Collett and Gyles Venfield who were the Joint Lords of the Manor of Naughton in 1608, Naughton being only three miles from Upper Slaughter.

SIR HENRY (JOHN) COLLETT (1520-1592) Yeoman of Over Slaughter/Church Warden

<u>Born</u>: 1520 (Over or Upper Slaughter, Gloucestershire, England)

<u>Married</u>: 1540 (to Joan Hanks (1520-1598); after Joan's death to Edith Arnold (15201597?).

<u>Died</u>: 1592 (Charlton Kings, Gloucestershire, England)

<u>Parents</u>: Thomas Collett (1480-1556) and Alice Thomas (1485-1557)

<u>Children</u>: Listed in his will were: Alice Collett (1541); Elizabeth Collett (1545); Thomas Collett (1547); John Collett (1548); William Collett (1551); Jane Collett (1553); Anthony Collett (1554); and Henry Collett (1556) all born in Over Slaughter.

Henry was a Yeoman of Over Slaughter and Church Warden of the Parish. He is buried in the churchyard of Over Slaughter. Historically, a yeoman is a servant in a royal or noble household, ranking between a sergeant and a groom or a squire and a page. In this context it likely means someone doing good, hard, and valuable work for a cause, in this case the community of Slaughter. A church warden is a lay official in a parish or congregation of the Anglican Communion. They are typically elected by the church parishioners. A warden in this case was legally responsible for all the property and movable goods belonging to the parish church in Slaughter.

His will of August 20, 1591, in the 33rd year of the reign of Queen Elizabeth of England, France, and Ireland, Defender of the Faith, was proved in 1592. It named his eldest son Thomas Collett as sole executer. All of his children were named in the will, except his youngest son, Henry. Thomas Collett, being the eldest son, was allowed to reside in one half of the house occupied by his stepmother, Edith, until her death, at which time it became his property. It stated that Edith would get nothing if she didn't agree to this provision. They will also provide ten pounds and the best bed in the house to wife Edith; ten shillings to the poor of the village; three pounds to each of seven of his eight children; and a plough and a pair of harrows to his son Anthony.

When first researching Sir Henry on Ancestry, I found a listing of several wives having the same marriage date. I have since concluded by looking at English records that the above information in my estimation is accurate. In the process I examined the legality of having multiple wives during that time period recalling Henry the Eighth. Note that the Bigamy Act of 1604 made bigamy in England a crime. Prior to that time polygamous relationships may have been permitted. Note that Henry VIII of England, who was King of England from 1509 until his death in 1547, had six marriages. This was the period after the break with the Roman Catholic Church and formation of the Church of England. Note also that during this period, most marriages were arranged by the parents of the marrying parties.

An English site provides some clarity with remarriage

The website www.british-history.ac.uk has the well documented history of Naunton Manor from 1066 up to 1962. The history provides in part that in 1591 the manor passed to John Talbot, who married Eleanor, daughter and heir of Thomas Baskerville, and sold it to Giles Venfield and others when Venfield and John Collett were Joint Lords of the Manor and that Collett's half of the manor passed to Henry Collett in 1642.

REV. JOHN COLLETT (1548-1650) Inheritance of Naughton Manor in the Cotswolds

Born: 1548 (Over Slaughter)

Married: 1583 (Elizabeth Venfield of Naughton); Katherine Sanders; Susan Cheney

Died: abt 1650 (either Over Slaughter or Broadwell, Gloucestershire, England)

Parents: Sir Henry (John) Collett 1520-1592 and Joan Hanks (1520-1598)

Children: Ann Collett (1586-1637) from Katherine Sanders; **Sir John "Thomas" Collett** (1578-1659) from Susan Cheney

In 1591 John Collett with his brother Thomas Collett and Richard Pratt were listed as Trustees of the Lands of Upper Slaughter which were purchased and conveyed for the church and relief of the poor. John was then Joint Lord of the Manor of Naughton with Giles Venfield, who was probably John's brother-in-law, being his wife's brother. As the firstborn son, he inherited the home from his father, Sir Henry John Collett (1520-1592). It is located in the Cotswolds, perhaps the most picturesque area of England, west of Oxford and south of Birmingham. There is a plaque inside St Peter's church in the village with the heading "Benefactors" acknowledging his contribution.

SIR JOHN "THOMAS" COLLETT (1578-1659) Move from Gloucestershire to Huntingdonshire

Born: August 3, 1578 (Little Gidding, Huntingdonshire, England)

Married: 1600 (to Susanna Ferrar (1682-1667))

Died: March 29, 1669 (Little Gidding, Huntingdonshire, England

Parents: Rev. John Collett (1548-1650) and Susan Cheney (1552-)

Children: Mary Collett (1600-1680); Thomas Collett (1601-1675); Anna Collett (1602-1639); Elizabeth Collett (1602-1657); **William Collett** (1605-1660); Hannah Rebecca Collett (1605-1653); and John Collett (1616-1621)

Sir John "Thomas" Collett was baptized on August 3, 1578, at Ashchurch, Tewkesbury, Gloucestershire. Ashchurch is near Naughton Manor in Slaughter, which may explain the christening there. The family apparently then lived in Huntingdonshire which is east of London some distance away. The family may have moved to Little Gidding as a result of Sir Thomas' father being a minister and possibly assigned to a different congregation.

WILLIAM COLLETT (abt 1605-1660)

Born: abt 1605 (Badbury, Wiltshire, England

Married: abt 1648 (Mary Komm)

Died: 1660 (Badbury, Wiltshire, England"

Parents: Sir John "Thomas" Collett (1578-1659) and Susanna Ferrar (1580-1657)

Children: William Collett (1651-1714); Richard Collett (1656-1721); Robert Collett (1657-1661); and **John Collett** (1659-1729)

It may be noteworthy that William was the second son of Sir Thomas Collett. He is the first Collett male for some time not to have Sir as a title. It is probable that he inherited little except some religious fervor from a father who was a reverend.

[**I am including** the following information regarding George Collett who was likely a first or second cousin of William Collett (1605-1660) also living in Wiltshire and who preceded our line in coming to America. When putting together her recollection of family lines a great aunt "to the best of her recollection" stated that the Collett family came from England and established a "colony" in America. The person filling that role was likely George Collett (1616-1689) who played a significant role in early Pennsylvania. His heirs also wound up in Loudon County Virginia contemporaneously with our known family members.]

GEORGE COLLETT (1616-1698) Founding of Pennsylvania Colony with Wm. Penn

Born: March 16, 1616 (Highworth, Wiltshire, England)

Married: (Elizabeth Corless, December 21, 1636, Swindon, Wiltshire, England)

Died: January 15, 1698 (West Marlborough Township, PA)

Parents: Stephen Collett and Elizabeth of Highworth

Children: His eleven children were: John Collett; Francs Collett; George Collett; Elizabeth Collett; Robert Collett; Stephen Collett; Anne Collett; Mary Collett Pennock; Joseph Collett; Susanna Collett; and Benjamin Collett.

After 1656, George Collett and his family settled in Clonmel County, Tipperary. He was forced to pay for the maintenance of the local priest in Clonmel, as they were Quakers. (WikiTree). [My DNA study shows an Irish connection in what may be an appropriate percentage.] It is interesting to note that in the Smead line, Sir Richard Woodhull Smithe/Smead (1574-1638) was located in Ireland for a period of time.

Family history as related in a letter from Alma Whitehouse reflecting her discussion with her mother Grace Collett Johnson (1888/9) "Near as Mother could remember" says "Sir Henry Collett was a direct descendant. He came from England got a tract of land and started a Colony." In fact, research reveals 1250 acres of land located in West Marlborough Township (west of Philadelphia) Pennsylvania were granted to George Collett by William Penn. Sir Henry Collett (1520-1592), who is a direct descendant, is shown as passing away in Charlton Kings, Gloucestershire, England.

William Penn (1644-July 30,1718) was the son of the admiral and politician Sir William Penn. Penn was a writer, an early member of the Religious Society of Friends (also known as Quakers), and the founder of the English North American colony, the Province of Pennsylvania, which became the state of Pennsylvania. The democratic principles that he set forth served as an inspiration for the United States Constitution. His daring experiment in religious liberty, equality, and peace.

William Penn owed money to the king of England and received the Pennsylvania territory in payment in 1681. His goal was a "holy experiment" by a union of temporal and spiritual matters. Pennsylvania made guarantees of religious freedom, and kept them, attracting many Quakers and others, including George Collett (1616-1698). Quakers have been a significant part of the movements for the abolition of slavery, to promote equal rights for women, and peace. They also promoted education and the humane treatment of prisoners and the mentally ill, through the founding or reforming of various institutions. Quakers insisted God could speak to ordinary people, through his risen son, without the need to heed churchmen, pay tithes, or engage in deceitful practices.

The history of Loudoun County reveals that in 1722-1725, Quakers from Pennsylvania moved west of the Catoctins in Loudoun County and that in the 1740s, Quakers from the Philadelphia area, where farmland is scarce, concertedly settled upper Loudoun, from the German Settlement south to Beaverdam Creek. Quakers at Waterford name their Friends' Meeting, established in 1741, after the new county. In 1757, Loudoun was formed.

JOHN COLLETT (1659-1729)

Born: 1659-1729 (Veryan, Cornwall, England)

Married: 1688 (Ann Bland (1663-1751) in England)

Died: August 6, 1751 (England)

Parents: William Collett (1605-1660) and Mary Komm (1632-)

Children: **Abraham Collett** (1695-1754)

Note the move to Cornwall which had an active Quaker settlement and the name given to Abraham, which is a biblical name not otherwise common at the time.

ABRAHAM COLLETT (1695-1754) Scotland to Fredrick, VA

Born: 1695 (Scotland)

Married: 1715 (Magdalena (Magdalen) Hollock in TN, America); Jeanne Nihotte (1690-1780)

Died: 1754 (Fredrick, VA)

Parents: John Collett (1659-1729) and Ann Bland (1663-1751)

Children: **Abraham Collett** (1715-1782)

Speculation at best, but with a religious background, the development of the Quaker movement, and the family's move from Cornwall to Scotland, sets the stage for immigration to America.

Collett family tree information suggests arrival in the colonies from Scotland prior to age 20 in 1715 and marriage in Tennessee and birth of son Abraham in 1715, a move to Maryland at age 27 in 1722 and then later a move to Frederick, Virginia where he died in 1754. It is certainly possible that he could have connected with other related Colletts already in America before and as part of this journey. Another tree also has Abraham having the same birth and death dates and approximate locations but father as Lawrent, Mother Marie-Ann (same difference in birth dates and Ann as part of both names) with a son Abraham born in 1710 in Augusta, Virginia, close enough to suggest the same person with some factual errors in record keeping.

Frederick County is where Abraham Collett (1695-1754) lived and died at age 59 in 1754. Lord Thomas Fairfax of England who through combined grants at one time controlled over 5,000,000 acres of land in Virginia, including much of the land that became Frederick County.

On the date of Abraham's death in 1754, Colonel George Washington located his headquarters in Winchester before and during the French and Indian War. He resigned from military service in 1758 when he was elected to the House of Burgesses in 1758 and 1761, seventeen years being "elected" as the commanding general of the yet to be created Continental Army.

ABRAHAM COLLETT (1715-1782) Wife Celia [Catrina?] Ijenhuigen from The Netherlands

Born: October 3, 1733 (Frederick County, Virginia)

Married: 1735 (Catrina Ijenhuijsen)

Died: May 1782 (Frederick, Virginia) [an alternate is given as Washington, North Carolina]

Parents: Abraham Collett (1695-1754) and Jeanne Nihotte (1690-1780)

Children: **Abraham Collett** (1733-1782); Celia Cerene Collett (1735-1761); James Collett (1749-1807); and Isaac Collett (1755-1809)

DNA study showed 4% Netherlands - could wife Catrina Ijenhuijen be the source (a Netherlands Genealogie index is given as a resource). The Netherlands was a known hotbed of Quaker activity.

ABRAHAM COLLETT (1733-1782)

Born: October 7, 1733 (Frederick County, VA)

Married: abt 1759 (Mary Styers (1740-1783) North Carolina; abt 1777 (Margaret W Wakefield (1747-1783))

Died: November 4, 1782 (Washington, Tennessee)

Parents: Abraham Collett (1715-1782) and Catrina Ijenhuijsen (1720-1780)

Children of Mary Styer (1740-1783): **William Collett** (1762-1820); Ruth Collett (1764-); Ann Collett (1766-); Abraham Collett (1781-1847); and Isaac Collett (1783-1859)

Children From Margaret W. Wakefield (1747-1783): Elizabeth Collett (1769-1856), Rachel Collett (1771), and Charles Collett (1773-1855)

There is obviously an overlap in birthdates for the children listed for the two wives. Washington County, Tennessee is Tennessee's oldest county, having been established in 1777 when the state was still part of North Carolina. This would explain the location of some events being in North Carolina which were prior to 1777.

At age 45, on November 23, 1778 Abraham is listed on the US Revolutionary War Rolls (1775-1780).

WILLIAM COLLETT (1762-1820) South and then west to NC and KY

Born: 1762 (Rowan County, North Carolina)

Marriage: abt 1781 (Susannah Bellew (1766-1840))

Died: 1822 (Clay County, Kentucky-burial Essie, Leslie County, Kentucky or Parkersburg, Wood County, West Virginia)

Children: Elizabeth Collett (1780-); Sarah "Sally" Collett (1782-1844); Abraham Collett (1782-1844); **James Collett** (1788-1864); Christopher (twin) Collett (1790-1878); Emily (twin) Collett (1790-1870); William Collett (1791-1881); Oliver Collett (1793-1814); Hiram "Henry" Collett (1796-1827); Samuel Collett (1799-1870); Elizabeth Collett (1802-1850); and Nancy J Collett (1843-1885)

Children were born in Knox, Kentucky (1782); Burke County, North Carolina (1782-1791); Buncombe County, North Carolina (1793-1796); Virginia (1799); and Leslie and Clay, Kentucky (1802-1814).

Burke and Buncombe Counties are adjacent to each other east of present-day Charlotte, North Carolina. Knox, Leslie, and Clay Kentucky are across the North Carolina state line in the eastern part of Kentucky, with Frederick County lying to the north in Virginia, west of present-day Washington DC.

JAMES COLLETT (1788-1864) Leesburg, Loundon County, VA

Born: April 1788 (Leesburg, Loundon County, VA)

Married: Feb 16, 1809 (Mary Molly Carter (1786-1860), Leesburg, Loundon County, VA)

Died: October 10, 1864 (Warren, Knox, Kentucky)

Parents: William Collett (1762-1820) and Susannah Bellew (1788-1840)

Children Born in Virginia: Melville James Collett (1811-1880); Presley Collett (March 31,1812-November 23,1868); Hiram Collett (1814-1878); George Admiral Collett (1814-1860); **John Collett** (Dec. 6, 1815-Oct. 4, 1875); Harriet A Collett (1818-1890) (possibly Kentucky).

Children Born in Kentucky: William Collett (Dec. 8, 1819-Sep. 26,1873); Mary Carter Collett (1825-1899); and Elizabeth "Anne" Collett (1828-1879).

James and Mary's children were born both in Loudoun County, Virginia and in later years in Kentucky where William Collett (1762-1820) had lived. Upon his father's passing in Kentucky in 1820, it appears that James and Molly returned to their extended family in Kentucky.

Subsequent marriages of some of their children occurred in Warren County, Ohio meaning that some members moved to Ohio prior to 1834 when Presley was married. James Collett died in Warren, Knox, Kentucky on October 10, 1864.

Son William enlisted October 1, 1862 in West Virginia during the Civil War, serving as a First Lieutenant mustering out in Richmond, Virginia. This would have been at the same time as James Collett (1845-1939) who is clearly in our line would have been serving in the Indiana Regulars for the North.

JOHN COLLETT (1815-1875) Leesburg, VA to the founding of Collett, IN

Born: November 22, 1815 (Leesburg, Loudon County, VA)

Married: March 11, 1841 (Sarah Ann Osborn Collett, Warren County, OH); 1856 (Rebecca Beck Osborn, Collett, IN)

Died: October 4, 1875 (Collett, IN)

Children: John Collett and Sarah Ann Osborn Collett had the following children: **James William Collett** (Cpl.) (1843-1903); David Wells Collett (1850-1924); Presley G. Collett (1852-1914); Rebecca J. Collett (1847-1868); and Margaret Ann Collett (1842-1883).

<u>Children</u>: John Collett and Rebecca Beck Osborn Collett had the following children: Joseph R. Osborn (stepchild); Lydia S Osborn (stepchild); and Alice (Allie) Margaret Collett.

(Sir) John Collett (November 22, 1815-October 4, 1875) was born in Leesburg, Loudoun, VA He died in Jay County, IN, and is buried in Zoar Cemetery in IN. John Collett's parents were James Collett (married February 16, 1809 – Leesburg, Loudoun Co., VA and Mary Collett. [Ancestry shows John Collett's parents as William Collett and Ann Callitt, and there is a conflict on birth dates on the various sites.] He was known to be of English heritage. He married Sarah Ann Osborn (1819-1854) on March 11, 1841 in Warren County,

John Collett first appears on record as one of four sons of James Collett and Mary Carter and was born in Leesburg, Loudon Co., VA, on 6 December 1815. No further data was found for him until 1841, when he married Sarah Ann Osborn, as documented in Warren Co., OH Marriage Records, 1834-1854, p. 178. She was a sister of Eber Samuel Osborn. See Osborn in a separate section of this book.

John moved from Warren County, Ohio, to Jay County, Indiana, between 1845 and 1847 with his wife and two children, Margaret Ann and James William, where he operated a farm.

After Sarah passed and John Collett had a large family to take care of, James Collett went to live with his uncle on his mother's side in Warren County, Ohio. After about three years this uncle died so he returned to live with the family in Indiana.

While he was away James' father, John Collett married [Sarah's sister?] Rebecca Beck Osborn (1822 Huntsville, Tenn.-Sept. 25, 1967). From a prior marriage Rebecca had two children, Joe and Linda. John and Rebecca had a daughter Martha Alice (Allie) Collett (1864-). Allie married Alfred L. Barber on September 20, 1888 operating a grocery store in Collett.

Sarah's brother, Eber S. Osborn (1823-1887), buried in Camden Cemetery, served in the Civil War (Pvt.) for the Union army in the 23rd Veteran Reserve Corps. It was his son who homesteaded north of Vantage on the Columbia River. (Uncle Ben Osborn to James Robert Vrooman).

After the death of Sarah Ann in 1854, he remarried to Rebecca Beck (Osborn) in 1856. She brought two children to the family, Joseph R. Osborn and Lydia S. Osborn from her prior marriage to James Osborn. John and Rebecca had one child, Alice Margaret ("Allie"). The Osborn family is dealt with elsewhere in this book given their likely travel West with the Colletts and intermarriages.

John Collett platted "Collett", Jay County, Indiana on February 13, 1872 and sold lots there. It was located along the railroad then under construction and had a station for the G.R. & I. Railroad and a grocery store operated by his daughter Allie and her husband Alfred L. Barber. With a population of 125 Collett served as a trading and Shipping Point. Today, a small church building remains, as do a few residences along the narrow farm to market access road.

John Collett died October 4, 1875 in Collett, Jay County, Indiana. He is buried in Zoar Cemetery, at the intersection of CR 133 and 160, 1—1/2 miles South of Collett, alongside his wife Sarah Ann and with many of his family members nearby. The cemetery is well tended and lies in an area of intensely farmed, slightly rolling country. There are a number of trees on the property.

JAMES WILLIAM COLLETT (1845-1903) Civil War Veteran/College Professor

<u>Born</u>: July 20, 1845 (Warren County, OH)

<u>Married</u>: March 21, 1867 (Portland, Jay County, IN - Tibatha Elma Baar January 9, 1849 December 20, 1939)

<u>Died</u>: January 5, 1903 of pneumonia, buried in the Lyon, Colorado cemetery

<u>Children</u>: James and Tabitha Barr had the following children, all born in Jay County, IN:

James Alfred Collett (July 9, 1868); John Wilson Collett (November 4, 1870-February 4, 1933); Janie Collett (1873-1873 died at two months); Mollie Lavinia Collett (1876-1883); William Henry Collett (August 31, 1878); Charles Eber Collett (March 8, 1882-1973 Denver, CO); Viola Sara Collett Osborn (Nov 20, 1879-June 13, 1956 married to Samuel Eber Osborn, November 3, 1898 Ellensburg, WA); **George Anthony Collett** (June 16, 1884-Sept.1, 1958, Walla Walla, WA); Esther Angeline Collett Twist (Feb 16, 1886-Aug March 15, 1968 Lyons, CO); Grace Melvia Collett Johnson (Aug. 11, 1888-Oct. 29 1989, Port Angeles, WA); Minnie Alice Collett (October 23, 1890-Apr. 4 1932, Grand Junction, CO)

The John Collett family settled and farmed in the NW corner of Pike TWP, Jay Co., IN, about 1846.

John William Collett was 19 years old when he enrolled as a musician in Co. H, 130th Reg., Indiana Volunteers on February 29, 1864, and was later mustered into the Union Army on 10 March 1864 at Kokomo, IN. He was described as being 5'7", with dark complexion and hazel eyes. He saw action in many battles in Georgia, Alabama and Tennessee and the campaign of the Carolinas. During this time, he was wounded in the shoulder and also reached the rank of corporal. He was mustered out on 2 December 1865. Source: Indiana Military Record document, and Compendium of The War of The Rebellion, pp. 1156, Co. H, 130th Regiment Indiana Volunteers.

While in the service, on 2 February 1865, he purchased 80 acres of land from his father, John, for $2,000. (Jay Co., Indiana Book of Deeds, I 232). Curiously, he sold this same 80 acres back to his father on 11 April, 1866, for $1,000. (Book of Deeds, S-385)

Tabetha Elma Baar Collett

On March 21, 1867, he married Tabitha Elma Baar (January 9, 1849-December 20, 1939), who was also from Ohio, in Portland, Jay County, Indiana. His marriage to Tabitha Elma Barr (89) is recorded in Book C-C, pp 124, Jay Co. Marriage Records as 21 March 1867. She is 18, he is 22. (Tabitha Elma Baar's father served on the same Civil War regiment as James Collett.) Tabitha Elma Barr's sister Allie owned oil wells in Kansas.

James attended college in Jay County, Indiana and taught school there for 15 years. In 1896, at age 51, he moved with his wife, 3 sons and 4 daughters to Lyons, CO, leaving two sons in Indiana. In route they stayed in Nebraska for a short time, arriving in Lyons, Colorado on June 16, 1896.

Homestead Lyons Colorado

Son, William Henry Collett

Having been a teacher for fifteen years, James Collett became a professor at Boulder College from 1896 to 1898. Boulder College was founded in 1896 and is about 14 miles from Lyons.

James Collett suffered a debilitating injury in 1898 and was having a difficult time making a living. He took his son George out of school to help the family. They operated a rented farm, and cut and hauled posts and poles for sale to farmers in the lower valleys below Lyons and also supplied much of Lyons with cut and split firewood. He and his sons Charles Eber and George Anthony built a house up in the mountains near a sawmill, and freighted lumber and supplies throughout the area as far as Longmont, all using teams and wagons.

During the depression of 1900, his military pension appeared to be his major source of income; he spoke in one letter of being able to buy warm clothes for his son George [then 16] and himself from this source. On February 18, 1900, in a letter to Samuel and Viola Osborn he stated:

"Have a deep snow on, the first deep one this winter. George and I went to the place for two wagon loads of hay; we had to leave one load, put 4 horses to one load to bring it home. The teamsters are using 4 horses to haul a small two-horse load. . . . [neighbor Bud Weese] is getting out posts for us, up at the cabin in Coffin Top Gulch, at 4 cents apiece. We have hauled 4 loads of these posts, and taken their supplies to them, hauled 85 at one load in this snow. We took 80 of Bud's posts to Plattesville, where we went for hay; got 12 ½ cents each for them. Have another 40 of our own here yet, will take them soon. Expect to furnish Mr. Barker 700 posts at 15 cents each, and 500 small corral poles for fence stays at 12 ½ cents each. . . . he then references a Mr. Smead [likely Chester Lyman Smead or Warren Smead, Lillie's father] wants to sell me a good Norman horse; a little heavier than Charlie; asks $50. Will take posts for him; has two or three more young horses as large, and larger than Charlie, all for sale. George and I can get a little ahead by hauling while winter lasts. We were both in rags, nearly freezing, until my pension check came. I got a new warm suit, with an all wool under shirt, good thick drawers, felt boots, and heavy wool socks for George, also good warm mittens as he does most of the driving. Got warm underwear for Ma and Esther, new shoes for Gracie and Minnie and saved some money to send to you." The letter is addressed to Mr. S.E. [Samuel Eber] Osborn in Laketown, Utah, prior to their move to Washington State. Although there is additional detail in the letter it is clear they were barely getting by, having to barter loads or wood poles and hay in miserable weather, and incredibly thankful for the further detail contained in the letter, to have new warm clothes. It also shows the relationship with the Smead family, which was well known for their horses as noted in the description of Lyman Chester Smead contained in the section on the Smead family.

A deeply religious man, he purchased an organ and organized a small church with a congregation of 12-20.

By July 1902, his health was failing, and he was blind in his left eye. This information is in his letter to Samuel Osborn and daughter Viola dated 27 July 1902, one of a number of letters he wrote through the years to family. The letter included: "The prospects for crops are not so promising as we have always had some since we have been here, and there is not the usual amount of snow on the range, and there is not more than half the usual supply of water. We have a grand crop of fruit of all kinds. Hay is higher in price; Alfalfa $5 per ton; wild hay, timothy and etc. $8 per ton, meat is high. I suppose you are where you can catch plenty of Salmon now, and kill game which will help your meat supply, if you have time to get them. I fear you are in for a whole lot of hard work, if you can get a home, and if you were a strong man, you could clear the land, but it breaks a man down. I hope you will not get sick. We pray to God every day for him to keep you in health and to care for you." He was likely commenting on Viola and Samuel Osborn's decision to homestead at Brushy Creek on the Columbia River.

A letter to Sam and Viola dated 25 Jan., 1903, from Tabitha Elma (Barr) Collett transmits word of her husband James' death on 5 Jan., 1903, of pneumonia and possible complications. He was buried in Lyons, arrangements by the G. R. Patron. He and his wife, Tabitha Elma Barr, have visited the gravesites of both he and his wife, Tabitha Elma Barr.

In other correspondence with her daughter Viola, Tabitha Elma Bar (who outlived her husband by more than thirty years, dying at age 90) relates "I run the fellow that lives in the other end of our house away from my chicken house with the shotgun one night and it not loaded only just a cap on it but he did not know it." It also states that the minister Mr. Chatfield lost his wife and baby last week (childbirth deaths were fairly common).

GEORGE ANTHONY COLLETT (1884-1958) Lyon's, CO to Whidbey Island, WA

Born: June 16, 1884 (Collett, Jay County, IN)

Married: 1916 (Ellensburg, WA - Lillie Lenora Smead Collett)

Died: September 1, 1958 (Walla Walla, WA)

George Anthony Collett

Children: **Mary Georgia Collett** (December 14, 1922-Culdesac, ID); Josephine Omar Collett (February 26, 1929-Ellensburg, WA); Howard Stubblefield (stepchild, July 2, 1909-April 17, 1995); Arvilla Stubblefield (stepchild); and Emory Stubblefield (stepchild).

George Anthony Collett was the ninth child of James William Collett and Tibatha Elma Barr. He was born in Jay County, Indiana June 16, 1884. In addition to his older brothers and sisters he had three younger sisters.

His daughter, Josephine Collett Lackman related to me her father's first recollection of his childhood. With twelve children in the family and living in a rural area as a young child, he wandered off into the woods on his own. He was wearing a type of dress as he was not yet potty trained. The circumstances of his separation were not clear, perhaps other family members were collecting the wild fruits, consisting of plums, grapes, pawpaws, blackberries, gooseberries and the like which were plentiful in Jay County at the time. Perhaps he found himself in the wild pea vines and rye in the area which made it difficult for a toddler to see where he was.

In any event Indians were passing through the area and stumbled upon the child. They were likely Miamis or possibly Wyandottes, Pottatamies, or Shawnees. Not finding any people in the vicinity they rescued the child from harm as Jay County still had numerous wolves, wild cats and bears. The wolves were particularly dangerous attacking both livestock and wild game. George recalls that the Indians treated him kindly taking him into their wigwams and treating him as one of their own. Some years later word reached the settlers that there was a young white child living amongst the Indians at which time George was reunited with his family.

Josephine related that her father always looked with great kindness on Indians. Much later in life local Indians in the Ellensburg area, members of a local tribe, would visit him accompanied by their families to discuss legal problems they were having.

Much of what is known of George Anthony Collett comes from the recollections of his daughter, Mary Georgia Collett (Abel) by letter of 17 January 1989:

"My father shared a couple of experiences while his big family still lived in Indiana (until June 1896). The winter was long, food was scarce, but little George found a hidden treasure under the wild plum trees. If he'd dig under the fallen leaves there were dried plums, oh, so good for that hungry little boy.

"There was an Indian village close by the Collett homestead in Indiana. Young George and a young Indian boy became playmates and friends. George visited his friend in this village and was invited to share from their stewpot that smelled so inviting. After the meal his friend asked if he knew what they had eaten. George said, "No, but it was good"! His friend laughed and told him it was a dog!

"In spite of the fact that his father (James William Collett) was a teacher, George had only three grades of "formal" school. The big family and his father's ill health required George's help when he was a boy. Letters written to older sister Viola (Sarah Collett) by their father attest to George's sacrifices for the family. Driving the team to bring out lumber, fence posts and hay for the stock even in the bitter Colorado cold was his lot.

"Just because his formal education was short didn't mean his mind wasn't better than average. I still remember that he could figure the board feet of lumber in his head, faster than I ever could on paper, or by calculator!

"George Collett's kind, loving manner won him many friends, but all children and animals particularly loved him. He had time for them. My early recollection was of George working out and staying at his employer's during the week. He did manage to get home Saturday night and to spend Sunday with his family, as well as coming home one night mid-week. Mama (Lillie Lenora Smead) and little Mary (about 3 yrs.) had a happy contest to see who could get to Daddy George first for that happy home-coming hug and kiss.

"After younger sister Josephine Omar Collett came along, Mama had a bigger job of making Shirley Temple curls for two girls on Sunday mornings. Josephine's hair was naturally curly but Mary had her hair set with rag strips to create curls. George had a ritual of making the Sunday morning pancakes, so Lily had "hair time" for the girls. For many years, those pancakes were extra special because they were made dollar-sized for two little girls. Hot home—made maple-flavored syrup went along too, of course.

"In my childhood Halloween meant finding tricks to play. My Dad told of getting with a friend and rigging a low rope across a path they knew an old man would take to reach his home cabin. After dark, the two mischievous fellows managed enough animal sounds to spur the old man to a good run before he reached the rope. They stayed just long enough to know the rope had been hit then they made themselves very scarce.

"A Halloween I remember, my friends were gathered in our yard after dark trying to think up some trick to play, when around the corner of the yard came bear sounds and the figure of a big bear lumbered toward us. Kids scattered, but somehow that bear was familiar. Yes, it was George in his full-length bear coat to liven up our evening.

"About this same time Mama and Daddy received word that brother Howard Stubblefield who had gone to work in Portland OR was very ill with pneumonia, before wonder drugs that was serious business. The family bundled into the car to try to get there "in time". On that trip, Daddy George fixed 12 flat tires. That meant jacking up, taking the wheel off, and the inner tube out, finding the leak and covering the hole with a cold patch before all could be reassembled and the tire pumped up by hand. Never once did Daddy George have bad words or ever complain. George's life was made up of much hard, conscientious work, mostly for other people. He and stepson Howard both worked for John Clerf on his big Kittitas Valley ranch at one time. Howard told of being out with the boss on more than one occasion and being told they shouldn't hurry as George would do the milking chores, although not his job, if they didn't get back in time. And he did." [Howard Stubblefield, who confirmed this event, added that George was very good at irrigation and did this work for Clerf.]

"Family get togethers were special for George as he had a chance to get to know the grandchildren as they came along. We had a picture of him milking his goat and squirting milk into the grandkids and the cat 's mouths! The kids loved Grandpa and Grandma's Whidbey Island country acreage where they learned to dig "Gooey ducks" (Big clams).

"George's final years were plagued by asthma brought on by hand digging water wells for neighbors on Whidbey Island. He'd use a forked stick for "water witching". When his asthma would be worst, he'd head for Emory (stepson Stubblefield) and Marguerite's in Walla Walla where their turn of the century house and farm atmosphere always made him feel at home.

"George's sister Esther came out from Colorado to visit sister Grace (Collett Johnson 99); sister Viola (Collett Osborn 95) also managed to come from Ellensburg. God was good and permitted George good enough health to join them for a wonderful visit to Port Angeles. Shortly after this we received an urgent call for help to get Daddy George back to Walla Walla where he was more comfortable breathing.

"I'll never forget the trip, nor I'm sure will Marguerite. She took the three children and our three boys with her in her Volkswagen Bug for the trip to Walla Walla, so we'd have room to make a bed for George in the whole back seat of our Chrysler -Mama, Howard and I in front.

"He died at home Sept 1, 1958, and is buried in Walla Walla WA, where he was at home. George's family may not have been rich in money but there was always plenty to eat and plenty of love, acceptance and understanding. His stepchildren, Arvilla, Howard, and Emory, were always as much a part of his family as were his own Mary and Josephine. What more could you ask?"

George Collett recalled a story of the family taking in an Indian boy one winter. It was exceptionally harsh and the Indian boy showed him how to dig up fruit (native plums?) frozen under the leaves which they lived on through the winter.

According to Josephine Collett Lackman (George's youngest daughter) a bullet came out of his chest when she was seventeen. Although the circumstances aren't given, he had been shot by his older brother Charles.

While in Kittitas and Ellensburg he worked a variety of jobs including riding "shotgun" on wagon shipments in the area. His shotgun had a "hair" trigger with only a slight squeeze to get a shot off. He also worked on the building of the railway snow shed at Lake Kaches, crossing the lake on ice to get to work.

George and Lillie Collett at their home on Whidbey Island, WA

One of his sisters had owned and operated a small log type hotel next to the highway east of Easton near the Roslyn turnoff. The building was destroyed to make way for the widening of the I-90 freeway.

Per his daughter Mary, George Collett was proud to be from the Collett's of England as opposed to the Collet (one "t") from France.

MARY GEORGIA COLLETT (1922-2016) WAC during WW2/Private Pilot

Born: December 14, 1922 (Culdesac, ID)

Married: May 2, 1942 Seattle, King County, WA Howard Hadley; King County-Ed Abel

Died: June 12, 2016 (Walla Walla, WA)

Children: James Eldon Hadley (July 27, 1946-Ellensburg, WA); George Howard Hadley (May 22, 1948-Ellensburg, WA); Kirk Jackson Hadley (August 19, 1949-Ellensburg, WA)

Mary Georgia Collett

Note: The following was written by Mary Hadley for a newsletter of the Rio Verde Retirement Community where she lived for a time. She separately prepared pages of notes containing more details of her life. I have included this information in brackets in an attempt to supplement.

My parents were both from pioneer Colorado families. Grandpa Collett was a Civil War veteran and became a professor.

Both parents moved west separately. Mama married and had three children. My father was a handsome bachelor until at 32 he was reunited with his Colorado neighbor. I was born at my grandmother's farm in Nezperce, Idaho. [Culdesac in Nez Perce County. While there, she formed a bond with Jim Bond, whom she thought highly of.] When the family moved to the Kittitas Valley, it was by horse and wagon along with the animals and children. [The children include the three Stubblefield children in addition to Mary.] At three years my favorite place was in the shade of the wagon. A sister [Josephine] came along when I was about ready to start school.

Mary Georgia Collette

[Mary would return to her grandmother's home for visits. She recalls receiving a wind-up merry go round for Christmas, skinny dipping in the lake on the property and Mary's sister, Josephine told me of Jim Bond having snow swept off the lake one winter so Mary could go ice skating. Lillie's cousin Bill Walker (author of "The Longest Rope") would sometimes stop by and entertain with his fiddling.]

I went to Ellensburg schools and graduated in 1940. [A Junior High teacher introduced her to drama. She was in school plays, in speech class with an "A" for her triple "E" club sweater. She also learned to play the piano, perhaps from her father who played both the piano and violin.] We had a 62nd reunion this past June. With the help of a $50 scholarship, I attended Central Washington State College before going to Seattle to work full-time in a drug store.

My special fellow, Howard Hadley, was in the Army at Ft Lewis, and it became wedding bells for us in Seattle in 1942. [Mary's mother, Lillie, did not approve of Howard and refused to attend the wedding, although he earned his way into her heart in later years]. He went to the South Pacific that first year as the country was at war. My answer to pressure to not stay alone in the big city was to join the war effort as a Navy Wave. Ginger Rogers was there for our swearing in ceremony; then off to Hunter College for boot camp. My billet was on the 7th floor and we were not allowed to use the elevators. After Navy schooling at Indiana University, I was promoted to Storekeeper 3rd Class and eventually to SK 2nd Class while stationed in Oklahoma. The Navy allowed me to muster out when my husband returned stateside after years in the South Pacific.

Our home was made in the Ellensburg area where our three sons were born. While in the Ellensburg area, I took advantage of my G.I. Bill of Rights and took flight training, ending with my private pilot's license-a Highlight of my Life.

Tour of the United States in 1953

In 1954 we moved to Auburn and became part-time farmers. It was here that kids' school activities, PTA, and church participation became more important.

When the youngest son went to school, I felt I could think about working again. An opportunity arose and my husband and I started "Hadley Floor Covering" located in the Van's Furniture Building first until growth necessitated building our own building. At the end of 10 years, we decided we were working too hard and the boys weren't interested in taking over, so we sold out.

When we moved to Tucson, I was able to work again in a quality furniture store. It was here that my husband of 36 years and I parted company.

Maui, Hawaii had a job for me and a chance to start over. Condominium furnishings were a challenge and I had a chance to enjoy the Islands and climate for seven years before retiring.

Ed Abel had been our real estate salesman, and it wasn't long until we decided two could have more fun than one. We were married and lived here for 10 years from 1990 until his death in 2000.

The constant love of my life has been traveling; to Mexico and Alaska with an airstream trailer; by auto to the National parks; to Europe for a 45-day tour; another tour to Japan, Thailand, China; a trip to New Zealand and Australia; three cruise vacations, one through the Panama Canal, and two tries to get the fall foliage tour right as well as two trips to Western Samoa. I'm still ready--all you have to say is "Let's Go" and I'll say when.

It was a privilege for me to represent Auburn as runner-up to Queen Charlotte at this year's Good Ole Day celebration.

I feel blessed to have been able to live at such an interesting time in history, in this country and with good neighbors and friends.

[At Beth and my last visit with Mom, her parting request was for us to take her back to Italy. Had she been physically able to travel it would have happened. My first memory of her (if babies have memories, mine is a picture) was a picnic under a tree on a blanket at two months old. We had flown in a private plane and landed in a field. I don't remember if mom or dad flew us there as both were pilots.]

Mom has been referred to as a lady, a person with grit and many other things. My memory is of a person of determination and a sense of adventure.

Growing up dirt poor in a strict evangelical home left mom at times feeling like she grew up on the wrong side of the tracks. No makeup and long dark dresses set her apart from her contemporaries. Her home life was filled with contrasts, her gentle, patient loving father who could tame wild animals and have them eat from his hands, her mother with vigilant prayer meetings, strong opinions and a loaded shotgun next to the back door. (Our uncle Howard wound up with the shotgun.) Mary Collett Hadley chose to be cremated and have her remains placed in her father George Collett's grave.

Mary was in high school with her younger sister Josephine

JOSEPHINE OMAR COLLETT (1929 – 2024)

<u>Born</u>: February 26, 1929 (Ellensburg, WA)

<u>Married</u>: March 22, 1946 (Poulsbo, WA., Donald Ralph Lackman (December 14, 1925-January 21, 2001))

<u>Died</u>: December 25, 2024 (Sonoita AZ) Buried at Cochise Memory Gardens in Sierra Vista, AZ

<u>Children</u>: Susan Marie Lackman (September 7, 1948); Donna Joe Lackman (August 8, 1954); Rebecca Ann Lackman (November 10, 1955) and Edwin Thomas Lackman (July 7, 1960- January 20, 1993)

Josephine Omar Collett

Josephine with her husband Don raised their family in Bremerton, WA. At one time Josephine relates she was the senior civilian administrator of the Bangar Naval Submarine Base based in Washington state. After retiring she and her husband Don Lackman traveled for many years in a motorhome stopping to assist in charitable endeavors including the Mobile Missionary Assistance Program (MMAP), finally settling in southern Arizona where they constructed a home.

OSBORN

Viola Sarah Collett Osborn was George Collett's older sister. She and my grandfather George were to remain close and to spend their lives in proximity to each other. Viola became a member of the Osborn family by marriage. The Osborn and Collett families were joined by marriage earlier, as John Collett (1815) and Sarah Ann Osborn (1819) were married on March 11, 1841, in Warren County, Ohio, prior to starting their lives in the town they founded, Collette, Jay County, Indiana. Viola and her husband Eber Samuel Osborn were cousins. George Collett spent time at their Brushy Creek homestead on the Columbia River. The Collett's and Osborn's lived in Ohio and Indiana together, likely traveling in the same wagon trains west.

The following are segments of James R Brooman's book "Collett and Osborn Families 1975- 1995" Whirlwind Press, Albany OR. Addressing the lives of the Osborn family members most closely tied to the Collett's.

EBER SAMUEL OSBORN (1823-1887) Civil War Veteran/OH to IN (with the Collett's)

Born: About 1823 (Warren Co., OH)

Married: About 1865 (Mary Louisa Thomas White)

Died: 1887 (Montpelier, Blackford Co., IN)

A SKETCH OF THE LIFE OF EBER SAMUEL OSBORN

(Assembled March 8, 1994 by James R. Vrooman)

Born 171 years ago, in Warren Co., Ohio, Eber Samuel Osborn has left few tracks in the sands of time. What we know of this direct ancestor and his times follows:

He is a brother of Sarah Ann Osborn, who became a member of the Collett family by marriage to John Collett. Records show him, at age 27, in Warren Co., OH. Verbal history passed down by Viola Sarah Collett (Osborn) suggests that his parents came from New York or New Jersey; no records have been found to support this.

His first marriage was to Jane Lewis; there were at least four children of that union.

Eber's marriage to Mary Louisa Thomas (White) is documented in her handwritten record and in the Madelia, MN Census. She brought two children to this union. Samuel Eber Osborn is a child of that marriage.

Viola Sarah Collett (Osborn), in speaking with her granddaughter Mae Morey, recollected that Eber had a third marriage, in Ohio, to a woman he had known for years; this was an unhappy relationship, and he returned to Jay Co., IN. He was also reputed to be a concert violinist and travelled a "Circuit" for income.

A copy of the official document outlining his Civil War service is on hand with the Patron. It confirms his place of birth and describes him as "5'-11 1/2" high, Dark Complexion, Grey eyes, Black hair, and, by occupation when enrolled, a farmer." He was awarded pay and Bounty on 8 July, 1865, and additional Bounty on 19 December, 1868, per "Act of July 28, 1866."

As detailed in FGR 161 and 153 Documentation, Eber applied for a Disability pension on 4 September 1886, 21 years after his discharge, claiming "Chronic diarrhea which was contracted in the service at Lexington, State of Kentucky, in February 1863." The request is signed personally by Eber S. Osborn in a clear hand.

On 8 February 1887, the Pension Office returned a form letter to Eber, asking for a physician's testimony as to his illness. The accompanying envelope shows that this was mailed 11 February 1887, in Washington, D.C., and received in Montpelier, IN, on 14 March 1887. Stamped on that envelope is "Unclaimed" "Return To Sender" and a handwritten comment, "Person addressed dead." The documents detailing the above were discovered and copied at the National Archives in Washington, D.C.

Although Eber died at Montpelier, he is interred in Pennville, IN, about 5 miles south of that town. Pennville, IN, was originally named Camden. Thus, when we were told that Eber S. Osborn died in Camden, IN, it was actually Pennville. To add to the confusion, a present-day Camden is in northwestern IN, many miles from Pennville. He is buried in the "Old Camden Cemetery" under a military headstone. As one approaches Pennville from the East, it is the second cemetery on the left. His marker is one of the first on the right as one enters the cemetery.

His father, Eber Samuel Osborn married Mary Louisa Thomas (White) about 1865.

SAMUEL EBER OSBORN (1868-1927) Playing a Stradivarius/Living with the Sioux

Born: March 6, 1868 (Yorktown, Delaware Co., IN)

Married: November 3, 1898 (Viola Sarah Collett-Boulder, Boulder Co., CO)

Died: March 3, 1927 (Ellensburg, Kittitas County, WA)

Children: 13, listed under Viola Osborn

Samuel E. Osborn, hereinafter referred to as Samuel, was born March 6, 1868, at Yorktown, Delaware Co., IN. That same summer, the family moved to Madelia, Watonwon Co., MN*. His father, William Osborn, was born about 1800 in either New York or New Jersey and married Samuel Eber's mother on June 25, 1818 (Warren County, Ohio). His mother died in Warren County, Ohio about 1871 (no proof of this date) when Warren would have been three. His father died when Samuel is believed to have been 11 or 12.

Samuel told his daughter Mildred Osborn (Vrooman) that he met his future wife, Viola Sarah Collett when she was a baby in College Corner, Jay Co., IN. That places him in that area in late 1879 or early 1880. He would have been 11-12 years old then. There was, according to Louis Trowbridge (543) of St. James, MN, a "plague of grasshoppers in the early 1870's" which may have contributed to Samuel's father's move back to IN.

After his father died in Jay Co., IN, Samuel next surfaced in February 1891 at Valentine, Cherry Co., NBC as follows:

Samuel and Viola Collet Osborn

Feb 2, 1891, Samuel borrowed $32.00 from F.O. Query. As security, he offered "One set heavy work harness, 1 bay horse, 3 years old, named Billy." Mar 30, 1892, Samuel borrowed $13.75 from D. E. Sherman, due Nov. 1, 1892. July 25, 1893, he borrowed $55.00 from the Walter A. Wood Harvester Co. paid Jan 18, 1895. As security he put up: 160 acres in his own name located in sec 19 and 30 TWP 34 Cherry County, miles NW of Valentine. With 65 acres improved and personal property in the amount $500.00, Jan 18, 1895, he borrowed $65.35 from Walter A. Wood Harvester Co., paying in full May 19, 1896. Cosigner on this note was his cousin David W. Collett (son of John) and Sarah Ann Osborn. Security was I1 blue horse 6 yrs. old Liger 1 black horse 6 yrs. old 4 white feet, 1 set work harness, 1 Sping Wagon.

Thus, Samuel is in Valentine, Nebraska or thereabouts from February 2, 1891 to May 19, 1896. He had a homestead and had improved 65 acres of it by July 1893. He probably was freighted into Fort Collins, CO, during the latter part of this time. Note that the airline distance between these two cities totaled more than 460 miles, through the sand hills of Nebraska and across several major rivers.

His loans to the Walter A. Wood company were probably to purchase wagons used for this purpose. We have a picture of him with David W. Collett and his family and an Indian around a wagon, listed as being in Valentine. He was known to have considerable friendly contact with Indians in that region, and spoke some of their language; Mildred Vrooman recalls Samuel telling her that he sometimes came home to his "soddy" home to find the stove going full blast and many Indians sleeping on the floor. Times were not easy; a history of Cherry County (Valentine) says, in part:

"When the nineties arrived, a change came over the country. A severe drought in 1890 ruined the crops, causing many people to become destitute. The session of the Legislature which met in 1891 appropriated $200,000.00 for relief of the people. This drought was followed by a depression, which created a panic in 1893, which was also the driest year on record in Cherry County. It even exceeded the great drought years of 1934 and 1936. To add to the misfortune of the settlers, a hot wind on July 26, 1894 made an almost total failure of the corn crops.

"Interest on borrowed money was high, and lending agencies charged from ten per cent per annum to two per cent a month for short time loans. (Samuel paid 10% on his) In 1895 the Legislature appropriated $250,000.00 for relief, and in addition to help given by the state, the G. A. A. sent special relief to the Civil War Veterans. Many settlers who had made or could make final proof on their claims secured loans on them and left the country.

"By 1896 the tide of fortune began to turn, and that year Nebraska produced a corn crop which was a record breaker. The yield per acre that year has never been excelled and is only equalled by the crop of 1944. Corn was then only ten cents a bushel, and many people used it for fuel. Wheat was only twenty-five cents a bushel. All through the nineties, prices for stock and farm products were low. Calves sold for six dollars a head at weaning time; yearlings for ten dollars and cows from twelve to seventeen dollars per head. "According to a letter from his daughter Mary Elma Osborn (Wirsching). now in possession of his daughter Elsie Jane Osborn (Morey). Samuel sold horses to the Army that he had rounded up and broken".

A letter is on file from James William Collett to Samuel dated August 23, 1898, placing Samuel at Greeley, CO. There is the impression that he had been in Greeley for some time, working for wages. "One dollar a day, $30 per month, steady work". He was obviously in contact with the Collett family living in Lyons at that time.

Samuel married Viola Sarah Collett, November 3, 1898 at Boulder, Boulder Co., CO. A news item has them returning to Greely. Howard Stubblefield was told by Viola Sarah that she and Samuel were cousins. From the common ancestor, William Osborn, sprang Eber Samuel Osborn and Sarah Ann Osborn. Eber Samuel m. Mary Louisa Thomas to whom Samuel E. was born. Sarah Ann Osborn married. John Collett and their son, James William Collett, married Tabitha Elma Barr. Viola Sarah Collett was a child of that marriage. Samuel and Viola's eldest son, Elmer William Osborn, was born in Plattville, Weld County, CO, a short distance from Greeley in 1899.

They next appear at Laketown, Rich Co., UT. James W. Collett wrote to them there on 20 Feb., 1900. They were still there in September of that year, as mentioned by James W. Collett in a letter of 10 Sept. 1900 to his son John in Indiana; "Viola and Sam are still in Laketown, Rich Co., Utah. Sam and some other men have gone over into the Big Horn valley looking. We had a letter last week." Conditions were desperate in these years, with drought and economic hardship throughout the area.

The family moved about 50 miles East to Kemmerer, Uinta County, WY, before 6 Jan., 1901, when the second child, Mary Elma, was born (Note that Uinta County was divided in 1912 and Kemmerer now lies in Lincoln County.) They were still there on 4 March 1902, when child Grace Ellen was born. (One letter dated 27 July 1902 was addressed to them at Frontier, a coal mining town near Kemmerer) Samuel operated a butcher shop at Kemmerer and worked as a mine machine engine operator, probably at Frontier, while in that area.

By November 1902, the family arrived in Kittitas County, WA, traveling by covered wagon, and took out a desert claim on Brushy Creek, located 30 miles north east of Ellensburg. The Brushy Creek homestead was known by several names as Brushy Creek and Quilomene Creek drained into the Columbia River close to each other and there was a place known as Dry Gulch a short walk away. It had been an Indian meeting place for many summers, and a collection of arrowheads and other stone artifacts found there is now held in a museum.

Although little is known of this trip, much can be surmised. First, the three children ages 2, 1, and an infant, would have been a handful to care for on such a journey. Geographically, they were faced with crossing two mountain ranges, the Washatch and Blue mountains, and negotiating the Snake River drainage in Idaho, in summer heat and dust. Samuel had much experience to draw on for this trip, noting his association with horses and that he had a few years previously "freighted" between Valentine, NB, and Fort Collins, CO, an airline distance of over 440 miles.

One of several possible routes from Kemmerer, Wyoming would have to follow the Bear River (present route 30) to Pocatello, Idaho, then track the Snake River through Idaho (generally along the route Interstate 84, the Oregon Trail) and NE Oregon's Blue Mountains near Pendleton, across the Columbia River and on into eastern Washington. Samuel probably scouted the Brushy Creek area before applying to the Yakima County Seat for his Desert Claim. Total distance for this trip, at a minimum, was 625 miles. For instance, at 20 miles per day, such a trip, without layovers, would take over a month. One can assume improved wagon routes at that time, but negotiating mountain passes must have been slow going, even then.

Their claim lay on the N 1/2 •of the N 1/2 of Sec. 22, TWP 19 Range 22 E, Wm Meridian; the 1910 survey is on file. By 1910 a complete irrigation system was in place and fields of grass wheat, barley and alfalfa were producing, along with orchards of many kinds of fruit, especially peaches, apricots and quince. A team of horses pulled the wagon loads of fruit to Ellensburg, where there was high demand. About 1917 or 1918, Samuel bought his first truck, used for fruit hauling into Ellensburg, and for general freight and farm use.

It took them eight years, until 1910, to prove up and get the deed. In 1913 Samuel bought the Wooster ranch on Quilamene Creek. In 1913, Samuel built a large house on the Quilamene property to accommodate his growing family and moved there from the Brushy Creek home, a distance of two miles. He expanded his farming practices to include the new property.

Along with a neighbor, Court Rothrock, Samuel built a school house in about 1907, the Dry Gulch School, Dist #37. School started there in 1908, and continued until 1925. This information, along with pictures of the school, and several classes, and the school census forms for 1910, 1911 and 1921 is in possession of Elsie Jane Osborn, who has done extensive research on this subject, and is the author of the sections on the Osborn family found in Volume I "A History of Kittitas County Washington 1989".

Samuel was chairman of the Board of Directors of the school, served as a Kittitas County Assessor, a census taker, and served on juries. He had a deep interest in Indian artifacts and had a fine collection of arrowheads, which are on display in museums in Eastern Washington. In 1926, he was employed at the Northern Pacific Railroad roundhouse in Ellensburg. In 1927, just a year after moving to Ellensburg, Samuel died of influenza during an epidemic. The family had moved to town to provide schooling for their children.

In an interview with Howard Stubblefield on May 12, 1986, he recalled that "Sam Osborn was a tall, rangy man, with a moustache; kind of an executive type, not in a hurry, kind."

As an addendum to this article on Samuel, a letter written in February 1993 by Benjamin F. Osborn, Samuel's 4th son, in response to a request for details of Samuel's life is included verbatim. It is a story filled with love and respect, and says much about the kind of person Samuel was:

"As a youth, the sons of Samuel Osborn spent a lot of time with their dad. Now, I will try to tell you some of the things I remember. It was such a thrill for me to hear Dad talk about his youth and younger years. Being a youngster with a certain amount of wanderlust, his life sounded exciting and, needless to say, also filled with hardship.

"As I remember, Dad's mother died from childbirth when he was born. His father raised him alone until he was 11 or 12 years old. As the story goes, Grandpa had been married before and had some children (I don't know how many) and his wife died. He then married a younger woman (Dad's mother). The children disapproved of her, so they left home and moved away and Dad had no contact with them ever.

"In his early childhood, being raised by his father, the two of them played the violin together (So Grandpa must have taught him how to play). Grandpa had a Stradivarius. When Grandpa died, Dad was only 11 or 12 years old and was left with a guardian, apparently appointed by the authorities. This guardian was a woman who smoked a corn cob pipe. One of Dad's jobs was to fill her pipe then get a charcoal from the fireplace and light it. He hated this chore and didn't care much for her either. So one day he collected the violin he had inherited and his personal belongings and put them outside the door, ready for a quick exit. When the time came to fill her pipe, he added a grain of black blasting powder, so when the live coal was added, the pipe blew up. He ran out of the door with a stick of stove wood behind him that she had thrown. He never went back and never saw her again and was on his own at that young age.

"Dad said he lived with the Indians for quite a while. (I presume it was Sioux) after he was alone and had to fend for himself. I do know he had learned many of their habits and customs and could speak the Sioux language fluently. Somewhere, he learned to snap a black snake whip. He could pick a fly off a horse's ear. He could shoot a gun as well as Wyatt Earp or Wild Bill. He seldom aimed — shot from the hip! He was an excellent rider and broke wild horses for his own use. I'm wondering if some of these skills were learned from the Sioux.

"As I recall he never spoke much about his life between the stay with the Indians and when he married Mother. I suppose he was moving around trying to make a living.

"After he and Mother got married, they became "frontiersmen". They left for the west in a prairie Schooner and a team of oxen. They homesteaded along the way, and when people moved in around them, they sold out and traveled further west, then homesteaded again. It was really hard, and along the way they were running out of money and supplies and Mother talked him into selling the Stradivarius violin which was worth a lot of money. They did replace it with another violin.

"By the time they reached Washington State 4 or 5 years later, they had a spring wagon and a lively team of horses. They homesteaded on 160 acres on Brushy Creek. Dad called it the "Lone Pine Ranch" because of one lone pine tree. This was in 1902. Shortly after that, Dad built a log house. I was born there in 1908 and have a picture of the front of •the house and me at about 2 years old. I barely remember when Dad bought the Quilamene Ranch (I was 5 then). I do remember people coming from all over to help Dad build this big house. "I started school at Dry Gulch but only went there a couple of years, then we went to school in our log house on Brushy Creek because it was closer and there was only our family plus one. I have a book (Penrod and Sam) given to me by Mrs. Lamb on

April 29, 1921, and I was in the 6th grade. She lived with us and taught at the old log house on Brushy. I guess as you mention Dist. #37 It probably takes in the whole area.

Bushy Creek WA Homestead

"I remember, while there, Dad farmed the Booth Ranch down on the Columbia River. He put up a windmill to pump water for irrigation, and raised cantaloupes to sell. He took them by wagonload to Ellensburg. He had an agreement to work this property but did not sign any papers as his word was his bond. I don't know how long he farmed the Booth Ranch but when he left, he sold the windmill and it was set up down by the Vantage Ferry Dock for several years.

"Another point of interest was that every winter Dad trapped, mainly for coyotes. I remember him taking 2 pack horses loaded with skins, several times during the winter as the snow was so deep it was impossible to take the wagon. He had his own technique for catching the varmints and did quite well, bringing in some extra income during the slow months.

"Dad was a very versatile man, and as a boy I thought he could do just about anything and everything and worked hard at every endeavor. Talk about living at home. Dad had his own blacksmith shop, shoeing all the horses. Also, he was a cobbler, fixing all the shoes of the family. Mother made all our own clothes on an old treadle sewing machine, and cut all our hair. I'm sure they had to work hard to support 13 kids, but to my knowledge we never went hungry. There was always plenty to eat and plenty of love, laughter and entertainment. Dad would play his violin and this was always a thrill. Mother had a beautiful voice and her favorite song was "Rock of Ages". In later years there was an organ (Al said he got it for her). I had left by then, but heard her play on visits, so she must have learned to play in her early years. Charlene (Al's daughter) has the organ now.

"In addition to the orchards and hay fields Dad also raised cattle, sheep and hogs. Each fall we butchered 15 or more hogs for our own use. In the spring, he sometimes sold to a man called "Hog Raising Red" over 100 6-week-old pigs at $6.00 a head. The cattle grazed all winter on bunch grass, besides us feeding them. Most farmers sold their cattle in the fall, but Dad waited until spring and received a prime price for them because they were so fat and in good shape after feeding on this bunch grass. We had over 100 head of sheep and each year a man would come and shear them, and Dad would sell the wool. My job was to round up the sheep and bring them back to the corral each day after school. Dad taught me how to butcher the yearling when I was 10 or 11 years old. I then butchered one every week for us to eat. My experience and knowledge of working with our own sheep helped me greatly when I went to California as I worked on sheep ranches, lambing every spring for several years.

All in all, Dad taught me many things that have helped me throughout my life. I had a great respect and love for this man who died in the same room I was in, during the flu epidemic in 1927. If I could be granted one wish, it would be to be like Samuel E. Osborn, my Dad. (By Benjamin F. Osborn)"

VIOLA SARAH COLLETT OSBORN (1879-1956) Brushy Creek Homestead

<u>Born</u>: November 20, 1879 (College Corner, Jay Co., Jackson Township, IN.

<u>Married</u>: November 3, 1898 (Boulder, Colo.- Samuel Eber Osborn (1868-1927)

<u>Died</u>: June 13, 1956 (Ellensburg, Kittitas Co., WA)

<u>Children</u>: Viola and Samuel Eber had 13 children: Elmer William Osborn; Mary Elma Osborn; Grace Ellen Osborn; Mildred Osborn; Alfred Samuel Osborn; Oliver Burt Osborn; Benjamin Franklin Osborn; George Russell Osborn; Raymond LeRoy Osborn; Cecil Lewis Osborn; Elsie Jane Osborn; Hazel Eunice Osborn; and Jennie Viola Osborn

One of Viola's daughters, Hazel Osborn McFarland, had four girls and a boy and lived in Kirkland, WA. Another family friend, Chuck Richardson married into the Osborn family.

Viola Sara Collett Osborn

Viola Sarah Collett Osborn was born on 20 Nov 1879 in College Corner, Jay Co., Jackson Township, Indiana. Her parents were James William Collett (1845) and Tabitha Elma Barr (1849) married March 21, 1867 in Jay County, Indiana. She grew up in Northeastern Indiana, where her father was a teacher. The family moved to Colorado in June 1896, when she was 16. Her high school diploma, dated June 1, 1897, from Colorado Public

Schools, Boulder District, is on file. According to letters on hand from her father, she played the church organ on occasion and was of the Methodist faith.

After marriage to Samuel Eber Osborn on 3 Nov 1898 in Boulder, the family moved first to Plattsville, CO, then to Laketown, UT, and then to Kemmerer, WY. Their first three children were born during this time. These were difficult years of depression and drought in this area. The family left WY and arrived in Kittitas Co., WA by Nov 1902. Times were hard at first; her daughter Mildred (170) recalls that a trunk of Viola's personal effects and books arrived from Lyons, CO, but they were unable to pay the freight, and lost it.

Her family remembers her as a competent, positive person with great strength of character. She would have needed all of these traits to manage the very difficult trip to WA, travelling by horse and wagon with three small children. A discussion of this trip can be found in the "Sketch of the life of Samuel Eber Osborn" included in this volume.

George and Viola with family in Brushy Creek WA

For the next 24 years, the family lived on and developed a desert claim and a homestead in the Brushy Creek and Quilamene Creek area, alongside the Columbia River upstream from Vantage, WA. They made a living farming and selling produce and animals in Ellensburg, WA, 30 miles away. She bore ten more children there, while keeping house, teaching school on occasion, and making a home for her family. All but one of her 13 children grew to adulthood.

The family moved to Ellensburg, WA in 1926, so as to be near high schools for the younger children. She lost her husband during the 1927 flu epidemic and was left with medical expenses, no income, and five children at home. Somehow, she weathered these problems and lived in a small home in town, where her life was centered on her grandchildren, her church, and many friends. Her grandson James Robert Vrooman remembers her as a short lady of medium build, with a happy face and outgoing personality. Even at advanced years, her hair remained shiny black. To quote her daughter, Mildred Vrooman, in the final paragraph of an article about memories of her mother:

"She was still a very busy, independent person, always determined once she made up her mind to do anything. I had always thought she had the highest courage and the most beautiful black hair of anyone. Certainly, she displayed great courage and fortitude during the final painful six months of her life. Her seventy—six years were full to overflowing with her great interest in literally everything. She was greatly missed!"

Memories of My Mother, Viola Collett Osborn

Daughter of Tabitha E. Collett

My earliest memories of my Mother are inseparable from a feeling of warmth, security and happiness. I recall our gathering about her to hear the stories of her growing—up years; her beautiful alto voice singing the hymns and old ballads of the Civil War period. My Father played his violin as she sang. Having been raised a devout Methodist; hymns were often heard in our home.

Since both of our grandparents had served in the Civil War, stories of that time became a part of our lives. My paternal grandfather had never recovered his health from the illness that pervaded the camps.

The two families had known each other for several generations. My Father often said Mother was his only girl, as he had known her since she was eleven days old. Since he was eleven years older than she, one can well believe that! Always full of spirit and adventure, he was to become involved to some extent in the frontier life of the times. It was a challenging way of life for him and also an opportunity to achieve financial security. Knowing her as an older woman, I feel she had to some extent developed the courage and determination that sustained her through the many difficult times she encountered in later life.

When I think of those early years, when we were young, I find myself unable to separate the person she was from the feeling of self-confidence, the courage, and determination that seemed to shine from her. Those same qualities must have been the sustaining values that carried her through the many traumatic and even tragic times of her life.

As a young girl she grew up in an age when grade school graduates accepted the fact that if further education was the goal, they must be prepared to pay for it through their own efforts.

By working after school and on Saturdays, she managed to graduate from Boulder High School. To be in church with her family on Sunday, she rode her bike up the many steep grades to the nearby town of Longmont. At times the graveled roads proved her undoing. At least once the bike wheels sank deeply into soft gravel, throwing her. There she was found lying unconscious by a man passing by on a wagon. I am sure she found some humor in that experience as she did in many later events that were frightening to her children. Perhaps in that way she was demonstrating and teaching us.

At nineteen she married the man she had known all of her life; a year later a first son was born. He was a delicate little fellow, with seemingly small desire to hang onto life. Eighteen months later a sturdy, determined baby girl arrived.

Within a year, they were to embark on a several-year wandering in hopes of saving the life of their firstborn. Medical opinion of that time frequently leaned towards a change of scene, live outdoors, and sleep under the stars. This was what they were told to do if they were to raise the little boy.

So, the long trek began slowly heading toward the Northwest.

Finally reaching Wyoming, they settled for a time in the mining town of Kemmerer where my Father opened a butcher shop. With miners fully employed, business was good and the family prospered. A third child was born. It is interesting that her clothing came from a small one room board building placed on a corner lot and owned by James C. Penny, the first of the mighty business chain of that man.

By this time, the second child was larger and stronger than her brother; when she headed for the street, all he could do was hang on to her dress and scream for Mother. Hopefully, she arrived in time.

They left that area when mining slowed down and continued west. Another mining town, a short stay, then on to the growing young town of Ellensburg which later became known as a university and agricultural center. On their arrival, Father was put in charge of laying out the city streets and sidewalks (board, of course). They must have stayed there for two years or so; surely Mother was to have her last bit of town life for some time.

The urge to have a place of their own led them to take up a homestead approximately 30 miles from Ellensburg. The spot they chose for their future home was a relatively inaccessible place since all travel was by horse and buggy. With the two fine horses left from the large number Father had before his marriage, they somehow, with much labor and determination, brought this property to a high level of production and built a solid home for their children. The once frail child grew to manhood there. He was slender and tall, able to hold his own.

Mother was often alone for several days at a time with full responsibility. Father was given the task of acting as Assessor and Census taker each year or so. It was during one of those absences that an event took place that became a prized family story. I can vividly recall Mother facing up to a possibly drunk sheep herder, a lonely man Father had permitted in and loaned magazines to on occasion. He came to the door and asked to come in. Of course, she could not let him in, even if sober, when Father was away. We children gathered round her long skirts, her very firm "you cannot come in, my man is not at home. "When he continued to insist, she took down the ivory handled Colt 45 always kept hanging high near the door, and said, "If you do not leave now, I will shoot you so full of holes. " Needless to say, we were terrified she would shoot him for she always did what she said she would. Bluff or not, he did leave though not as far as she thought. In a very short time, we followed and found him napping a few hundred yards from the house. We watched carefully until he finally left. We weren't at all sure she would not carry out her threat. Some 25 years later, at a family reunion, we told this story to her, to her great surprise. "I didn't know he hadn't gone." We had kept the secret well. The sanctity of the home and protecting the children were her responsibilities.

Another delightful memory picture stands out clearly even yet. She was seated at the ever-busy sewing machine in front of a bank of sunny windows, singing as only she could, and Father standing near her playing his violin. He had come in for a short break; possibly, he had heard her and wanted to be near her. There was much love in that home.

So far, I have not mentioned her personal appearance. Her personality was so much a part of that. Much shorter than my tall slender Father, she had very black and curly hair, which became ever more lovely with greater age, bright pink cheeks and hazel eyes that could sparkle with either humor or anger.

We were a bookish family; she loved poetry though I wonder how and when she found the time for it. Always with needlework in hand and knitting with fine yarns, she made gloves for her youngest runabout. On winter nights she sat near a corner table under the lamplight knitting with red yarn tiny gloves to go in the Christmas stockings.

She was a disciplinarian when it came to improper language; we never heard it so that was not a problem really. She would not abide name-calling. "Coward," said in anger to another, was sure to bring a spanking. She had taught school for two years or so; finding a family with teenagers, who had never attended school, was more than she could stand. What a trial it must have been, testing even her great patience. However, out of that time came a lasting friendship with one of those young people, the one who went on to school and eventually became a fine chef and professional cook. Since Mother was an excellent and imaginative cook, they found a real challenge in outdoing each other. A new cake recipe had to be baked, tested for quality in texture and in every other way. Her standards were high both in cooking and in the clothing she made for her children. Both showed the same desire for excellence in workmanship and in the many finishing touches she used. Her love for her friend Myrtle, whose infrequent visits must have been filled with "girl talk" as well as the exchange of recipes, filled a real need in her life.

She taught us a love of gardening, both flowers and vegetables, to appreciate order and beauty. Since almost all the food we required was produced, canned, preserved, or stored, it was a never-ending task. I can well remember weeding and aiding in processing while still very young.

The years passed, children grew and left home for school, work, or marriage. Those ready for high school were forced to be away for long periods, usually home for some summer months. I must have been an early-bloomer. I can recall pestering Mother to teach me letters. Since the school at that time was held near our home, in self-defense I expect, she let me start at four. At any rate, I left the nest at thirteen for high school. I never really lived at home again and never really knew my Mother very well after that for the next ten years or so. The pressures of school and work left little time.

Tragedy struck the family, my Father's death, coming just a year after their move from the homestead to a place near schools and the city, was devastating to my Mother. She was left with overwhelming medical expenses and a bout with pneumonia which added up to a dreadful burden for her. However, she picked up that burden and worked her way through it. Even with five school age children, she managed somehow.

She was to bear the loss and grief of her eldest and her youngest, and finally four more were to precede her in death. The five little grandchildren from the dead daughters were such comfort to her. Eventually she was to have twenty grandchildren and several great grandchildren. They seemed to keep her young in spirit and zest. She could identify with them, enjoy, and be enjoyed.

For many years she had lived in the city with a son who, while keeping watch, let her plan and live her life as she desired. She had purchased a home at some distance from the University. Some years after her death as that school continued to grow and spread, it finally took in the lots where her home had been.

She was happy there; her life was centered around her grandchildren, her church, and her many friends. Her beautiful yard was full of blooms for she had always loved flowers. She was still a very busy, independent person, always determined once she made up her mind to do anything. I had always thought she had the highest courage and the most beautiful black hair of anyone. Certainly, she displayed great courage and fortitude during the final painful six months of her life. Her seventy-six years were full to overflowing with her great interest in literally everything. She was greatly missed!

By Mildred Vrooman

Viola's niece, Josephine Collett Lackman, recalls that there was an Indian burial ground on the Brushy Creek homestead. Although sacred to the Indians, the Osborn's collected fruit boxes of Indian burial artifacts from the burial ground. They were quite valuable even then; some were provided to museums, and others were sold to private collectors. They served as Viola's source of income after Samual died as there were no government pensions. One wonders, male members of that family all died of "accidents" an Indian curse?

SMEAD

The surname Smead may derive from the Old English pre-7th-century "smethe," meaning smooth, and was a topographical name for someone who lived on a piece of smooth, level ground. It could also have originated as a nickname for the same word "smethe" meaning someone of amiable disposition. Various spellings include Smeed, Smeeth, Smead, Smeathe and in our case even Smythe and Smith. Smith was a very common name in early English and American history, including the formation of the Virginia Company. There are numerous Richard Smithe/Smith preceding our confirmed Smead line. Due to proximity of birth places and overlapping dates and religious affiliations I elected to start with Richard Smithe/Smith (1499/1500-1563) appearing below.

RICHARD SMYTH (Smith) (1499/1500-1563) Theologian

Born: 1499/1500, (Worcestershire, England)

Married: unknown

Died: July 9, 1563 (Douai, France)

Parents: unknown

Children: Sir Richard Cornelius Smithe/Smith (1550-1630)?

(From Wikipedia) Richard Smyth (or Smith) (1499/1500, Worcestershire, England – 9 July 1563, Douai, France) was the first person to hold the office of Regius Professor of Divinity in the University of Oxford and the first Chancellor of the University of Douai.

Oxford University Library

Educated at Merton College, Oxford, and taking his MA degree in 1530, he became Registrar of the University of Oxford in 1532 then (by royal appointment) its first Regius Professor of divinity in 1536. Taking his doctorate in divinity on 10 July 1536, he was subsequently made master of Whittington College, London, rector of St Dunstan-in-the-East and then Cuxham, Oxfordshire, principal of St Alban's Hall, Oxford, and divinity reader at Magdalen College.

Some (possibly unreliable) accounts have him renouncing Catholicism and the authority of the Pope at Oxford and (on 15 May 1547) at St Paul's Cross on the accession of the Protestant Edward VI. However, even if the accounts are reliable, soon afterwards he became a Catholic again and was thus replaced in his professorship with Peter Martyr. He and Martyr were to hold a public disputation in 1549, but fled to Leuven before it could be held.

On release he left to become professor of divinity at Louvain Belgium, returning on the accession of Mary to become canon of Christ Church and royal chaplain and take part in proceedings against Thomas Cramer, Nicholas Ridley and Hugh Latimer. Regaining most of his benefices, he lost them all again when Elizabeth succeeded Mary, and was briefly imprisoned in the House of the Archbishop Mathew Parker. On release, he again fled to the continent, this time to Douai, where Mary's widower, Phillip II of Spain, appointed him dean of St. Peter's church and then, on Phillip II's inauguration of the University of Douai, France, on October 5, 1562, the university's chancellor and professor of theology. The University of Douai was established in 1559 and in 1887 transferred as the University of Lille. Its foundation was confirmed by Pope Paul IV. Its history notes that its first chancellor was Richard Smithe/Smead and its formation coincided with the accession of Elizabeth I and the reimposition of Protestantism in England. It was at one time one of the largest and most significant universities in France.

Works

Assertion and Defence of the Sacrament of the Altar (1546)

Defence of the Sacrifice of the Mass (1547)

Defensio celibatus sacerdotum (1550)

Diatriba de hominis justificatione (1550)

Buckler of the Catholic Faith (1555–56)

De Missa Sacrificio (1562)

Refutations of John Calvin and Christopher Carlile,[1] of Philipp Melanchthon,[2] John Jewell,[3] and Theodore Beza, all published in 1562.

SIR RICHARD CORNELIUS SMITHE/SMITH (1550-1630)

Born: February 28, 1550 (Chillingham, Staffordshire or Somerset, England)

Married: Anne Gifford (1555-1583)

Died: September 20, 1630 (Shrewsbury, Shropshire, England)

Parents: unknown

Children: Sir Richard Woodhull Smithe/Smead, Richard the Great, / 1st Earl of Cork Boyle (1574-1583)

Wife Anne Gifford (1555-1583) died at age 33 in Shrewsbury, Shropshire, England. Place of birth Shrewsbury is in the same region as Worcestershire where Richard Smyth/Smith (1499/1500-1563) was born.

SIR RICHARD WOODHULL SMITHE/SMEAD, RICHARD THE GREAT 1ST EARL OF CORK BOYLE (1574-1638)

Born: 1574 (Naughton, Suffolk, England)

Married: Lady Elizabeth Mary Boyle (1572-1635)

Died: April 8, 1638 (Dorchester, Suffolk, England)

Parents: Sir Richard Cornelius Smythe/Smead (1550-1630) and Anne Gilford (1555-1583) or (alternate Sir Thomas 1 "Customer [Cornelius] Smythe (1522-1591) and Dame Alice Alicia Judde (1535-1593)

Children: **William Smead** (Smith) Sr. (1587or 90-1638); Katherine Smith (1597-unknown); and Catherine Smythe (1610-unknown); [other account includes Sir Percy Smith/Smythe; Catherine Smith; Dorothy Smyth; and Alice Smyth]

Son William Smead was born in Naughton, Suffolk, England in 1590. Wife Lady Elizabeth Mary Boyle died March 26, 1635 in London, Middlesex, England

Sir Richard married Mary Boyle, the sister of Richard Boyle, 1st Earl of Cork. Richard Boyle (1566-1643), also known as the Great Earl of Cork, was an English-born politician who served as Lord Treasurer of the Kingdom of Ireland. Her parents would have been Roger Boyle and Joan Naylor. Richard Boyle became one of the most powerful landed and industrial magnates in 17th-century Ireland. Mary Boyle was born circa 1572 in Canterbury, Kent, England. Her husband is described as Captain Sir Richard Smyth. Sir Richard Smydth, Knight, was of Ballynatray, County Waterford, and Rathcogan, County Cork. He was High Sheriff of County Waterford in 1613.

Sir Richard, as a Captain, aided in the command of the defeat and expulsion of the Spanish at Castle-Ny Parke, County Cork.

WILLIAM SMEAD (Smith) (1590-1638) Arrival in Massachusetts in 1636

Born: 1590 (Naughton, Suffolk, England)

Married: 1623 (Judith Stroughton (1599-1678) in Naughton, Suffolk, England)

Died: September 26, 1638 (Northampton, Hampshire, Massachusetts

Parents: Sir Richard Woodhull Smithe/Smead Richard the Great 1st Earl of Cork Boyle (1574-1638) and Lady Elizabeth Mary Boyle (1572-1635)

Children: John Smead (1621-); and **William Smead** (1635-1703)

At age 40, in 1630, William Smead, his wife Judith and son William arrived in Massachusetts. After his death at age 48 on September 26, 1638 his will was probated in Plymouth, Massachusetts. His body was returned to England for burial on May 3, 1639 in Wiltshire, England.

WILLIAM SMEAD (1635-1704) Phillips War/Queen Anne's War - Raid on Deerfield

Born: January 1, 1635 (Coggleshell, Essex, England)

Married: October 31, 1658 (Elizabeth Lawrence (1635-1704) in Dorchester, Massachusetts)

Died: January 1, 1703 (Deerfield, Franklin, Massachusetts) or February 29, 1704 (killed in the Raid on Deerfield

Parents: William Smead (Smith) Sr (1590-1638) and Judith Stoughton (1599-1678)

Children: William Smead (1660); Elizabeth Smead (1662); Judith Smead (1664-5); Mehitable/Mirabelle Smead (1667-1704); Samuel Smead (1669-1730); **John Smead** (1670-died in infancy); John Smead (1673-1720); Ebenezer Smead (1675-1753); Thankful Smead (1677-1704); and Wait still Smead (1679-1704).

His wife, Elizabeth Lawrence (1635-1704), was baptized in Hingham, Massachusetts, on March 6, 1641. His wife, on another family tree, is listed as Judith Stoughton (1599-1678), who was killed in the 1704 fire of son Samuel's home during the Raid on Deerfield. In any event his wife died in the raid.

The emigrant ancestors were widow Judith Smead and her son William. They came in 1636 and settled in Dorchester, Massachusetts. William was but one year old at the time. Prior to 1660, the family had settled in Northampton, Mass., and removed from there to Deerfield about 1673.

Upon the death of his mother, William Smead was put under the care of John Pope. Pope died April 12, 16 6, leaving by will unto William a conditional bequest requiring that he learn Pope's trade, and that he dwell with Pope's wife until his time was out. In any event, William was made a freeman in 1660 at age 25, bought a house in 1671, and was one of the early permanent settlers before his death in 1704.

He was in Deerfield at the time of King Phillip's War (1675-76), which pitted native Americans against English settlers. Metacomet or King Philip, the name given him by the English. The immediate cause for the outbreak of the war was the trial and execution of three of Metacom's men by the colonists. Metacom and his men began attacking and destroying English settlements and kidnapping and killing English settlers. For a while, it looked like the colonists might have to abandon the frontier and withdraw into a handful of fortified seaside towns. Attacks took place at Plymouth, Longmeadow and other places in Massachusetts and Providence Rhode Island was burned. Connecticut troops repelled an attack on Hadley, Massachusetts. Many of the Indians were captured and sold as slaves.

King Phillip's War has been called the United States' most devastating conflict. One in 10 soldiers on both sides were killed, 1200 colonists' homes were burned, and vast stores of foodstuffs were destroyed. The effects of the carnage and property damage were felt for years by the colonists. The war's ramifications for Native populations of southern New England included not only loss of life and for some enslavement, but the continued erosion of sovereignty, land rights and communities as well.

In 1704 the Raid on Deerfield occurred during the Queen Ann's War on February 29 when French and Native American forces under the command of Jean-Baptiste Hertel de Rouville attacked the English frontier settlement of Deerfield, Massachusetts just before dawn. They burned part of the town and killed 47 villagers including William and Elizabeth Smeed, and left with 112 settlers as captives including Williams's son Mehitable, whom they took overland to Montreal. Some died or were murdered along the way, and 60 were later ransomed by family and community. Others were adopted by Mohawk families and became assimilated into the tribe. In this period, the English and their Indian allies were involved in similar raids against French villages along the northern area between the spheres of influence.

SAMUEL SMEAD (1669-1730/1) Family Members Killed During Indian Raid

Born: May 27, 1669

Married: March 17, 1698/99 (Mary Price, killed in the 1704 attack); April 18, 1707 (Mary Weld who's first husband David Alexander was also killed in the 1704 attack)

Parents: William Smead (Smith) (1635-1704) and Elizabeth Lawrence (1635-1704)

Died: January 1, 1730/1 (killed)

<u>Children</u>: Sarah (1700); (killed in 1704 attack); William (1701) (killed in 1704 attack); Mary (1708) (married William Carr 1735); Sarah (1709-10); William (1712); Marcy/Mercy (1714) (married Ebinezer Nims, who had been captured in the 1704 attack, in 1735); and **Samuel Smead, Jr**. (1718-1809)

His house, valued at L50, was burned February 29, 1704; his mother, Elizabeth Lawrence Smead, first wife Mary Price and two children, Sarah and William, were smothered in the cellar; his father was also killed-see Raid on Deerfield under William Smeed 1635; a house lot was granted him in 1719, but he probably lived and died in Wapping January 1, 1730. He married Mary on March 17, 1698, daughter of David Weld.

SAMUEL SMEAD, JR (1718-1809) 1746 Siege of Fort Massachusetts

<u>Born</u>: February 25, 1718 (Deerfield, Franklin MA)

<u>Married</u>: November 28, 1743 (Rebecca Severence (March 4, 1728) from Deerfield, Franklin, MA)

<u>Died</u>: May 15, 1809

<u>Parents</u>: Samuel Smead (1669-1780) and Mary Weld

<u>Children</u>: Ezra Smead (1744); Samuel Smead (1746-early death); Samuel Smead (1748); Rebecca Smead (1752); **Nims Smead** (1754); Electa Smead (1756); Joseph Smead (1759); Polly Smead; and Rufus Smead (1764)

Removed from Deerfield to Montague, Franklin, MA, and assisted in the organization of that town in 1751; was a Tory during the Revolutionary War.

Near Deerfield where Samuel Smead lived with his family was Fort Massachusetts, the westernmost in a line of forts built by British colonists to protect the northern border of Massachusetts from French and Indian forces in 1745. It was constructed on the banks of the Hoosac River in what is currently North Adams, Massachusetts by a company of British soldiers led by Captain Ephraim Williams. It consisted of a wood stockade with a guard tower at each corner and a central blockhouse which was designed to be defensible if the walls were breached.

Samuel Smead's cousin John Smead (b 1702-John of John of William) was stationed at Fort Massachusetts in 1746. It was the site of the Siege of Fort Massachusetts, in a battle in King George's War between the twenty-one garrisoned British troops and almost a thousand allied French and Indian soldiers that resulted in the burning of the fort and the capture of the British forces and their families on August 20, 1746. According to Reverend John Norton, who was among those surviving, in his narrative "The Redeemed Captive" Captain Williams was away on business and around half the soldiers were ill at the time of the attack. Surrounded by so many forces, it was deemed impossible for a messenger to get through and ride to the fort at Deerfield for reinforcements. The British held the fort for 36 hours before surrendering to the French captain due to a lack of shot and gunpowder. The terms of surrender were that they should be prisoners of the French only, that children be allowed to remain with their families and that they be exchanged at the first possible opportunity. The first term was not heeded, but in Norton's account they weren't treated with cruelty and Indian troops carried those who were too sick or wounded to walk.

John Smead, with his wife and five children, was among those captured and was carried to Quebec, Canada. They were exchanged as prisoners of war, but only fourteen, ten men and four children lived to be traded back to the British a year later. The fourteen included John Smead and his children, arriving at Boston, August 31, 1747. John Smead was killed by Indians near the mouth of Millers River, just seven weeks later.

John Smead's youngest daughter, Mary, at about age six at the time of their capture, on the first night was wrapped in a blanket by a French soldier and soon fell asleep by his side; during the night she awoke and crept out into the darkness in search of her friends, whom she expected to recognize by feeling the hair of the sleepers; after some search she found two men lying near together, whom she took be her brothers John and Daniel (then 20 and 17), and so she cozily nestled down between them and was soon asleep; the Frenchman, missing her, went out with a blazing torch to find her; who can picture the dismay of the child when, by its light, she saw her companions to be two hideous Indian warriors instead of her brothers. She was quite willing to return to the tent. She came back motherless and was brought up in the family of Reverend Woodbridge of Hadley.

On the second day of this march, August 22, 1746, another child was added to this captive family; she was named Captivity. A litter was made of poles and bearskins on which the mother and child were carried. Captivity died in Canada on May 7, 1747.

NIMS SMEAD (1754-1781) MA to VT

Born: October 23, 1754 (Montague, Franklin, MA)

Married: October 23, 1783

Died: March 26, 1781 (VT)

Parents: Samuel Smead (1718-1809) and Rebecca Severence

Children: Elisha Smead (July 23 1874); **Chester Smead** (August 28, 1786); Elizabeth Smead (Jan. 9, 1789); Electa Smead (July 1, 1791); and Rufus Smead (Jan. 31, 1794).

Nims Smead was born in Montague, MA which is just a few miles from Deerfield. His parents were original settlers in what is now Montague Center which was established in 1754. It consists of five villages one of which is Lake Pleasant. It is tucked into the hills of Franklin County with pastoral rolling countryside. In the early 1800s grist mills and a sawmill were established there, perched over a series of waterfalls.

CHESTER SMEAD (1786-18) VT, NH to Eldred, IL

Born: August 28, 1786 (Swanzey, Gheshire, NH)

Married: October 25, 1810 (Lydia Rugg (1788-1870))

Died: Illinois?

Parents: Nims Smead (1754-1781) and

Children: **Chester Lyman Smead**; Emeline Smead Eldred; Carolyn Smead Scott and perhaps others.

There are multiple references to Smeads in Vermont during this time frame. Many moved from Massachusetts and other places at the end of the Revolutionary War in 1783 when a floodgate of settlers moved to Vermont in search of cheap land. Finding the soil poor for farming there was a mass exodus from Vermont by 1830 resulting in a move west to Illinois.

The family settled in Green County, Illinois. Daughter Emilie married James John Eldred, after which the village of Eldred, Illinois, was named. The village was founded due to its location in the Illinois River Bottoms, which combined the values of a river and bluff-sided village. The founders were known to be primarily of Scotch-Irish ancestry.

Eldred Mansion

The James J. Eldred home is a grand, Greek Revival ranch house. During the 1860s and '70s, James and his wife Emeline had a reputation for hosting grand parties at their "Bluff Dale Farm." The three Eldred daughters, Alma, Alice and Eva all died of illness at home in their beds. Both Alice and Eva were 17. Alma was only four years old. In 1999 the home was listed on the National Register of Historic Places, and in recent years the Illinois Valley Cultural Heritage Association has made great strides in restoring it.

CHESTER LYMAN SMEAD (1822-1915) Early (1859) Pioneer of Colorado

Born: February 27, 1822 (Weybridge, Addison, VT)

Married: Chester married Mary Ann Portwood on February 17, 1848 in Greene County, IL (Marriage Book 1, Page 84, License #2499).

Died: June 13, 1915 (Lyons, Boulder County, CO-buried Hygiene Cemetery, Hygiene)

Parents: Chester Smead (1786-18), Lydia Rugg (1788-1870)

Children: Oma Arvilla Smead Mott (1844-1899); Chester Lyman Smead III (1848/49-1882); Marion William Smead (1856-1927); **Warren A. Smead** (1862-September,1935 in Ellensburg, WA); Emma Caroline Smead (1864-1919); and Rufus Harrison Smead (1864-1913)

Chester Lyman Smead at his cabin

There may have been an additional young son not listed here who died while crossing the plains.

He moved to Illinois in 1836 at age 14, marrying Mary Ann Portwood twelve years later at age 26.

Family history lore has an uncle of Mary Ann Portwood as a discoverer/explorer of the Mammoth Caves in Kentucky.

Chester Lyman Smeed and Mary Ann Portwood left Illinois for Colorado with their sister Carolyn Scott, while his sister Emeline Eldred and her family remained on their large farm in Illinois. They crossed the plains in an ox-pulled cart. On their way west (believed by Lillie Smead to be in 1858 or 1859 as work started on her Grandfather's cabin in 1859) one of their young sons was run over by a wagon wheel and died. Not having available wood to make a casket, they dismantled part of the wagon for this purpose and buried him on the plains. Lillie Smead inherited an old trunk from this crossing which passed to her son Howard, and then by Howard to one of his children.

Per a lengthy article in the Denver paper on his death, in 1859 Chester Smead started for Pikes Peak but failed to reach their destination, instead remaining in Missouri (Indiana?) for a year. The following spring the trip across the plains continued by ox team. After arriving in Boulder, which was then a small fort, he continued on to Longmont, then known as the little village of Burlington. He selected a piece of land on the upper St. Vrain River to make his home. In 1860, he then sold this property to J.W. Goss and went further up the river, where he constructed a comfortable log home (the first home may have been constructed of sod). There he turned his attentions to ranching and cattle raising. Hay he raised was hauled into the mountains, where it was disposed of at a good profit. His cattle ran on the ranges during the summer and were rounded up in the fall and driven to Denver, where they were disposed of. He helped skin animals whose hides were converted into clothing and rugs. On his ranch he also raised corn, wheat and garden crops.

In advancing years, he built a new house where his "hands" lived, while he remained in the cabin. His wife, Mary Ann Portwood died when he was 60, and he "batched" thereafter while caring for his invalid son (Rufus?) who died at age 50.

One of the first settlers in the St. Vrain Valley in 1859 he homesteaded near present day Lyons Colorado (prior to the formation of Lyons). The homestead is on fertile land which was part of the prairie on his arrival.

Lyons lies at the base of a canyon 14 miles from Boulder at the confluence of the North and South St. Vrain creeks which shortly downstream join the Platte River. It is at the base of the Rocky Mountains on the edge of the plain that stretches past Denver. In the 1860s families came from the eastern United States and settled in the foothills with ranches and farms. Fort St. Vrain was nearby and active during the Indian unrest. The Plains Indians including the Ute Nation and the Cheyenne, Arapaho, Comanche and occasionally the Pawnee were attracted to the vast grasslands ideal for hunting bison. The Utes were the last tribe forced into an Indian reservation after the Colorado gold rush. The town of Lyons was founded in 1880 by Edward S Lyon for the potential quarry of its red sandstone outcroppings. Lyons was (and still is) known for its supply of red sandstone facing many historic buildings in the area and further afield, served by the narrow-gauge railway brought in to transport the sandstone.

Chester was known to be of a quiet and peaceful disposition, making friends easily. He was known to get along with the Indians who were frequent visitors in the area when other white men were at war with them. He was known to raise fine horses.

DENVER ROCKY MOUNTAIN NEWS (Colorado), Sunday, March 3, 1912:

Longmont, Colo., March 2. - C. L. Smead, living on a farm seven miles west of Longmont, last Wednesday celebrated his ninety-second birthday by inviting several pioneers to spend the day with him.

Smead enjoys the distinction of being the oldest man in the county, and few in the state are as old as he. He came to the St. Vrain Valley in 1860 and homesteaded 160 acres of land, where he built a log cabin. Later he erected a large house on the place which is used now by his tenant, while he makes his home in the cabin which is more than fifty years old.

Smead is in good health, physically and mentally. His mind is clear and his memory excellent in recalling happenings and dates. He spends a great deal of time reading and is well posted on all events of the day, and is ever ready for argument when he converses with one who disagrees with him.

Smead spends his time, aside from reading, doing light chores about the place and doing the housework for himself and his youngest son. The son is in poor health. The father looks after him as he did when the boy was a baby. He refuses the assistance of his other children, who have offered him a home with them, and says he prefers to live out his days in the cabin.

The old man is a frequent visitor to Longmont. He lives more than half a mile from a railroad station, and whenever business calls him into town, he makes the trip by train, walking from his home to the railroad station. He never fails to come to Longmont each fall when the pioneers hold their annual reunion.

He does not use tobacco or liquor in any form, and says he fully expects to live to be more than 100 years old.

Smead has four living children - Mrs. Charles Bird of Lyons, Marion Smead of this city, W. Smead who makes his home with his father, and another son living in the West.

Chester L. Smead, who lives two miles east of Lyons, was 89 years old last Monday, and quite a number of his old-time neighbors and friends reminded him of the date by calling at his home and spending the day with him. A bountiful supply of everything good to eat was taken along by the visitors and a good time in general was indulged in during the evening.

MIDDLE PARK TIMES (Colorado), June 25, 1915:

C. L Smead, a pioneer of 1859 and said to be the oldest man in Boulder County, died in his original log home, nine miles west of Longmont, at the age of 96 years. A broken hip, suffered a few weeks ago when rolling off a cot on a porch, resulted in his death.

Mrs. Smead died in 1906 at age 81. Their daughter, Emma Bird, then took care of Mr. Smead until the time of his death at age 93 on January 21, 1915. Mr. and Mrs. Smead both lie at rest in the Hygiene Cemetery.

WARREN A. SMEAD (1862-1935) Last Indian Raid in Lyons, CO

Born: February 2, 1862 (Boulder County, CO)

Married: December 20 1883 (Fort Collins, Larimer, Colorado to Della Green (aka Greeno) (1866-1939)); December 22, 1898 (Fort Collins, Larimer to Lucinda Alice Driskell (1875-1954); 1924 (Nez Perce County, Idaho to Ella Baker (1882-); and August 14, 1931 (Lyons, Boulder

County, Colorado to Cora Phibbs) [I had some difficulty confirming Della's marriage to Warren as her last name in records varies from Green, to Greeno, to Greenough and some family trees erroneously list Warren's second wife Lucinda Driskell as the mother of Della and Warren's children].

Died: September 15, 1935 (Ellensburg, Kittitas County, Washington

Parents: Chester Lyman Smead, Jr (1822-1915) and Mary Ann Portwood (1826-1906)

Children: Warren and Della Greeno Smead had two children: Lillie Lenora Smead and Herbert Smead.

Warren Smead was the third white (non-Indian) child born in Boulder County, Colorado.

Warren Smead

His first home was known as Lyons, Boulder, Colorado Territory and also as Saint Vrain, Boulder, Colorado Territory with a residence post office of Burlington and then a third as Pella (likely Pella Crossing), Boulder, Colorado. All three addresses given were physically proximate to each other and, in all likelihood, are reflective of the family's ranch, which was in the country outside of both Lyons and Saint Vrain near Pellas crossing, all in what is now Longmont, CO. The ranch and its buildings are described under Chester Lyman Smead, Jr. above.

He had younger siblings Emma Caroline Smead born when he was two in 1864 and Rufus Harrison Smeed when he was six in 1913. He also had an older sister Oma A. Smead (1859- 1899) and two older brothers Marion William Smead (1856-1927) and Chester L. Smead III (1849-1842). His Brother Chester died in Boulder County when he was 20.

His daughter, Lillie, related to me that Warren, her father, was taken and sold by the Indians, and he was with them for quite a while when he was a baby. Warren's father, Chester made a trade with the Indians (most likely horses) to get him back. Chester was a friend to the Indians, and this was all done without too much fuss.

It appears that Warren remained in Colorado until coming west with his son Herbert and daughter Lillie in about 1904.

Articles written by Warren Smead reflecting his youth include the following: The Lyons Recorder, L.T. Hartcorn, editor and publisher.:

INDIANS RAN OFF ALL THE HORSES IN THE LYONS COMMUNITY BUT ONE

Posse followed and killed one brave but failed to get the stock back. This was the last raid in this territory, says Smead pioneer, who was here at the time of the event.

Warren Smead, third child born in Boulder County and pioneer resident of Lyons, has a vivid memory of early days and has given an account of the last Indian raid in the community for readers of the Recorder.

Warren Smead was born February 2, 1862, and his parents moved to the old Smead farmstead in 1866, where the boy remained for a great many years. The old Smead place is now the McFadden farm.

There was at that time between what is now Hygiene and Estes Park a man teacher, who "boarded" around riding his horse from place to place. His horse was taken in the raid and he had to walk until he could get another.

Why no whites were killed in the raid has never been explained. The Indians were probably a bunch of young braves out for plunder and not in a big force. But they got all the horses except one colt, which belonged to Dr. Dow who lived on the Montgomery place and the mother broke back and returned. She was the only horse in the entire territory. Later, it seems, a team got out of the bunch being run away, but one of the animals got into a burning straw stack and was killed.

There was evidence that the Indian raiders had been camped on the Big Thompson and made a race from there. They went back that way and out of the country. They were over well on their way before a posse could be mounted from outside, but Dr. Dow finally headed a party, which ran across a straggler of the party at the Colard ranch on the little Thompson and they annexed his scalp.

The Indians were numerous in this section in those days, Smead states. At one time they had 500 horses on a meadow where the Bullock farm now is.

THIS INDIAN WAS LOOKING FOR HORSES THAT DAY, NOT PAPOOSES

(This is the second of a series of stories in the Lyons territory in the early days, recounted by Warren Smeed for the readers of the Lyons Recorder, September 4, 1931.)

Because a certain Redskin was looking for horses to steal and was not out for papooses on this particular day, Mrs. Susie Miller, mother of Mrs. Alvin Weese, and Warren Smead were not brought up in a Sioux wickiup as they might otherwise have been.

Just because there were some Indians out looking for scalps to hang on their belts and horses to steal, was no good reason why mothers of these two babies should not hitch up the oxen and go out after wild plums, grapes and berries to put up for winter.

It was so in the early days of this territory. These women got up earlier than usual, put their babies on comforts covering a bunch of hay in the back of the wagon and prodded their cattle along up the St. Vrain to where Lyons now stands.

There was plenty of wild fruit in the vicinity, so they put the babies under the wagon and having seen no signs of Indians for some time, they felt safe to wander about in the vicinity, filling tubs and boilers with the fruit.

But there was an Indian in the territory that their sharp pioneer eyes failed to see. He was lying upon the ledge just west of what is now the main part of town and watched their every movement.

For some time, he lay there debating as to whether he should interfere with their property, then went back to camp, reporting that he could have gotten papooses but wanted horses instead. This circumstance was reported by a friendly Indian later.

Warren Smead's aunt lived in Eldridge, Township of Ganeer, Kankakee County, Illinois, a town named for her and her husband. It is near the Kankakee River. It could have once been known as Eldridgeville and established by J.C. Eldridge.

Warren married Della Greeno (aka Adelia "Della: Greenough) in Fort Collins, Larimer, Colorado, on December 20, 1883, when he was 21 and Della was 17. (Note that Greeno and Greenough are phonetically the same and used interchangeably.)

Della's father, William J Greeno (1832), had enlisted in the Union Army in 1862, serving during the Civil War with the Unass'd 2 Missouri Cavalry. He and Rachel Martz Green were married before the war on January 8, 1852 in Wapello County, Iowa. Their daughter Della was born August 4, 1866, and their brother William (born July 1864) when she was two. They were both born in Missouri, although it appears that the family moved to Colorado after the war, which was the location where Warren J Greeno was receiving his military pension, eventually passing in September of 1875 in Loveland, Larimer, Colorado, when Della would have been 11.

Della and Warren's children Herbert Warren Smead (1884-1966) and Lillie Lenora Smead (1886-1986 at over 100 years!) are both shown as being born in Colorado although Josephine Lackman, one of their granddaughters, is emphatic that they were born in Idaho and their births were recorded when they returned to Colorado.

What happened between Warren and Della's marriage in 1883 and Warren's subsequent marriage 15 years later to Lucinda Alice Driskell (1875-1954) on December 22, 1898 in Fort Collins, Larimer County, Colorado isn't entirely clear although his daughter Lillie related that he was a builder in Fort Collins and accompanied her and brother Herbert to Oregon in 1904.

Della's brother William (1864-1948) married Ella Frasier on January 23, 1896 in Union, Oregon. Union County borders Joseph and Wallowa Lake which came to play significant roles in family history, particularly that of Della's daughter Lillie Lenora Smead. He and his family lived in Imnaha, Wallowa, Oregon at or shortly after his daughter Mabel Greeno's birth in 1899. Imnaha is a tiny, tiny place and also the location of the Stubblefield homestead described elsewhere under the Lillie Smead and the Stubblefield trail portions of this book. Family lore has Della having a homestead both at Imnaha, Oregon and what is now Whitebird, Idaho. It may well be the homestead in family stories was her brother William's, although it is quite possible that she had an interest in it.

By 1920 both Della and William Greeno were living in Lewiston, Nez Perce, Idaho. My aunt

Warren Smead's son Herbert was living in Joseph, Idaho County, Idaho on May 4, 1910. Son Herbert was a farmer and horticulturalist who among other things developed new strains of walnuts. He was a longtime resident of the Lewiston, Clarkston ID area. Father Warren had a farm near his son for a number of years perhaps in the 1920 's and 30.

Records indicate that Warren Smead was living in 1900 in Lyons, at age 38, but may have moved to Joseph, Idaho by 1910 (although it could have been Joseph Road, Whitebird, Idaho). This was after his mother, Mary Ann Portwood, died in Lyons in 1906. He was then in Yellow Pine, Idaho, as shown on the 1920 census, and married Ella Baker in February 1924 in Nez Perce County, Idaho, moving to Pataha, Garfield, Washington, at age 68. The move to Joseph and the Lewiston area in Nez Perce County was likely to be closer to his children, Herbert and Lillie, whose mother, Della Greeno Smead, lived in those locations. Son Herbert is shown as living in Joseph, Yellow Pine, Pataha, etc. He returned to Lyons, Colorado in 1931 to marry Cora Phipps. He passed away on September 15, 1935, in Ellensburg, WA.

There were overlaps during this period with William Greeno's family, with, for example, his daughter Ella Greeno [Greenough] Frasier living in Imnaha, Wallowa, OR, Union, OR and Lewiston, Nez Perce, ID.

LILLIE LENORA SMEAD (1886-1986) Homestead near Imnaha, OR/Carousel Proprietor

Born: April 19, 1886 (Loveland, Laramie County, CO)

Married: Newell Stubblefield (1906); George Collett (August 1916-Ellensburg, WA); Joe Stevens

Died: May 2, 1986 (Walla Walla, WA, buried near Langley, Whidbey Island, WA)

Parents: Warren Smead (1862 – 1935) and Della Greeno (1866 – 1938)

Children With Newell Stubblefield: Arvilla, Howard, and Emory

Children With George Collett: Mary and Josephine

Lillie Lenora Smead (April 19, 1886 Loveland, Laramie County, CO- May 2, 1986 Walla Walla, WA, buried Whidbey Island, WA) and George Collette (June 16, 1884 Collette, Jay County, IN –September 1, 1958 Walla Walla, WA) were married August 1916 in Ellensburg, WA.) They were both from near Lyons, CO.

Lillie lived a colorful but difficult life. She was a small woman (under five feet tall), strong willed and determined. She was Pentecostal with lots of "Praise Jesus" and daily prayers.

Much of Lillie Lenora Collett's early life is captured in her own words using a check register page as paper. Minor edits have been made to correct some misspellings, add punctuation as the phrases ran together without paragraph breaks, etc. There were a few words that were difficult to read but I believe we have pretty fully grasped the content of her story. Other provisions in quotes are reflective of an interview I did with her captured then on cassette tape and subsequently transcribed.

Lillie's words:

January 14, 1960, Today is a stormy, disagreeable day. I worked pulling nails for 2 hours, came back to the trailer house, got an iron barrel, dug a hole, and fixed my dog a good bed, covered it with galvanized tin, he has a door, as he overshadows one most of the time.

I have thought for a long time that I should write a brief outline of my life, especially to give an account of the homes I have helped to make and own, beginning at my first and earliest childhood home.

I was born in a log hut in Larimer County, Colorado, in what is known as Rattlesnake Park. This place is found above Loveland and close to Bald Mountain. There was no doctor present on this occasion. At an early age my father and mother homesteaded in Wyoming when the cattle war was on. About all I remember about this home was a very large home made of clapboard; at least when I was so tiny it seemed so to me. I was hiding in it when playing hide and go seek with my brother, and again I was such a small ball. I remember I would roll myself up in bed. One day my brother was setting a rabbit trap and caught my finger. Jim Bond made a little toy gun for me and himself out of a board. When the antelope would and my brother and I would shoot at them.

Then my next remembrance was I found myself at Smead's on St. Vrain River, Boulder Co., Colorado, and my father and mother lived in the milk shed and the old log house with a big fireplace, which was built in 1859-60 -100 years ago. The milk shed was covered with the flat wide flagstone they quarry there, and three of these flagstones formed one whole side of the building.

The saddest and most important event I remember was when I was five years old, and I was standing out under a tree. I will never forget the spot where my mother bid me farewell, and I never saw her again until I was 12 years old. It must have been very soon after all this that the chip room, the mop, and the dishrag were also put into my hands. My granddad was there, and I can't remember when there were not one to three old men hanging about for their board and room free, and that called for extra work.

My grandmother was a very hard worker and helped plant and raise a garden, pick and stem gooseberries, which means pick squash bugs, potato bugs, and tomato worms. My brother helped to do some of these things, but he, being a boy, seemed to escape from the greater part of it. He had a pet badger and would go to the big ditches and fish and swim, catch butterflies and roam the hills. He brought many a good mess of fish home to us. He loved to tantalize and tease and got by with a lot of it. My grandmother cooked and made her own soup in a large kettle outside. My brother and I took turns stirring it, and I was barefoot, and he took the paddle. We stirred the crackling and hog entrails we made soup out of, dished out a portion of them, and threw them on my bare feet. I know he didn't realize what he was doing, this was just one of his tantalizing pranks.

My pastime (when there was any) was spent picking Johnny Jump Ups, playing with my pet lamb, hunting turkey nests, gathering mushrooms, playing in the straw with my brother and cousins that spent about as much time at my granddads as they did at home. My cousin Jessie always had stomach aches when it was time to wash dishes, and most always got by with it. Her mother and my grandmother did not like my mother and loved to say mean things about her in my presence. This made me very unhappy and I grew very bitter over it. They had a dislike for me on account of my mother and life was usually one round of unhappiness. Only when my father would come to see us (he usually was many miles away working) but when he came, I was one happy little girl. He would take me up and usually called me pet, I always called him "pa". They would never let me know he was sending any money home to take care of my brother and me, but after I got older, I realized it, the hard-earned money that supplied the whole bunch, aunt and kids, and me included.

Usually, once, sometimes twice a year, my father would take my brother and me to where my mother's brother lived. This was my birthplace. Uncle Marion and Aunt Mati Greeno have 2 girls around our age, and I lived from one time or year to the next to get there. It seemed like heaven to me to be carefree for a little while. And oh, I can see us all playing hide and go seek and blind man's bluff, yet I was small and could dodge so easily and make my getaway. I can hear my uncle Marion laughing yet.

I enjoyed going to school which helped break the monotony, but remember the dishes had to always be washed before my brother and I took off to walk or usually as he was long legged and when I would get out of breath and couldn't keep up, I'd spin some kind of interesting yarn or story for a few minutes to hold him so I could catch my breath. We had the same teacher for many years "Florence Chapin" and this one school was the only one I ever went to. I remember my brother used to get in many fights. He was nearly two years older than I was, but he had a sis that stood by, and I had more or less learned to hold my own by being with no one to take my part, and I would fight for my brother.

Of all the things that happened in my young life, I am grateful for a teacher who read a little out of the Bible and sang a hymn before she started the day. And I am grateful to be kept in school until I at least got an average education.

When I was 12 years old, my mother came to see my brother and me. It was after supper that she walked in on us. I recall there were several sitting around the old fireplace having a good chat and I was out in the kitchen washing dishes alone when she came to the kitchen door. She told us afterwards that she always felt that when she found me, I would be washing dishes. I often think of the big batches of light bread to feed all the strays that lived off from my folks and I can't remember any of them ever lending a hand. I could make light bread when I was 12 years old as good as I can now. How much younger. Wash days were hectic, my brother had to help do that, but escaped, and we didn't have electric washers and ironers either.

I usually had one Sunday summer dress and one good winter dress a year, and the rest of mine was Mother Hubbard's, which was what I always wore to school. It was all the kind my grandma could make, and I was always so happy to get a new one. She used to sometimes braid my hair into pigtails so it would be curly and fluffy, and I could be pretty occasionally. I remember my first skirt. The skirt was black and the waist was red, with flannel, and I was ever so proud. I thought I was a young lady for sure. I was a little past 12 years old.

Well, it wasn't long after my mother returned to Oregon that my father remarried and lived away from my grandparents. It was a sad day for me as my stepmother wanted me and what for? Well mostly to do the drudgery and let her play, and that is what she did most of the time. She was fickle and unstable and not good to my father, herself, or anyone else. I managed to stick it out until turning 18. I told my Dad I would stay till I was 18 then I was gone. She left him so many times during that time that he was growing weary and ready to let her go for good.

So, when I got ready to go to Oregon, he was ready too, so he, my brother, and I all left Colorado at the same time. We first stopped up at the Sumpter mines close to Baker City, Oregon. The snow was about 12 feet on this level, and it was in March, and people had tunnels into their mines and homes. This was in 1904 and that same spring I left and went to Imnaha, Oregon to be with my mother. It was quite a change in routine and way of living. My mother had cattle, and there was a lot of riding on horseback to be done. That year around the third of July there was an awful water spout which washed most of her orchard and fertile ground away. All her chickens but one old hen which was on driftwood when found. We all took to the high ground and escaped, building a fire under a big pine tree until most of the storm was over. The pavilion we had built washed away, had it been the 4th instead of the 3rd, we would have all drowned. After this my mother decided to go to Idaho and run her cattle. We crossed Snake River which was wide open for 640-acre homesteads. And I don't know and never did know how many acres and homesteads my mother owned when she sold her cattle and left but anyway, I got my share of riding the range, camping in the wide-open spaces, being scared of cougars, which would be mostly people trying to run us off but once in a while the real thing.

At the age of 20 years on March 13, 1906, I was married to Newell Stubblefield, thus my first home was a new cottage in Enterprise, Oregon, where we were married. I was proud and loved to keep it clean but soon afterwards my husband moved to Chico, Oregon which was about 35 to 40 miles out. He drove the stage from Enterprise there and I run the Post Office.

But alas! alas! a terrible thing happened to me, as a horse ran away and I was thrown hitting my head as I landed on top of my head, and the speed of the animal as I tried to jump and did jump to keep from being rolled over the bank into the river as my saddle was turning and I had no bridle on my horse. My spine was pushed several vertebrae past the other and all out of line. The doctors failed to help, and I suffered it out until my first child was born. I was hauled back to Enterprise on bedsprings and managed to make it through by a very narrow margin. The doctor did me no good, and for four years and six months, I was very poorly and most of the time I was in bed.

My husband and I decided to make a change again, and I was hauled on bed springs for many miles trying to get to where my father and brother's homestead was in the vicinity of where I had helped my mother. It was a rugged trip as the Snake River was as far as we could travel with a tram and wagon. We made camp on the river and sandbank. Baby and I stayed there while Newell and Herbert, my brother, swam the horses across the Snake River, got a little rowboat, and got our supplies and ourselves finally all on the Idaho side. From there on, Newell carried the baby and led the horse I sat on, and we managed to make it about ½ way up the long, steep, rugged mountainside before night overtook us. Newell had to clear a place on the side of the mountain in the slide rock to make our bed. With my back broken and hardly able to sit up but for a short while at a time, the 2nd day we got to my brother-in-law's place, and he was always very congenial and made life as pleasant as possible. After resting up we started out again up Divide Creek to my father's place traveling the same way and rested there a few days.

Newell got a tent set up on our 640-acre homestead, thus my 2nd home. We had a rugged time, managed to keep warm and had Bannocks (type of bread), beans and potatoes some of the time to eat. The snow was around one foot to 18 inches. The most tragic thing that happened was that our puppy went mad, and the baby and I had been confined to the tent with him while he was going through the early stage. He followed Newell to work the first time when he became really bad, consequently lay out in the woods all night, and the coyotes surrounded him. After that a real panic of coyotes, cattle, horses, hogs and people with the disease. Newell set the baby in my arms in a tree on a limb for safety while he got a horse to find and kill the dog.

When my log cabin was finished and I could shut the door, it looked better and meant more to me than any mansion ever made could look. As time went on a little boy "Howard" came to "Wild Cow". The name of our 640-acre homestead. 4 ½ years have gone by, and I got to visit a good Osteopath doctor, which straightened me out a lot. Nearly a month before I could walk after the baby boy came and good fortune came my way when I got my back helped but not entirely well.

An opportunity afforded itself for us to move to a lower climate and I took a desert claim on what is known as Sulphur Springs on the Snake River--- thus my 3rd home. Many unusual things happened. Newell drove the Lumberton horses back from Eureka Mines on the Snake River over the most rugged and dangerous trails there are anywhere. Once on top of a steep mountain, before going down to the river, the horse rolled with lumber tied to her sides and turned somersault after somersault until she got to the bottom, and to his amazement, she was not injured or killed. The lumber caught the weight, her ribs were broken, her eye was out, but she lived.

It was at this homestead that our 3rd child was born, "Emory", his father naming him. In the meantime, Newell got a wild idea to mortgage our homestead and buy a Jack and a bunch of horses and nurse horses (mules). The children and I raised a garden and killed any rattlesnakes. Arvie and Howard were very young but they learned to catch our saddle horse or horses many times. We all rode the same horse but they eventually had a gentle old mare "Old Seeley". We usually rode to the garden and always to "Wild Cow", our homestead. We didn't have many neighbors and what we did have would pull pranks on us to scare me out and get the land. We made a real ride of thirty miles just in time to telephone my filing money into the land office in Lewiston, Idaho. They went partway on horseback, then took a car, but the telephone let them do it.

The children were getting to school age and things had to change. I finally had a couple, the name of Van Poole, come and offered to trade me their lovely home in Grangeville for my desert claim because it controlled so much land and accounted for water. This was the only really nice home I ever had, but I did not get to even stay all night in it, thus my 4th home, as Newell would never consent for us to live there. The outcome was a 160-acre place in Harney Valley, Oregon. Cold and bleak place with an old log cabin thus my 5th home.

Something has happened at the mismanagement and misunderstanding, something that cannot be understood or put into words, only to say a lack of faith and confidence. When our homestead went, love and confidence went with it, the trials of sickness, and unwillingness to give and take, in other words rebellion of heart brings separation. I found myself weighed and found wanting, not knowing God and being controlled by the devil on the part of both Newell and me. And thus the 6th home is 14 miles from Parnia, Idaho in farming country. My health is run down, and financial difficulties have arisen after a period of around two years. We are losing our home when it is about ½ paid for and through sickness I find myself going to Cultesac, Idaho to stay a while at what was originally known as Cultesac Faith Home, my mother backing it financially and otherwise.

[Her notes fail to directly include her separation and divorce from Newell as depicted elsewhere in notes from my conversation with her, when she walked away to live in a tent with the children trading a horse for a carousel on Wallowa Lake, Oregon. Some family members say the cause of the separation was long spells when Newell refused to talk to her and others Newell's tiredness with her constant preaching.]

After a course of time, our little Mary was born, her father being away and never seeing her until she was around 8 months old. All the while I am learning my lessons that God's ways are not my ways and he is looking for a shielded vessel to become pliable, to be the clay and let God mold, break and make me after his pattern, and be able to say not my will be God but thy will be done. The Lord is intervening in both our lives. He is also "George". After this experience, and I being faced with death, I promised God if he would come home, I would die for him if that is what it took, and was gasping my last, stricken and bedfast, and repent before I could be revived and brought back. Thus, George, my husband and father of my baby, came to realize after much suffering that it doesn't pay to want to go his way and serve the devil, and our home is established again.

We find ourselves traveling in a covered wagon and mule team from Culdesac, Idaho, to Ellensburg, Washington. Seven years have passed since our little Mary was born, we have been visited by another baby girl, little Josephine, at home in Ellensburg, and further, we have a 15-room apartment house that George is building in Kittitas, Washington. Making the 8th home.

From the apartment house bring up to the 9th home we bought in 1947 ten acres on Whidby Island making it our home until sickness drove us to travel. In the meantime, we are buying and using two trailer houses for our home 2 trailer houses which brings us to the 10th home. In the years 1958 and 1959, I myself obtained a cabin on my Placer mining claim at Tepoca, California, helping to build it, and now it brings the number to 11th home. On this date, I find myself living in another trailer, which I helped buy, and I also call my home the 12th home. While I occupy said trailer house I am working on a cabin, building a home for someone. It is located on Vanetta and Bob (Arvilla's daughter and husband) and Elmers (Emory's boy) claim.

I have been asking myself whether I have made my life count. This is a brief biography of Lillie Lenora Smeed Stubblefield Collett's life. January 14, 1960.

Beginning from 1960, bringing up to date 1968, many interesting and venturesome stories to tell, especially my mining experience at Tecopa Mineral Health Springs. In the past 10 years being left alone, my husband passing in 1958 I have accomplished dehydrating the mineral water at these famous health springs into a bath salt to be shipped all over the world. Dedicated to my family if Susie will make some copies Lillie Lenora Collett

Her parents, Warren Smead and Adelia Della Greenough (aka Greeno, 1866-1969), separated when Lillie was five. Lillie then returned to live with her grandfather, Chester Lyman Smead, on his ranch near Lyons, CO. Lyons is a few miles south of Loveland, where Lillie was born. She did not see her mother again until she was 12 when her mother visited. As Lillie said "She came back to see us kids. She stayed all summer and then had to go back to her home in Oregon. And she wanted me to go with them, and I told her I was always good and I used some good sense and I was not going to kid either. I told her that would not be right, and Jay, they had taken care of me, my Grandfather and Grandmother, and my father and it would not be right for me to run off and go with her to her home. I used my judgment at that time and I got a pretty good education by staying there with Grandpa and Grandma. I went through the ninth grade, which was a pretty good education in those days. I stayed with them all through until I was 18."

With respect to her grandfather Lillie said "My Grandfather Smead was a man that got along with everybody and you never heard of him having a fuss with anybody. He was awful good natured. Nobody ever went through there hungry or needed anything when he didn't take them in. He fed more old dogs. I washed more dished for old cowhands than you could shake a stick at when I was a kid you know."

While in Lyon, living with her grandfather, Lillie met George Collett, whom she was to marry years later. Lillie recalled with respect to George Collett that "Yes, his people, we were all there together in Colorado. Played hide and go seek together and everything else you can think of." Lillie's favorite cousin was Oma Gidson, daughter of Vinnie Mott Gidson and Oma Arvilla Smead Mott (her grandfather's sister).

In the meantime, while Lillie was growing up in Colorado, her mother Della Greennough acquired a large homestead in Idaho and possibly a second (likely her brother's) in Oregon on opposite sides of the Snake River. She became relatively wealthy. After her divorce from Warren Smead, Della Greenough Smead had a "common law husband," as Mary Hadley put it, Jim Bond, who helped manage Della Greenough's properties and crews.

Family oral history has Jim Bond being a "cousin" of Della's. The 1920 US Census lists Jim Bond and Della as cousins living in the same household with three lodgers. Della and Jim were the same age, both born in about 1867, although his place of birth is given as Iowa. His occupation was listed as a partner in the boat industry, acting as an employer. His mother's birthplace is given as Indiana. It is not inconceivable that the Colletts, Osbornes, and other families described in this text were part of shared wagon trains coming west.

The town of White Bird, Idaho, was founded in 1891 when Lillie was five. It is located on a small portion of Della Greenough's White Bird homestead. White Bird is on White Bird Creek not far from its confluence with the Salmon River. It is near the Salmon River crossing point for the Lewis and Clark expedition. It is also the location of the Battle of White Bird Canyon in 1877, which was the first fight of the Nez Perce War and a significant defeat of the U.S. Army. Chief White Bird was a leader of the tribe. Its elevation is 1581 feet; however, above the city, the summit of White Bird Hill is 2700 feet. It is a small town with a current-day population of about 95 in a beautiful setting, having steep cliffs and rapids along the Salmon River. White Bird, on Lillie's mother's homestead, is where Howard Stubblefield was born.

Nez Perce Indians

Della and Jim Bond had been able to buy the homestead for $100 when the original homesteaders were going broke. White Bird is about thirty miles as the crow flies from the Imnaha homestead. At that time there were a number of ferries crossing the Snake River.

The Salmon River intersects with the Snake River a few miles downstream of the confluence of the Imnaha River with the Snake River. Although there has never been a road through the steep canyon through which the lower reaches of the Imnaha River flows, there are signs of a path along the side of the river that could have been traversed on foot or by horseback.

My mother Mary Collett Hadley recalled "Grandma Smead" having another homestead near

Imnaha, Idaho, on Lightning and Little Sheep Creeks. This could have been the location of Della's brother William's homestead. These creeks drained into the Imnaha River from the west, not far from the Stubblefield homestead on Horse Creek entering the river on the east side. It is probable that the Smead's knew their Stubblefield neighbors and that was where Lillie Smead and Warren Stubblefield met.

In any event when Lillie was 18 (in 1904), her father Warren, brother Herbert and she traveled to Oregon. Warren and Herbert took up work in a mine in the mountains above Baker, Oregon while Lillie went on to visit her mother in Idaho. Later Lillie's father and brother visited Lillie and established homes near Lewiston, Idaho.

Della's home at that point is believed to be in Culdesac, ID is in the Nez Perce Indian reservation. Culdesac lies on Lapwai Creek which empties into the Clearwater River which at Lewiston, ID merges with the Snake River. It is about 55 miles from the White Bird homestead. It was a nice home with a wide breezeway on a hill with a small lake on the property nearby.

Lillie Lenora Smead about 1904

[May 12, 1904 news article] "Mrs. Della Smead is made happy by the presence of her daughter, Miss Lillie Smead, who came from Lyons, Colorado. On a visit, Mrs. Smead was introducing her daughter to friends in Bell City on Sunday, as the young lady is very prepossessing in her appearance and manner. We do not wonder that her mother was smiling and happy for her."

Mary Hadley remembers that Lilly's cousin, Bill Walker, would sometimes entertain them with his fiddle and song. Billy Walker lived in Lewiston and listed his occupation in the 1870 US Census as mule skinner. A muleskinner was a muleteer or mule-driver. He is remembered for his wonderful book, "The Longest Rope – The Truth About The Johnson County Cattle War" by D.F. Baber, as told by Bill Walker, Copyright 1940 by The Caxton Printers, Ltd, Caldwell, Idaho.

James "Jim" L. Bond (April 20, 1866, Wapello, Iowa – October 23, 1953 Lewiston, Nez Perce, ID). Della's cousin and common law husband was a talented engineer, among other things, designing some of the ferries providing transportation across the Snake River. He also helped manage Della's properties. Stealing of timber was a frequent problem. Jim Bond and Della Greenough had a child, Elsie (a redhead), born August 16, 1891. One story reported from multiple sources has Elsie and Lillie camping on their own in or near a family barn. Hearing a mountain lion (cougar) they threw their bedrolls into the hay loft where they hid staying quiet. Elsie married Albert Joshua Poole, who my mother and a cousin referred to as "gunslinger" and "outlaw" who was in hiding from the law. Stories are of Elsie being "crazy" (her parents were first cousins so that might have had an impact). When Lillie was visiting with her daughter

Mary Elsie had one of her "fits". Lillie told my mother (Mary) to hide under the bed with Elsie coming after Lillie with a knife. Al Poole was a part of the notorious Poole Gang (see Appendix).

There is also a note from J. Stubblefield, 11/16/1905: "Don't buy new shoes when you can have your old ones made as good as new. Bring me your work. Satisfaction guaranteed." This would have been prior to Lillie's arrival, but it confirms that Lillie's mother was acquainted with the Stubblefields.

While in Idaho with her mother, Lillie worked in a dress-making business. Her mother, Della, wanted her to go take care of her mother who was sick. This would have been at the Imnaha property. There she no doubt met her first Husband Newell Stubblefield.

Despite her mother's wishes, Lilly married Newell Stubblefield in 1906 at about age 20. Their first home was at the Stubblefield homestead on Horse Creek near its juncture with the Imnaha River north of Imnaha, Oregon (45 degrees 40" 43.1 N, 116 degrees 46" 06.1 W). The homestead was originally established by Newell's father, Billy and is described in the story of Billy's colorful life. It's in the Hells Canyon Wilderness area, beautiful with its mountains, steep cliffs, but not overly hospitable for farming, with ditches from upper Horse Creek carrying water to the orchards and gardens. It was composed of a full section, 640 acres. Their home consisted of two cabins connected by a covered breezeway, outbuildings and a small structure constructed over the creek where they could keep things cool. They had a small orchard where they raised peaches. They had a cow, some beef cattle, horses, mules and chickens.

The homestead was called "Wildcow," As Lillie related "the last wild cattle was killed on that creek where we homesteaded. They killed the last; they had wild cattle over there, and they killed the last ones; they exterminated them right there on the creek where we homesteaded."

The nearest town was Imnaha, only a few years old at that point. The name Imnaha means "land ruled over by Imna"; Imna was a local Native American subchief. It is the easternmost settlement in the state of Oregon at the confluence of Big Sheep Creek and the Imnaha River. Its elevation is 1978 feet. Its post office opened January 4, 1885, but the townsite was not established until 1901, and was platted in 1902.

[The following is per Mary Hadley, April 8, 1998]. Summer about 1915. The young family had found a homestead with a house and a peach orchard. While Lillie, the young wife took care of the three little children, her husband walked to the nearby community of Imnaha, Oregon where he was a blacksmith. Lillie had her eyes on that peach orchard as a cash crop. Unfortunately, others too remembered those luscious peaches. As the peaches were about ready to pick, she found local fellows were helping themselves. Lillie politely asked them not to take advantage, but she got busy building a fence just in case. A day or two later, the showdown came, and the intruders were met by a feisty little lady with blood in her eye and a very big gun! Fortunately, they got the message. But that wasn't the end of the story. Next, she found the road was a shortcut from Wallowa Lake to the Snake River for the Nez Perce Indians. Being a smart businesswoman, Lillie decided half a cash crop was better than none and invited the Indians to help themselves. After eating their fill, they were on their way. There was still time to get the rest of the crop to market. [There was another story that when Newell was home catching the Indians after their peaches, he threatened to sick his dog "Bogus" on them. Bogus was known to hate Indians.]

Lillie and Newell's time together was tumultuous. Lillie said "[Newell] inherited from his granddad a stubborn, rebellious disposition." She acknowledged that she too was stubborn. One problem was that after giving birth to three children she broke her back. She told me, "A horse ran away with me and landed me on top of a big rock, and for four years and six months, my back was broken. vertebrae and it was all out of place." This resulted in Newell having all the work to do . . ."He washed the baby's diapers, he done all the cooking, he had to make a living and half the time we never knew where the next meal was coming from and my mother was mad at me because I married him . . . and he got on how anyone would get so much up and down, up and down, up and down, go down the trail, go to milk and have a fight with the old cow and come in and take his fight out on me and me sick and he wouldn't speak for a week at a dime and was discouraged too." Their trials trying to make a living from the homestead added stress. I asked if they tried raising horses. She responded, saying, "Yeah, that was what broke us. He got, you see there was no money there. He has no money, that's why he would work out herding sheep or something. He would try to make a go at raising turkeys and he and I worked hard all one summer, what little I was able to do, you see they had to drive the turkeys about 35 or 40 miles to market and we sent those turkeys to Cottonwood to the market and his brother came back bringing a sack of sugar. He blew that money, and most of it was for whiskey for him and this other fella. That's all we had out of our summer's work." I asked and then you raised horses after that. She said "Well yes, he ah, there was an old man over there that had a jackass and he figured that he could get a bunch of mares and he would raise mules and that's what he went and did. . . but he never got good with them. He had a lot of, quite a few horses, and I traded five, I guess, mares, but he did no good with them. Everything he did, Jay, was a failure. [but] nobody worked harder than he did."

The family appears to have then moved from the homestead to Joseph, as the children were reaching schooling age. Lillie related after not being able to talk with Newel for weeks at a time and after ten years of marriage "finally I said it's enough, it's enough, it's enough, and when I was able to walk, we was living up in Joseph, that was five miles from our home town of Enterprise and I would walk five miles down there to Enterprise and found me a lawyer and told him I wanted a divorce that that was it." Having a lifetime to reflect back on this period, she went on: "Jay, if I were to do over again, I would have better sense than to do that, but I was mean too. I was as mean as he was. That's the reason I got my divorce from him for he was a good man. He didn't, I don't think, he spoke but he didn't have a whole lot of other bad habits and was an awful good worker."

Newell and Lillie had three children: Arvilla Stubblefield (December 20, 1906 Enterprise, OR.); Howard Stubblefield (July 2, 1909 White Bird, ID); and Emory Stubblefield (1913 Hells Canyon area, OR.). Lillie, when Newell was away, she took the three children on horseback to Wallowa Lake near Joseph, Oregon. There she saw a man struggling with his mule which powered a wooden carousel, she persuaded him to trade the mule and carousel for her horse. She and her three children lived in a tent near the amusement park. She made more money than she had ever seen in her life! She stayed there for three years and was able to support herself and the three children off earnings from the carousel.

She then left with her three children for her mother's home in Culdesac. She said, "She took us, little kids in and gave us a home, all of us."

From Lillie's memory, "[George Collett] came from Colorado, you know, and then he came to his sister's place on the Columbia River, and he worked with them for a long time, but he came to see us, and I don't know where he went from there. It was quite a while before we got married."

George Collette (June 16, 1884, Collette, Jay County, Indiana –September 1, 1968, Walla Walla, WA.) and Lillie were married August 1916 in Ellensburg, WA.) [George's sister Viola Osborn lived in Ellensburg, which might explain this location, although Mary was born on December 14, 1922, in Culdesac, ID, where they were living with Lillie's mother, Della Greenough.] Their second child together, Josephine Omar Lackman was born February 26, 1929 in Ellensburg, WA

While in Culdesac George worked on Della's farm.

In 1925 George, Lillie, three-year-old Mary, and Lillie's three children from a prior marriage, Emory, Howard and Arvilla (Arvy) Stubblefield walked and rode a wagon from Lewiston, Idaho to Kittitas, Washington, a distance of in excess of 220 miles. The wagon contained their humble belongings from Culdesac, Idaho where they had been living with Lillie's mother, Della Greenough [Smead]. Notes suggest that the mules pulling the wagon may have been provided by Jim Bond.

When Newell found out about the marriage, he blamed George Collett of stealing his wife and set out to kill him with his gun. George went into hiding in various places, including staying with cousin Osborns on their Brushy Creek/Dry Gulch homestead north of Vantage on the Columbia River. Newell eventually remarried and had a large second family.

George, Lillie, daughter Mary, Josephine, and their stepsister Arvilla (Arvy) lived in an apartment building in Kittitas. I remember hearing from my mother about a black woman who helped care for Josephine, who was an infant at the time.

The family moved to South Pearl Street in Ellensburg in 1942, then to the Capitol Hill area of Seattle, where daughter Arvilla had a cobbler shop, and Mary Collett worked at a pharmacy across the street. In 1946 George and Lillie Collett moved to a small acreage on Saratoga Road near Langley, Whidbey Island.

Later in life, Lillie and George Collett pulled a house trailer to Tacopa, California, where she had a mining claim, mining salts and clay from the mineral-rich soil, selling both in mason jars.

I remembered Lillie into her 70s with a loaded shotgun next to the back door at her rural Whidbey Island home. She would drive an old pickup truck with loose steering and three on the floor with us kids aboard.

Grandchildren of Lillie Smead

Footnotes:

1. Lillie's cousin, Bill Walker tells the fascinating old west story of his kidnapping in "The Longest Rope, The Truth About the Johnson County Cattle War" by D.F. Baber, as told by Bill Walker, The Caxton Printers, Ltd. Caldwell, ID 1940.

2. Mary Hadley left notes from a Snake River trip at 7:30 August 11, Beamers Landing or Beamers Marine on Snake River Avenue, Lewiston, Idaho [there was mention of a hotel once owned by Della Greenough in Lewiston but don't know if that is it] as follows: Della's mother was Ruth Greenough. Ruth composed music and wrote Sunday School literature. In the Culddesac home a Mrs. Grooms, who was a pianist for the White House came from Washington DC to be healed at their home. Other family footprints include the names Myathenis and Gravis, and that cousins of Grandma Della Greenough Smead included John and Lillie, Edith and Leniu and two boys Robert and Clarence. Marion was Della's older brother Greenough, John Bear, Ike Bear, Clarence Bear, Jim Bond, Bill Walker (author of "The Longest Rope"), his brother Bob Walker. There are also notes that Johnnie Ames may have been a partner of Della and Jim Bond on a Snake River boat having a mail contract, which was sold to Pres Bruik.

3. Lillie relates that after her divorce Newell let the homestead go for nothing. "Just when he remarried, she never liked it over there and she wasn't a hillbilly like I was. I would put up with anything. She wouldn't.

And he bought it, sure it was worth some. He sold that, by God, he sold it to the people that got it; they told me they got over a million dollars worth, over a million dollars for that place."

STUBBLEFIELD

NEWELL STUBBLEFIELD

Born: Not researched.

Married: Lillie Lenora Smeed (1886 – 1986). One additional marriage was not researched.

Died: Not researched.

Children: Newell and Lillie had three children: Arvilla Stubblefield (December 20, 1906 Enterprise, OR); Howard Stubblefield (July 2, 1909, White Bird, ID); and Emory Stubblefield (December 3, 1913, Hells Canyon area, OR). Newell and Lillie homesteaded near Imnaha, Oregon and lived there with their three children prior to separating in 1916.

Arvilla Stubblefield Strange (1906-1984)

Born: December 29, 1906 (Enterprise, OR)

Married: (Jason Vanburen Martin Strange; Dick Shultz three times (Died May 1988)

Died: May 5, 1984 (Langley, Whidbey Island, WA)

Children: Arvilla and Jason Strange had one child, a girl named Vanetta, born in 1928. She was six months older than her aunt Josephine Collett (daughter of her mother Lillie and George Collett.)

Avrilla Stubblefield Strange and daughter Vanetta

She spent her early years at the Horse Creek, Imnaha, Oregon homestead. Surely that is where her love of horses first developed. At age 10 her mother Lillie Smead Stuffield and father Newell Stubblefield separated. She accompanied her mother to Wallowa Lake, Oregon where they lived in a tent while her mother operated a carousel. In time she, her younger brothers, Howard and Emory and her mother Lillie moved to Culdesac, Idaho where they lived with her grandmother Della Greenough and Jim Bond.

After her mother remarried George Collett, she traveled with the family, which at that time included her younger sister Mary Collett, from Lewiston, Idaho, to Kittitas, Washington, on foot and wagon, holding their possessions.

She worked in a cobbler's shop where she met her first husband, Jason Vandermartin Strange. Dick Shultz was his apprentice. She had her daughter Vanetta in 1929. In Kittitas or nearby Ellensburg her youngest sister Josephine Collett was born six months later. She worked at a cobbler's shop in Seattle in the Capital Hill neighborhood (between 11th and 12th on Pine?) where the family lived in an apartment on an upper floor, and her sister Mary worked at a pharmacy across the street.

She moved to Langley, Whidbey Island, Washington where she operated a cobbler shop with her then husband Dick Shultz. It was a narrow space with a small reception area having a long overhead belt system providing power to numerous shoe making and polishing wheels. Stacks of wooden foot molds lined the shelves. Dick Shultz specialized in custom making shoes for people with deformed feet, one leg longer than another, etc.

While in Langley she acquired a small acreage where she provided horse rides to visitors, having several horses including her favorite Blue Lady. There was a tack building with saddles, stalls for the horses and such along with a small corral. This property overlooked Hat Island and Puget Sound, and although waterfront, was on a high bluff with access to the water very difficult, with any trail built swept away with the sliding hillside.

In time, the property was subdivided and sold as individual building lots. Her relationship with Dick Shultz was tumultuous; she divorced and remarried several times, together at the end, but with separate entrances to their home and living on separate floors.

She was always generous with her nieces and nephews, providing free horse rides when they visited.

Howard Warren Stubblefield (1909-1995)

Born: July 3, 1909 (White Bird, ID)

Married: December 31, 1933 (Portland, Multnomah County, OR to Doris Anne McNiece, 12-31-1912 DOD 11-2-1995)

Died: April 17, 1995 (Salem, OR)

Children: Dorothy Mae Stubblefield Frison DOB11-1-1934, DOD 10-7-2008; Blaine Howard Stubblefield DOB 12-17-1935, DOD 2-7-1990; Jack (aka John) Warren Stubblefield DOB 9-8-1948, DOD 7-24-1980; George Newell Stubblefield DOB 7-12-1940, DOD 1-12-2004; Patricia Anne Stubblefield DOB 3-31-1943 DOD 1-22-2004; Mary Jo Stubblefield Killingsworth Young DOB 9-22-1949

He was raised on the Stubblefield homestead near Imnaha, ID. After marrying Doris McNiece in Portland, OR in 1933 he worked as a cobbler while his wife Doris worked as a nurse. He then became a plumber-pipefitter at the pulp mill in Salem, OR. He had two matching mid 1950's Buicks, one a sedan and one a station wagon. Both pink with lots of chrome. He always wore a smile on his face. Their children were Dorthy, Jack, Blaine, George, Patty and MaryJoe.

Emory Stubblefield (1913-2008) Scrap Metal Dealer/Bailing Machine

Born: Dec. 3, 1913 (Hells Canyon area, OR)

Married: July 12, 1936 (Margurite Aneta Fundemark, Lapwai, ID)

Died: October 8, 2008

Children: Aaron of Walla Walla WA, Elmer of Walla Walla, WA; Albert, of Cheverly, MD, Lenora Thompson, of Merced, CA, and Lily Shoop, of Walla Walla, WA.

Emory Newell Stubblefield, 94, died Oct. 3, 2008 at his home in Walla Walla, WA Emory was born in the Hells Canyon region of Idaho on Dec. 3, 1913 to Newell Stubblefield and Lillie Smead.

Emory was raised by his father and later moved to live with his mother and stepfather, George Collett, near Boulder, CO. There, he attended grade school, but his family eventually returned to the remote Imnaha River area.

Eventually, the Stubblefields crossed the desert terrain by mule train to Ellensburg, WA, where Emory attended school until the tenth grade. He soon started his first junk yard, the trade of which he proudly proclaimed "came natural to him, like breathing."

On July 12, 1936, he married Margurite Aneta Funnemark in the Indian church of Lapwai, Idaho. He brought her home to Ellensburg for their honeymoon, swerving to hit a skunk en route to impress his new bride.

In 1942, the couple moved to Walla Walla, with their first child, Elmer, and remained there for the rest of their lives.

Emory bought the Offner homestead of ten acres and established a rendering business, considered a "critical mission" during the war.

The Stubblefields welcomed two more sons, Aaron and Albert, and in 1953, twin daughters, Lily and Lenora. That same year, their family home burned down while they were at church.

During the post-war years, Emory bought property near the railroad on 11th Street in Walla Walla to transport junk and established another successful business.

As a self-taught mechanical and hydraulics engineer, he designed and built his own second bailer which he and his sons operated from dawn until dark.

A firm believer in self-sufficiency, he also raised livestock for beef and cows for milking.

For many years, Emory bid on various work sites and oversaw the dismantling of heavy industrial operations such as the Hanford Nuclear Plant and several dam projects. His work was often dangerous and he suffered injury when huge beams fell on his hand or when he suffered third-degree burns from welding. It was usual for him to "tough it out" and refuse medical help.

Emory was preceded in death by his wife Margurite of 58 years, in 1994; two sons, Aaron in 1984 and Elmer in 1996; his older brother, Howard Stubblefield, of Salem; and his sister, Arvilla Schultz, of Whidbey Island, WA.

Emory planned his own funeral which was quite an affair. It included a small country band playing old-time country songs, his Hispanic workers in colorful shirts and bolo ties with their welding overalls, greeting guests as they arrived. The pine box serving as his coffin was strapped down on the back of a flatbed semi leading the funeral procession to the cemetery.

He is survived by his three children, Albert, of Cheverly, MD, Lenora Thompson, of Merced, CA, and Lily Shoop, of Walla Walla, WA; two sisters, Mary Abel of Auburn, WA. and Josephine Lackman of AZ.

APPENDIX I

The following Ford information does not appear to be directly related to our "blood" line. Originally, I thought they were directly related due to the gap in time from the end of what I could find of the below Fords and their frequent use of "Jacob" as a first name. In any event it provides an interesting context for the early years of the Hadley, Collett and Smead lines which arrived about the same time in the same general area and could well have known these Fords. Particularly several Headleys served in the Revolutionary War in Pennsylvania. Major Francis Headley would have been a senior commander and in all probability served directly with Colonel Ford.

WIDOW MARTHA "Foord" FORD (prior to 1600-1630) 1621 Fortune Passengers Join Mayflower Pilgrims

Born: (England)

Married: (In England -William Ford (deceased 1621)); 1626 (Peter Browne) Died: 1630

Children of William and Martha are shown as: John Ford (c.1621-soon after arrival in Plymouth and died shortly thereafter); Martha Ford (c. 1619-England);

There is also a reference to a William Ford (1604), being a son of William and Martha Ford, also on the Fortune. He would have been age 17 on arrival in Plymouth, Massachusetts Bay Colony.

In 1621, one year after the Mayflower," Widow Ford" left London with her husband William and children Martha and John in the small sailing ship Fortune leaving all she knew in England for a colony that just the year prior had been hacked out of the wilderness in cold, snowy northeastern America. Her dear husband William died prior to or shortly after the ship reached the Cape Cod coast on November 9, 1621. The Fortune was the second ship sent to the Plymouth Colony by the Merchant Adventured investment group, which sponsored her trip and had also sponsored the Mayflower. Martha and her two children were Pilgrims, held together in a community of faith. Their faith was tested again and again in the hardships they faced. Martha tried not to second-guess the decision to abandon their home in England for an untamed wilderness populated only by the survivors of their first winter from the Mayflower (and wild savage Indians).

The Fortune was 1/3 the size of the Mayflower, displacing 55 tons. It carried 35 passengers. The Master was Thomas Barton. She departed London in the fall of 1621 and arrived off Cape Cod on November 9, 1621, and arrived in Plymouth Bay by the end of the month. The ship only stayed at Plymouth about three weeks loading cargo, and departed for England on December 13, 1621. On January 19, 1622, due to a navigation error, Fortune was overtaken and seized by a French man of war, and those on board were held under guard in France for about a month, and its cargo was taken. Fortune finally arrived back in the Thames on February 17, 1622.

The identification of the 35 passengers comes largely from the 1623 Division of Land list and its distribution of lots transcribed by William Bradford. Martha Ford and Elizabeth Bassett were the only women aboard the ship. Records show that sixteen of the passengers were from the London area and three from Leiden, with the origins of the others unknown. It is curious to note that Leiden is not far from Lincolnshire where Henry Ford, father of John Ford (1850) (known to be of our line) was from.

William Ford, husband of Martha Ford, a passenger on the Fortune died prior to or shortly after the ship reached port. He apparently had a share in the 1623 land division under "Widow" Foord, when the 4 members of the family, including William (deceased), wife Martha, son John and daughter Martha received four acres.

In 1626 "Widow Ford" married Mayflower passenger Peter Browne. In the 1627 cattle division the family appears as "Peeter" and Martha Browne, with her Ford children, John and Martha Ford." She died in 1630. There are also listings for William Ford, son of William and Martha Ford (they may have had two sons, William and John or perhaps William from a prior marriage). He became a Deacon in Marshfield, Plymouth County, Massachusetts. Martha Ford was born c.1619. John Ford, born about the time of the Fortune's arrival, died soon thereafter.

WILLIAM FORD (1604-1676) Grist Mill / Constable

Born: 1604 (Olave Parish, Southwark, Surrey, England)

Married: 1632 (Marshfield, Anna Eames Ford – died 1684, Marshfield)

Died: September 23, 1676 (Marshfield, Plymouth, MA)

Per the Division of Land List of 1632, he came with "Widow Martha Ford" on the "Fortune" to Plymouth in 1621.

Children: He and his wife Anna Ford had the following children: Margaret Soule (1631); Andrew Ford (1632); Deacon William Ford (November 4, 1633); Rebecca Ford (1634); Michael Ford (1635); John Ford of Massachusetts (1637); Millicent Drake Ford (1637); Jeanna Ford; Joanna Ford; Nicholas Ford (1633 Europe) Rebecca Ford; and Martha Ford.

There is a possibility that William Ford returned to England for a short period. Settled on the east side of the North River near Gravelly Beach in what is now Salem, Massachusetts, about 1639. He was at Duxbury (which is very near Plymouth, Massachusetts) in 1643 and listed that year as able to bear arms. He was a miller. He moved from Plymouth to Marshfield (just outside Plymouth to the north) for the purpose of constructing and operating a mill in company with Josiah Winslow, Jr. known as Dunham's Mill. Propounded freeman at Plymouth June 7, 1651 (he may have been an indentured servant for a time) and admitted as such June 3, 1652. He served in various capacities such as highway surveyor and constable.

While serving as a constable in 1658, William, having arrested Widow Naomi Sylvester, was attacked by her daughters Naomi and Dinah, who rescued their mother. As a penalty their brother, William, was ordered to pay Constable Ford two pounds (Counsel Republic). On October 3, 1662 he was fined five shillings for allowing Samuel Howland to breach the Sabbath by carrying grist from the mill. Sold lands in Plymouth May 26, 1661. In 1665/66 he became a selectman for Marshfield the first of several times.

JOHN FORD (1659-1721) Early Settler Pennsylvania/First Forge in Morristown

Born: August 14, 1659 (Born: 1659 (Duxbury, MA or Bridgewater, Plymouth, Co, MA)

Married: December 18, 1701 (Elizabeth Freeman Ford (June 26, 1671-April 21, 1772))

Died: February 2, 1721 (Morristown, PN)

Children: Jacob Ford, Samuel Ford, and Experience Conger

John Ford (8/14-/1659 - 2/ 22/1721) was a carpenter and miller. On December 18, 1701 he married Elizabeth (Freeman) Ford (6/26/1671-4/21/1772). They had three children: Jacob Ford Sr. (1704), Samuel Ford and Experience Conger. John Ford, born in Duxbury, MA, 1659, settled in Woodbridge, New Jersey, before 1700, was a deacon there in 1709, and elder in 1710, and came to Morris County before 1724. He was the son of William Ford and Sarah Dingey. William in turn was the son of Widow Foord who was a passenger of the ship Fortune, a vessel of 40 or 50 tons which sailed from London, England July, 1621, with thirty-five passengers, arriving one year after the Mayflower after a long and tedious voyage, having been taken by a French man-of-war and released to the Plymouth Colony, December 1621 with scanty provisions. A list of the passengers is available along with the children that accompanied her.

They moved to Monroe (between Morristown and Whippany) from Woodbridge after being offered a large tract of land by a large landowner named John Budd. They operated the first known iron forge in Morris County on the banks of the Whippany River.

Sometime around 1710, a major landowner in Morris County, a man named John Budd, * made an offer to one of the wealthiest residents of Woodbridge in eastern NJ — John Ford (1659— 1721). The two men had met each other while they were in Philadelphia at a meeting of their presbytery (the governing regional body of Presbyterian congregations). According to the History of Morris County, "Budd offered Ford a large tract of land if he would remove to Monroe, between Morristown and Whippany, an offer which was accepted."

Once Ford, with his wife Elizabeth (Freeman) Ford and their children, had made the move west to Monroe (between Morristown and Whippany), he and Budd opened what is believed to have been the first iron forge in the county on the banks of the Whippany River. A historical marker today marks the site where this forge was located. The History of Morris County relates.

Mr. Green in his history of the Hanover church speaks of the old building in the Whippany graveyard as "about 100 rods below the forge which is and has long been known by the name of the Old Iron Works." It was no doubt a very small and rude affair, where good iron was made free from the ore by smelting it with charcoal, and without any of the economical appliances even of the bloomeries of a hundred years later. The ore was brought to it from the Succasunna mine in leather bags on horseback—the only method of transportation. A single horse, it is said, would carry from four to five hundred pounds fifteen miles in a day.

An early History of Morris County, NJ, published in 1882, states that "the first actual settlement by the whites was probably in the northeastern part of the county, near Pompton Plains." On June 6, 1695, a group of colonists led by Arent Schuyler (1662—1730) purchased from the native Indians all the land between the Passaic River on the south, the Pompton River on the north, and the foot of the hills to the east and the west. In November of that same year, Schuyler and his partners bought another 5,500 acres east of the Pequannock River, then in 1696 purchased 1,500 acres west of that river. Arent Schuyler was the nephew of our ancestral immigrant, David Pieters Schuyler (see separate profile, "The Establishment of New Netherland: Il—Fort Orange (Albany)", through David's brother Philip Pieterse Schuyler, another prominent early Dutch immigrant to New Netherland. In addition to being a land speculator, during his lifetime Arent Schuyler was a surveyor, an "Indian agent," miner, and merchant.

In addition, Puritans whose ancestors had earlier settled New England began moving south to eastern New Jersey (for example, to Newark and Elizabeth), and then moved further west across the Passaic River into Morris County. Whether this settlement began before or after Arent Schuyler's purchases elsewhere in the county is unclear. The 1882 History of Morris County states that these Puritan settlements were established "following closely upon the heels of the Pompton Plains [i.e., Schuyler party] settlers."

However, a historical marker (see photos) in Whippany, NJ, commemorates the "Settlement of Whippanong / Hanover Township" in 1685 as the "first settlement in Morris, Sussex, and Warren counties." The marker notes, "The first settlers were attracted by the river, iron ore, and the fertile land."

The settlement and development of the western portions of Morris County began in Ernest between 1710 and 1715.

ANDREW FORD (1620-1692)

[This is another Ford line at the same location at about the same time/possibly a relation of William Ford.]

<u>Born</u>: 1620 (England)

<u>Married</u>: 1648 (Weymouth, Norfolk, Massachusetts-Ellen Lovell Ford)

<u>Died</u>: March 4, 1692 (Hingham, Suffolk County, province of Massachusetts Bay (near Weymouth).

Andrew Ford (1620-1692) was born in England. He married Ellen (Lovell) Ford about 1648 in Weymouth, Norfolk, Massachusetts. Died March 4, 1692, in Hingham, Suffolk County, province of Massachusetts Bay.

Andrews's parents in England were Robert (Fourde) Ford and Elizabeth (Bourne) Ford. He arrived in Weymouth sometime between 1636 and 1641, at which time he had seven acres in the east field. Weymouth is the second-oldest settlement in Massachusetts, second only to Plymouth, Massachusetts. It was originally settled in 1622 by Thomas Weston, who had been a financial backer of the Plymouth Colony. It was a purely economic in motivation, the men without families, and failed in the winter with supplies running out. Another attempt was made at the site in 1624 with most leaving due to the harsh winter, but the few that remained formed the nucleus of a permanent settlement, incorporated into the Massachusetts Bay Colony in 1630, with the name changed to Weymouth in 1635 to with the addition of 100 families under the leadership of Joseph Hull. There was a level of conflict between the Puritans of Boston and the Pilgrims of Plymouth. JAMES FORD [son of Andrew Ford] Born: 1649 Weymouth, Massachusetts Bay Colony Died: between February 1693 and 1702 (Weymouth, Norfolk County, Province of Massachusetts). James Ford's site says that John Ford's father was born in 1659; however, it is unlikely, as it also says he was born about 1649/50 and would have been only 10, too young to be a father. Received through Andrew Ford's will 200 acres at a place called Quinne Poge, near Roxbury (Woodstock, Connecticut). 11 brothers and sisters.

JACOB FORD, SR. (1704-1777) George Washington's Headquarters

<u>Born</u>: 1704

<u>Married</u>: Hannah Baldwin Ford (1701-1777)

<u>Died</u>: 1777

<u>Children</u>: Jacob Sr. and Hannah had seven children: John Ford; Jacob Ford (1738-Morristown, NJ); Phoebe Ford Phillips (1729-1819); Sarah Ford Tuthill (1732-1811); Mary Ford Dunham (1734-1802; and Elizabeth Ford

(1743-1746); Jane Ford Tuttle (born January 29, 1736 in Morristown, Middlesex County, NJ) and deceased November 22, 1794 Rockaway, Morristown, N J buried in the First Presbyterian Church Cemetery)

Numerous forges were built along Morris County's rivers and streams. Several of these forges were built by John Ford's son, Jacob Ford, Sr., including one described in the History of Morris County as "located just north of what is now called Water street and near Flagler's mill, called the Ford forge."

Jacob Ford Sr. was the owner of the inn (for which he applied for a license in 1738) which became Washington's headquarters in Morristown. It is now owned by the New Jersey Historical Society.

Jacob Ford, Sr., apparently was held in particularly high repute by his fellow Morris County residents. Andrew M. Sherman, the author of the 1905 volume Historic Morristown, New Jersey, said of him, "He was no doubt the leading man in Morristown."

COL. JACOB FORD, JR. (1738-1777) Militia Colonel During Revolutionary War

Born: 1738 (Morristown, NJ)

Married: (Theodosia)

Died: 1777

Children: Judge Gabriel Hogarth Ford; Jacob Ford III; Elizabeth Ford DeSaussure; Timothy Ford; and Phoebe Ford.

Col. Jacob Ford, Jr. (1738-1777) was married to Theodosia. He was an American Revolutionary Militia Officer. He was the second son and sixth of eight born to Jacob and Hannah Ford of Morristown New Jersey. His children were Judge Gabriel Hogarth Ford, Jacob Ford III, Elizabeth De Saussure, Timothy Ford and Phoebe Ford.

As anger at the American colonies' British rulers grew in the 1770s, the Ford family became ardent patriots in the cause for independence from England. On June 3, 1775, a "Provincial Congress" for New Jersey passed an Act for the regulation of a militia for the colony. The act specified that two regiments and one battalion were to be recruited in Morris County. Jacob Ford, Jr., the son of Jacob, Sr., was appointed colonel of the county's eastern regiment. He would have been 37 years old at the time.

*At least two other officers in this regiment also were part of our extended family tree: Benoni Hathaway (1743—1823), 32-year-old nephew of Abraham Hathaway (1685—1754), was a captain and, later, lieutenant colonel; and Joseph Lindsley (1735—1822), 40-year-old grandson of John Lindsley (second husband of Elizabeth Freeman Ford), was a major.

In October 1775, the Continental Congress made its first call on New Jersey for troops to serve in resistance to the British forces. The Continental Congress asked New Jersey to supply two battalions, consisting of eight companies each. In January 1776, the Continental Congress followed this request with a call to New Jersey for one more battalion, and the New Jersey Provincial Congress promptly organized the requested forces.

By that time, back in Morris County, the eastern battalion under the command of Jacob Ford, Jr., had grown to about 800 officers and troops. Ford understood the importance of adequate gunpowder for the American soldiers to be effective. Early in 1776, Jacob, Sr., and Jacob, Jr., together had built a new mill specifically for the manufacture of gunpowder for the troops. In his 1905 *Historic Morristown, New Jersey,* Andrew M. Sherman wrote:

Ford's powder mill, as it came to be known, was erected on the Whippanong River…. The path leading to [the] mill was through an almost impenetrable thicket, and was so completely surrounded by trees as to render it very difficult of discovery by the enemy; indeed, a more isolated spot could hardly have been chosen.

(Today, the site of Ford's powder mill is marked by a historical marker. The site itself remains in a secluded wooded area, accessible only by walking a trail from Morristown's more populated areas.)

Sherman also noted that some historians before him had claimed that "most of the gunpowder used in the Revolution was made in this mill." Sherman doubted this claim, but did believe that "it may, however, be more in accordance with the facts in the case, to say that most of the gunpowder used in New Jersey during the Revolution, was manufactured in Ford's mill."

By the winter of 1776-77, independence from Britain had been declared by the 13 American colonies, but the war to secure that independence was not going well for George Washington and his forces. Between the July 1776 "Declaration of Independence" and December 1776, the British defeated the Americans in numerous battles in New York state. General Washington had been forced to retreat from one New York and New Jersey location to another.

In December 1776, British forces launched a major attempt to destroy Ford's powder mill, and thereby to destroy the American force's major source of gunpowder. Colonel Ford learned of the advancing British troops and marched his Morris County battalion east to Springfield, New Jersey. There, on December 14, they successfully engaged the British, soon forcing the Redcoats to retreat. Ford withdrew his battalion from Springfield, back to Chatham (on the eastern edge of Morris County), where he waited and watched the further movements of the British.

Also, on December 14, 1776, the American general, Alexander McDougall, as an emissary of George Washington, visited Morristown, and three regiments of U.S. troops arrived in Morristown just three days later. In his history, Andrew Sherman theorized that McDougall was in Morristown under orders from George Washington to arrange for a winter encampment of the American army in Morristown.

On December 22, 1776, Jacob Ford, Jr., arrived back in Morristown after ending their watch in Chatham, and on December 31, Ford and his successful forces were celebrated in a parade south of the village Green. Before the parade ended, Ford became seriously ill. He was carried from the parade by a couple of his soldiers and taken to his bed. He never again rose from the bed, dying on January 11, 1777, from "lung fever" (i.e., pneumonia). By order of George Washington, Ford was buried with the honors of war

APPENDIX II

WILLIAM KIRKHAM "BILLY" STUBBLEFIELD "The Stubblefield Trail" (A Story of Newell Stubblefield's Father)

Born: October 20, 1825 (Grainger County, Tennessee)

Married: Josephine Stubblefield (and others)

Died: March 22, 1909 (Enterprise, Wallowa County, Oregon)

The following recount of Bill Stubblefield's life is believed to have been prepared by great grandson Blaine Stubblefield:

The first American Stubblefields were descendants of four brothers who came from England. This story begins with William Kirkham Stubblefield, born in Tennessee in 1825. Billy or WK was from a wealthy family and lived on a plantation. He left home at the age of fourteen because his mother would not allow him to bring his hounds into the house or feed them under the table while the family ate.

Billy began to live an adventurous life, working on a Mississippi Riverboat as a stevedore and fireman. He was already strong and had his fellow workers put a 500-pound bale of cotton on his back. Billy hauled the cotton into the boat end on a bet but cracked the gangplank. All of his life he was to perform amazing tasks and stand out as an individual and non-conformist.

He worked for a while in the coal mines of Missouri, learning the sad songs of the miners that he sang all of his life and passed on to his children. Billy became a plantation overseer and had two hundred slaves under him, yet he hated slavery and refused to fight in the Civil War because of his aversion to slavery

Billy left Missouri. He had been strongly affected by the cruelty he saw. For the rest of his life, he reared back his 6'4" two-hundred-pound frame every morning and bellowed out part of an old slave song, "I'm glad I'm free."

Billy fled Missouri and walked to Texas. He wore a leather blacksmith's apron with huge pockets for his tools and carried a saw on his shoulder. Along with all of this was his buffalo gun "Old Betsy." He depended upon his prowess to survive and stopped in Indian villages for food. He also began to learn Indian dialects. Arriving in Texas, Billy camped along the Palo Pinto River until he built a log cabin and barn. This was in the wilderness area of Palo Pinto County where the nearest neighbor was one hundred miles away. He now had a wife and family and built a stockade around the house and barn for protection against the Indians.

WILD TURKEY

W.K. was awakened one early morning in his Texas wilderness home to the gobble of a wild turkey. Turkey, being a welcome addition to his large family's larder, he rose, donned his buckskins and began loading his flintlock rifle with birdshot, when his frontiersman's instinct told him to be cautious. This could be a Comanche Indian trick to lure him out of the stockade to within bowshot. Pouring a larger powder charge down the barrel, he rammed down instead a heavy fifty-caliber lead rifle ball.

For situations such as this, W.K. had a special secret arrangement, a hidden tunnel going under the compound wall where a ravine skirted the log perimeter of the palisade. The opening of the tunnel was covered by a large rock and completely hidden by brush. Billy went out through the tunnel, rolled away the rock, and, crouching low, cat-footed down the ravine to a vantage point where he could observe through the brush without being seen. He had not waited long when a war painted and feathered Comanche leaped up from a large hollow stump and gave the "wild turkey!' call.

Billy's blue eyes gazed the long rifle barrel as he lined the sights of the big fifty caliber gun at the spot where the warrior had popped up. As the rifle sights held rock-steady he ticked off in his mind the seconds of the Indian's timing. When the doomed Red Man jumped up for his next call, the gobble died in his throat with the rending thud of the big lead ball, dropping his lifeless body back down into the stump.

Instantly, another warrior, bedecked and brave, leaped up from a hiding place in the brush and took off running like a deer, chanting a death song as he ran, but he was in luck, or his medicine was good, for Billy could not get the ritual of reloading the flintlock rifle soon enough to prevent his escape. This fellow would probably try again to get him through Billy. Living in the Texas wilderness of that day was a hard, uncompromising life. W.K. always befriended Indians when he could, even taking in sick ones to nurse them back to health. He never harmed or killed Indians unless he was attacked. But the Comanche and Apaches were ferocious and implacable foes, determined to drive the white eyes from the plains, and they never gave up trying to do it.

Another dangerous skirmish with the Indians occurred while the family was living in Palo Pinto County. This time W.K. fled for his life and barely escaped.

THE WOODS COLT

While he lived in Texas, W.K. had taken in a retarded boy to live with his family in their wilderness home. This boy, Wilbur, about seventeen, was what was then called a "woods colt" a homeless waif who had just wandered in, his parents perhaps killed by Indians.

Wilbur loved hunting and woodsman-ship: he followed Billy everywhere, practically becoming his shadow. W.K. and Wilbur were out in the woods one late fall afternoon hunting turkeys, having loaded their big fifty caliber flintlocks with birdshot for the purpose. Their keen eyes searched the low trees. The older man's brown hair under his plainsman's hat was trimmed just short of his powerful shoulders, which were set on a muscular six-foot four inch frame, the fringed buckskin shirt enhancing his handsome appearance. The younger man too was dressed in smoke—brown fringed buckskin, wearing on his round shaped head a coonskin cap and a childlike expression on his moon face. Suddenly as they passed through a glade, Billy pivoted his lithe body to the right, freezing into an action ready listening posture. Wilbur whispered as he too immobilized himself, "What is it Uncle Billy?" In this moment six scurrying wolf-like shapes shot through the small clearing in eerie silence, their yellow eyes appraising the man things as they passed.

Cautioning the lad to silence with a hand signal, W.K. moved close to him and whispered, "Them's Injun scoutin dogs. Thar's prob'ly a Comanche raidin' party near. We'll have to make for the river. Ah knows whar thar's a drift we can fort up in," If his ruse worked, he reasoned, they would not only elude the war party, but would lead the Indians further away from discovering his family in the log fortress compound.

After several miles, Wilbur gasped, "Uncle Billy, ah'm a gittin' tard." W.K. clutched his arm and yanked him onward, growling, Keep them short, Iaigs a locomotin if yo' wont tuh keep yore ha' ar." As they kept up the swift jog, their moccasin-covered feet treading silently over the frosty ground, W.K.'s frontier-trained ear detected faint sounds of pursuit behind them. Exultant yelps of the warriors came as the scout dogs led them to the white eyes' trail.

As they neared the Palo Pinto River, the pair put on an extra burst of speed. Billy warned Wilbur, "Now when we tuh the river thar's a big driftwood bar we can wade out to. Don't stop. Hold yer rifle and powder horn high and wade right out thar. Hide durned good in them drift logs, but hold far and don't do no shootin less'n ah tell yuh to."

On coming to the river's edge, they slowed their pace so as not to splash as they entered the icy water; wading out shoulder deep in the swift current about one hundred feet to the bar in the middle of the river where they crawled in among the logs. Instantly they unloaded the birdshot from their rifles and rammed down the fifty caliber balls. Then they found natural loopholes for their rifles and settled down to wait.

In a short time, a party of about a dozen gaudily painted and feather-bedecked warriors burst out of the timber and onto the river's edge. They searched up and down the shore for a while and then gestured and pointed at the drift bar. Billy swiftly noted that none of the braves had firearms, being equipped only with yew bows and obsidian headed lances. (It is not known why these Indians, who were great horsemen were on foot, but possibly their horses had been stolen by Apaches as horse stealing was a perpetual game among Indian tribes.)

As the bold Red Men entered the water and began to wade toward the white eyes' hiding place, Billy studied the demeanor of the oncoming braves for a moment, making a split-second calculation as to which of the attackers was the leader. His practiced eye unerringly picked him out as he aligned the sights of the big rifle on the hapless warrior's head. The Indian's fierce eyes glared like those of an eagle as he boldly waded the strong current toward their driftwood ambuscade, his bow at the ready.

W.K. let the dauntless brave get half the distance to his driftwood breastworks before "teching off" his long-barreled Tennessee rifle. At the thunderous boom, the chief disappeared into the water as the cloud of black powder smoke rose in the air. Pandemonium broke loose as the dismayed warriors clutched their fallen leader and dragged him to shore, where for a time they scurried and darted about aimlessly. But the tumult gradually subsided as a new war leader took charge.

As W.K. swiftly reloaded his rifle in the gathering dusk, he pondered a scheme for escape. They could probably hold out till darkness, for the braves would not very likely wish to face the two powerful rifles again in daylight.

The Indians dispersed, gathered wood, and made a big fire around which a wild and furious war dance began. Billy soon deduced their intentions and told Wilbur, "The devils are a goin' tuh th'o' far brands out hyar and bum us out." Darkness came, and as the war dance gained momentum, shrill yells and blood curdling war cries rent the air. Billy knew the dance would soon reach its crescendo and the firebrand throwing stage. He instructed Wilbur to roll into the water on the side away from the firelight to drift and wade silently, letting the current carry them down stream, low in the water, carrying his rifle and powder horn high.

The vengeance crazed Comanche's launched their brands amid shrill war cries as the pair drifted in the icy water. After half a mile of drifting down river, under the moonless sky, Billy said, "We can't last any longer in this cold water, we'll have to chance it on getting out of here."

As they crawled from the river, the cold closed down on the miserable pair like a frigid vice, "We'll have tuh run for it or we'll freeze," warned Billy, as they ran through the frosty wilderness, their water-soaked buckskins froze on them, becoming like clanking armor. As the miles reeled off, Wilbur tired and began to stagger and wobble. Billy grabbed his arm, supporting and steadying him with his great strength, saying, "Slow the pace a bit boy, we cain't quit naow when we hain't got much further to go." With this encouragement, the lad got his "second wind" and they soon saw the welcome light inside the palisade wall.

After being admitted by the frightened family, Billy's anxious wife quickly heated tubs of water, directing W.K. and Wilbur to get in the wooden horse trough where she poured warm water over their frozen buckskins so they could get out of them. She wrapped them in blankets, gave each a shot of whiskey and put them to bed, saying, "Paw, don't you worry none about them Injuns attackin' us. The boys and I will stand guard tonight with the rifle guns."

Life in Texas was complicated. Since Billy refused to fight in the Civil War, he was also harassed by Confederate vigilante renegades. He knew that they wanted to force him to leave the area and then take over his property. The family was sent to Carroll County Arkansas while Billy remained hidden in the Texas wilderness. He tried to think of a way to outsmart the renegades and keep his property, yet he was under constant attack by the Apaches and Comanche. Finally, the situation became too difficult and Billy left Texas to join his family in Arkansas. He started growing sugar cane in Arkansas and built a sugar mill. They had a huge house with two stories and lots of windows.

Yet news of homesteads available in Oregon sparked Billy's pioneering instinct again, and he got the Oregon fever. Once more, the family moved to a wilderness area. Billy walked first from Arkansas to Oregon, established the homestead, and sent for his wife and children, who came to La Grande, Oregon, by train. There was homestead land available in many areas, but he chose to settle in a rugged, deep gorge in Eastern Oregon.

The new homestead was on Horse Creek, feeding into the Imnaha River. Billy chose a beautiful canyon. Rim rocks surrounded the upper walls, and the clear, rushing Inmaha River flowed through the canyon. Some grass grew on land benches in the hills, and willows and cottonwood trees lined the creek. The weather was extreme, with deep snow or oppressive heat, and always wind. It was an austere canyon, yet there was a definite, strong and peaceful quality.

The family settled on Horse Creek in 1884. By this time Billy had an immediate family of nine. There was Billy Jr. from his second family, Ira from his third family, and Mickel, StonHawon, Newell, Fancho, Brennan, Lydia end Eliza from his fourth. Billy had fathered a total of twenty-six children. Josephine, the wife he brought to the Imnaha, was his stepdaughter, whom he married when his third wife died. She lived three years in Oregon and died at age 39.

Billy was sixty when he brought his family to Oregon. He had white hair to his shoulders and a white, tobacco-stained forked beard. When his sons were angry, they called him "old fork beard." A plainsman's flat, crowned hat, fringed buckskins, and moccasins were his usual attire. Over his shoulder, he carried "Old Betsy" and a Bowie knife on his belt. The people of the Wallowa County area, surrounding his new homestead, called him Uncle Billy. He earned the name because of his appearance and he was the uncle of Frank Stubblefield, a founder of near Enterprise.

Billy and his sons and daughters began to build a ranch in the wilderness and it was a tremendous job. Their home was a Tennessee-style log cabin. Two cabins were connected by a breezeway, or dog trot, in the middle. One cabin was a living room and bedroom for the women; the other was used for cooking. The long loft, covering both cabins and breezeway, was a dormitory for the men. A vertical pole with wooden pins extended through a hole in the roof, and provided access to the upstairs.

On the side near the hill were a root cellar, granary, and smokehouse. A barn, blacksmith shop, and corrals were built nearby as well as a springhouse, near the creek. A one railing footbridge crossed the creek and stones were laid on the creek bottom for fording by horse and wagon. Hay was planted on land benches in the canyon, and a road was built, sighted and measured by eye, which had the precision of modern construction.

Many items were fashioned by hand. Tables, chairs, cradles, shelves, and bins were made, with rawhide used for the couches, chairs, and beds. The kitchen had a large iron stove bought in a store, but the butter churn was made by hand, as well as the bread mixing trough, which was a hollowed half log on legs. The boy's clothing was made with hearty canvas. Shoes and harnesses were fashioned from leather. All of these tasks were learned by Billy's sons, and they worked in his blacksmith shop, learning a trade right on the ranch. Domestic animals of every variety were acquired for the ranch: cattle, dairy cows, sheep, hogs, chickens, turkeys and geese. The most acclaimed part of the ranch however, was the produce. Billy mail ordered sapling trees which were shipped by rail to La Grande. He hauled them to his canyon ranch and planted orchards on the sloping hill near the creek; there were pears, peaches, and apples. A wonderful garden of every kind of vegetable was planted, including watermelons.

DAY LIGHT

None of the residents of the Horse Creek ranch ever needed an alarm clock. Uncle Billy saw to that. At the first glimmer of dawn over the high crests of the mountains, he would get into his clothes, make kindling shavings to start the fire in the ladder hole to the attic sleeping quarters, tilt his head back, and roar, "Day-y-y- light. Usually one of these thunderous, rafters shaking bellows was all that was needed. But if all the men and boys sleeping above did not appear in ten or fifteen minutes, he would get under the hole to give them another blast, "Git down outa thar." This brought any laggards down in a hurry, practically sliding down the ladder much as firemen used to slide down a pole.

The men and boys went out to do the chores before breakfast. Some of them in work and saddle horses from the pastures to be fed grain or hay; they put the heavy harnesses on the work teams and saddled up the stock riding horses and sometimes pack horses, for the tasks laid out for the day. Others fed and milked the herd of milk cows. The pigs, chickens, sheep, etc. were left to be taken care of after breakfast by the women and girls.

The women and girls came into W.K.'s kitchen-living room and started preparing breakfast. One of the mainstays for breakfast was sourdough pancakes and biscuits. The sourdough starter and milk for liquefying was stirred into a hollow in the flour in the open top of the flour sack and thinned according to whether it was for biscuits or pancakes. This was the standard way of mixing sourdough in the Snake River Canyon Country, not only in those days but even up into the 1920's.) The thinner sourdough batter for pancakes was ladled directly from the flour sack top mixing hollow to the range top griddle and served with farm fresh butter which had been churned in the big handmade wooden churn. The strong coffee, made in a huge granite-ware" pot, was freshly ground in a hand cranked grinder from whole coffee beans. The pot was usually not washed except sometimes when none of the men were around.

After breakfast there was no dawdling around. Everyone hustled out to their assigned task for the day. Everyone knew his job and although W.K. was the "Big Daddy" director, he was a fair man and he conferred regularly with his sons on what should be done and what was the best way to do a thing. He knew that he had taught them well and he respected their judgment, but when he rumbled out a decision, it was final.

Uncle Billy hauled fruit and garden produce to the nearby towns of Enterprise and La Grande with a train of two of three freight wagons. All of the produce picked from his garden was transported out of Imnaha Canyon by pack horses via the Stubblefield Trail. Billy and his two older sons Mickel and Ira worked many days to build the trail, a shortcut over the mountains. It began at Corral Creek which was another tributary of the Imnaha River.

A small log cabin was constructed at the top of the trail. It was a low, funny structure with a little door, and the family called it Buckhorn because of the nearby Buckhorn Springs. Sometimes Uncle Billy went to the cabin just to shoot grouse. Freight wagons were kept at Buckhorn and Billy harnessed the horses right over their pack saddles, an unusual custom. Provisions were stored at the cabin and were transported between La Grande and Horse Creek.

WAGON TRAIN

Uncle Billy hauled fruit and garden produce to the towns of Wallowa County with a train of two or three freight wagons. All of the produce had to be transported up out of Imnaha Canyon by pack horse via the Corral Creek Trail and transferred to the freight wagons kept at the Buckhorn cabin. The trips were made during the summer and fall when the garden and fruit harvests took place. Sometimes an entire trainload would consist of watermelons, cantaloupes, and muskmelons. Other trips would carry apricots, peaches, squash, tomatoes and pumpkins.

When the wagons arrived at their destination, a camp would be set up just outside of town where the crew lived while selling the produce. W.K. did not sell to wholesalers but the three wagons separated and each driver took a different section of town, selling directly to the householders, driving slowly through the streets, the tinkling bells on the manes acting as an attention getter. The driver called out his wares on each block while his assistant, one of the younger boys, went door-to-door carrying buckets of produce to show as samples.

W.K. drove the lead wagon, with the older boys or sometimes hired hands driving the other two. Uncle Billy was quite an attention getter himself - a giant of an old man. His white, shoulder-length, curly hair topped by a flat-crowned plainsman's hat, his forked beard tobacco-stained, he strode along ramrod straight, driving his team from beside the wagon, pants tucked into high leather boots, bellowing, "Git yore wartermillions and mushmillions, hyar!"

These trips were about the only vacation or diversion enjoyed by the boys away from the canyon country. They were especially delighted when their paw allowed them to buy ice cream or candy: licorice whips, jaw breakers, chewing gum or Sen-Sen. They liked to gaze in the store windows at the marvelous things displayed there. Sometimes they were allowed to buy a pocket knife or a dollar pocket watch. One hardware store window they always looked into because it displayed against a velvet background a nickel-plated, lever-action, twenty-two caliber rifle.

Occasionally when a pair of work shoes or boots was worn beyond W.K.'s ability to make further home repairs on them, the lucky owner got to buy a brand-new pair, thus becoming the envy of his fellows for weeks.

Having lived in the wilderness all of their lives, Uncle Billy's sons, even though they had to camp on the outskirts (this was not an unusual thing in those days), were exhilarated by the sights and sounds of "city life" in La Grande. One of their favorite sights was watching the trains come in at the railroad depot. Mickel, in later years often said, "I allus wanted to be a steam train engineer."

The family lived in tents during their stay since the wagons were filled with produce and covered with canvas. On the trip itself much of the camp food was supplied by shooting game and fishing. In the long trek along the beautiful Wallowa River, game was plentiful: ducks, geese, grouse, and partridge. Even red pine squirrels made a tasty dish. The river abounded in trout and salmon.

Instead of returning to Imnaha empty the freight wagons often hauled back supplies for the ranch blacksmith supplies, nails, fence wire. Hauling in supplies for other ranchers was also a profitable venture.

THE MEDICINE MAN

Uncle Billy was a gregarious and generous man, so his ranch soon became a stop-off place for travelers, not only for those who were comers and goers, but also for many who were comers and stayers. It didn't make much difference to him; there was plenty for all, including the Nez Perce Indians, who practically made the Horse Creek ranch their Imnaha headquarters and rendezvous. The Indians liked to trade for watermelons, corn, "tomsaswaki" (as they called tomatoes), fruit, berries and hay for their horses.

The Indians being there once saved Billy's life. He had blown his thumb to shreds from an accidental powder explosion while reloading shotgun shells. Mickel, only eleven years old at the time, had been sent to town, riding at a dead run a relay of horses borrowed from ranches along the way, to get Dr. Ault at Enterprise, the famous "Doc" of the Wallowa country.

But before Doc Ault could make the long journey to the ranch in his buggy, via Imnaha ridge, where he was met by young Pancho with saddle horses, infection had set in.

An old Indian herb doctor or medicine man, who could not speak a word of English, had been hovering around in great concern, jabbering persistently. But presently the old medicine man disappeared for several days. When he reappeared, he had with him a parcel of plants which he had gathered in the high mountains. He then pounded these plants into a mash from which he made a poultice and applied it to W.K.'s mangled thumb. By the time Dr. Ault arrived, the infection was gone and he had only to trim and sew up the wound.

Dr. Ault stayed at the ranch for several days ostensibly to care for W.K. The boys knew, however, that the Doc enjoyed being there so they treated him to hunting and fishing jaunts, hikes into the rim rocks, trail rides and swims in the river.

The Doc even participated in a watermelon steal with the boys, chortling with elfin glee as he escaped with the melons. He avoided W.K.'s wrath by worming under the barbed wire fence surrounding Billy's prize melons and tearing his pants on the fence in the getaway. Uncle Billy pretended ignorance of who the thieves might be, roaring into the darkness, "Ah'll let yo' fellers have a load of rock salt in yore paints afore yo' git any of them wartermillions."

PRETTY REDWING

One of the older boys, Mickel, had an Indian boy for hunting and fishing pal and he spent much time in the Indian village on the lower Imnaha. He even learned much of the Nez Perce language. The Nez Perce boy had a sister who had alluring liquid brown eyes, lustrous raven hair, and a graceful curvaceous body. Mickel called her Redwing.

One day Mickel said to his pal, "Why don't me and that purty sister of yours git married? (In later years when telling the story to his sons, he claimed that he was only joshing.) His friend didn't answer and Mickel had forgotten the Incident .in a few days. Not long afterwards, he was jolted by the sight of the whole Indian encampment filing up the Horse Creek trail on their best paint ponies, everyone dressed in his most colorful finery.

White buckskin fringed and beaded shirts, leggings, beaded moccasins and gauntlets, porcupine-quilled and beaded vests, and feather head dresses. The women were in elk tooth-studded shawls and fez-shaped woven hats.

"Holy smoke," thought Mickel, it looks like they're dressed up for a wedding. And he soon found out that's just what they were dressed up for his wedding. Mickel was then only fourteen and he wasn't about to get married, especially not to an Indian Girl, desirable though she was. In those bad old days, Indians were considered something less than human. If you married one, you were a "squaw man. "So Mickel panicked and went running to his paw, Billy, and told him his sorry tale. W.K., with considerable compassion showing on his face, "Wal, Ah'll do mah best, boy. Uncle Billy turned and went resolutely out to meet the Chief and convey the bad news that there would not be a wedding.

There was much indignation and resentment on the part of the Chief at this affront. There were furious gestures and angry chatter from the women. Many of the young braves fingered their knives with dangerous glints in their eyes.

W.K. had to use all the persuasion he could muster to mollify the Chief and his people, explaining the white-eyes boys just don't get married that young. It took an hour or so of parleying and gifts of plenty of watermelon and fruit to get Nickel .out of his predicament. And he didn't tell the story to his sons until some fifty years later.

And what about little Redwing? How did she feel about being a pawn in this game? Could she have been in love with Mickel? Dad didn't tell me. I wish I had asked more questions when I could have.

Music often echoed from the walls around Deep Canyon Ranch. Billy's wife Josephine filled the canyon with her beautiful voice during the few short years she lived there. After the long hours of work, the yellow lights of the ranch house were reassuring in the deep, dark canyon. Over the roaring river, the canyon walls would echo the music as the visitors shared the evening.

COUNTRY MUSIC

And the Library of Congress

All the Stubs of that family were folk singers and inveterate raconteurs. They knew literally hundreds of songs. Traveling miners, cowboys, sheep men and peddlers coming through would stay for a while at the ranch and exchange songs with the boys. One of the boys would say, "Write that one down fer me." After the long hours of work, the .canyon ranch house was often jumping at night with the ring of banjos, guitars, fiddles, accordions, or whatever instruments the travelers happened to be carrying, and the happy singing voices.

Many of these songs sung at the Horse Creek ranch were later recorded for the Archives of American Folk Song of the Library of Congress, by Blaine Stubblefield, Mickel s oldest son, while he was the Washington, D.C. Editor of Aviation magazine, a publication of McGraw-Hill. Blaine prevailed upon his father, Mickel to sit for many days at his old Corona portable typewriter and peck out hundreds of the old songs.

Three of these songs by Mickel are reproduced in the book, Our Singing Country, the .second volume of American Ballads and Folk Songs by John A. Lomax, Honorary Consultant and Curator of the Archives of

American Folk Song of the Library of Congress, and Allan Lomax, Assistant in charge of the Archive of American Folk Song of the Library of Congress, with Ruth Crawford Seeger, music editor.

The Stubblefield family proudly possesses one of those books given by Blaine as a birthday gift to his father, Mickel, on April 28, 1942. On the fly leaf of this book is a tribute to Mickel, from Mr. Allan Lomax in his own handwriting which says:

"Greetings to Mickel Stubblefield, one of the singing pioneers, who has helped to preserve the songs of this country and those brought from other countries. Your contributions have come to the Library of Congress through your son, Blaine Stubblefield, three of whose pieces are included in this book."

Actually, it was five songs from the Stubblefield's published in the book, Mr. Lomax meant three were Mickel's. The other two were Newell's. The three songs in the book sung by Mickel were: "Brennan on the Moor," an Irish ballad; "Way Out in Idaho," a work song sung to the same tune as "The State of Arkansas; and "Hard Times in the Country," a work song. Two other songs in the book, Blaine had learned from Mickel's younger brother Newell: The Low Down Low," a sea chanty and "If He'd be a Buckaroo," a cowboy ballad.

Thus, the music from Horse Creek ranch put the songs of the Wallowa County pioneers representing Western Americana into the Library of Congress, as well as being published in the book, Our Singing Country, for as long as our country shall exist.

There are five songs altogether in the Lomax book, including the bawdy ones, and many more recorded by Blaine in the audio archives of the Library of Congress.

Special Note: My grandmother, Lilie Smead Collett's, half- sister Elsie Bond married an outlaw name Albert Joshua Poole. The following information was provided by a distant cousin, Jean Gay Watkins (Scenski) Thomas.

APPENDIX III

ALBERT JOSHUA POOLE (1863-1955) Member of the "Poole Gang"-Train Robbers

Born: October 10, 1863 (Santa Cruz, Santa Cruz County, CA)

Married: August 31, 1908 (Elsi Myrtle Smead aka Bond)

Died: May 12, 1955 (St. Marie's, Idaho, buried in Masonic Cemetery, Canyonville, OR

Parents: Napoleon Bonaparte Poole and Sarah Cardwell

Children: Edward Poole (1909-);   Sarah Delora Poole Devault (Whitebird, ID June 28, 1910-1994); Desda Rowena Poole (Cottonwood, ID, November 8, 1911-2002); Alies Bond Poole (Salmon River near Cottonwood, ID, March 5, 1914-1968); Vernon Napoleon Poole;

(Cedarville, CA August 15,1917-1987); Albert Joshway Poole (Fallon, Nevada September 16, 1922-1971); John Joshua Poole (Cul-de-sac, Idaho April 24, 1926-1963); Ruth Moretta Poole (1930); Ermydean Mamey Poole (August 6, 1934 - died age one year, 11 months, 19 days); William Bernard Poole (St. Maries, ID September 19, 1934-1972)

Siblings: William Bosier Poole (December 2, 1859-1945); James Washington Westin Boole (December 22. 1861-April 21, 1949; Julius Lincoln Chalkline Poole (April 8, 1862-April 21, 1949)

Elsie Bond (daughter of Della Greenough and sister to Lillie Smead) on August 31, 1908 married an outlaw, Albert Poole. She was 17 and Albert was 45 (28-year difference). Family stories portrayed Al Poole as an "evil" man, an outlaw on the run from the law. Certainly, given the diverse birth locations of their children they seldom settled in one place for long. Many of these locations were near Elsie's mother's homestead in Whitebird, ID or her home in Cul-de-sac, Idaho where my mother Mary Collett Hadley was born in 1922.

JeanGay Thomas, a granddaughter of Albert Poole forwarded me copies of the following articles which appear to relate to a period when Albert Poole and his brothers were in their 20's:

Some relate to John Case who is sometimes referred to as a "cousin" although perhaps just a close friend met by one of the Poole's while in prison.

Outlawing may have been in their family, as a Poole was part of Jesse James' gang following the Civil War. As former military units for the South during the Civil War, they had access to and knew how to use weapons, had a sense of organization and were unhappy with their treatment after the war. It could be these sensibilities were instilled in Albert at an early age influenced by family members.

The following article may be of interest.

A TRAIN ROBBERY IN JOHN CASE'S HISTORY

By R. MICHAEL WILSON 10/1/2018

John Case was 22 years old when he arrived at the Oregon State Penitentiary on February 2, 1886. He had been sentenced in Clatsop County to serve five years on a charge of "larceny in a store." Case was released on January 9,

1889, after serving three years, but within a year he was back behind prison walls, this time from Multnomah County serving seven years for "assault with a dangerous weapon." He tried to hold up a mining camp single-handed but was arrested when a Chinese miner creased his skull with a hatchet.

James W. Poole arrived at the penitentiary from Douglas County, Ore., on June 20, 1890. He was sentenced to serve three years for manslaughter but won a new trial. Although Poole was acquitted of manslaughter this time around, he was found guilty of "obtaining money under false pretenses" and sentenced to serve another year. Case and Poole met before the latter prisoner was released on July 19, 1892. When Case was released two years later, the two men rendezvoused in Douglas County and spent the next year planning to rob a train. A third man also became involved.

Cow Creek Canyon was a lonely place in 1895, 30 miles south of Roseburg and eight miles south of Riddle in Oregon's Douglas County. The mountain passes in the canyon were of such a peculiar formation, with many sharp curves, that trains had to travel at a very slow rate of speed in the dry season and even slower in the wet season. On Monday evening, July 1, 1895, there was a bright moon, but the remote canyon was pitch-black. At 10:15 p.m. Southern Pacific's northbound train No. 15, the Oregon Express, heading for Portland, entered the canyon. The only light came from the engine's powerful headlamp. Fireman Everett L. Gray was stoking the engine, and a stowaway hobo was helping him. Suddenly, an explosion rocked the train. Thinking it was a warning torpedo, engineer J.B. Waite applied the brakes. As the train sat idling, three masked men quickly approached it. Case collected, at gunpoint, the engineer, fireman and hobo and kept them still. Meanwhile, his two companions patrolled the sides of the cars, occasionally shooting into the air or exploding a stick of giant powder.

Case took his three hostages to the express car and demanded that expressman Ralph M. Donohue open the doors. Donohue did so, but he was one step ahead of the robber; he had already removed the treasure from the local express box and hidden it under some goods. All the hostages climbed aboard with Case, who told them to keep their hands up while Donohue opened the local box. When the robber saw nothing inside worth taking, he ordered the express man to open the through safe. Donahue said he did not have the combination and, when threatened, added: "Well, you are simply wasting time. I can't and won't open it. The combination is not given to me, just because of such occurrences as this...." Case replied, "You're hot stuff ain't you!" but he didn't press the issue.

Case took his four hostages to the mail car, which mail clerk C.A. Hermann opened after the robber threatened to use explosives. Once inside, Cass demanded the registered mail. Hermann produced only three registered pouches, which seemed to be the entire lot. Case then asked for the local packages, and Hermann replied: "It's Sunday, you know, and I haven't many. They are scattered in those pouches." Case went through the pouches and took out only five packages, leaving unmolested 45 other pouches that were well hidden.

Next, Case took his hostages to the first passenger car. Donohue walked ahead with a lantern, followed by the hobo carrying an empty sack. The party went through the coaches from front to back. Once the party stepped onto the rear platform of the last car, Case ordered the trainmen to the front of the train. With sack in hand, Case followed them, but then kept walking until he came upon his two partners. The three holdup men then hurried into the brush and disappeared into the darkness. Their take was calculated at about $1,000 from the mails and $520.70 from the passengers.

The Southern Pacific Railroad offered a reward of $2,000 for the arrest and conviction of each robber. In response, several posses took the field, while Sheriff C.F. Cathcart and Riddle's constable, George Quine, rushed to the scene of the robbery. Quine, an amateur detective, began documenting evidence. At a camp near the tracks he found distinctive boot prints, one with two rows of tacks in the heels. The foot tracks led to where the robbers mounted, and the posse then followed the horse tracks to a more permanent camp. There they found the masks, which had been made from sugar sacks, and a rag from a flour sack used to bind a wound. They determined that the robbers had used giant powder sticks that were common to miners.

On July 2 Stilly Riddle rode into Roseburg and reported that three men, working at Nichols' Station 13 miles south of Riddle, matched the description of the robbers. He said that two of them were Jim Poole and John Case, and it happened that the lawmen were familiar with those two desperados. With suspects named, the posse went to search the home of Napoleon Poole, father of Jim and his brother Albert [note James was Albert's older brother by two years]. Napoleon let the lawmen search the place, and they found sacks and strings that matched what had been found at the robbers' camp. They also discovered both Jim's and Albert's boots, each with heel prints that matched the peculiar double tack design. Case himself was arrested later that day and identified as the man who had gone through the coaches, as his mask of light cloth had revealed his features. The Poole brothers were also soon apprehended.

After a preliminary hearing, the three men were taken to Portland, where a five-day trial began in mid-December. On Christmas Eve, after one hour's deliberation, the jury returned a verdict of guilty against Jim Poole and John Case but found Albert Poole not guilty. Everyone on the defense side was astonished by the verdict against Jim Poole, as the evidence against him had been weak. The judge declared, "I am frank to say that I am not entirely satisfied with the verdict." The prisoners were returned to jail while the defense attorneys filed a motion for a new trial, and after months of thoughtful contemplation, the judge set aside the verdicts and ordered the prisoners released without bond, setting the new trial date for June 28, 1897.

Upon his release, Case made his way up the coast, stopping at several cities until he reached Tacoma, Wash. On May 23, 1897, Steilacoom, Wash., streetcar superintendent Frank Dame caught Case trying to rob a streetcar and shot him dead. Three men who knew Case positively identified his corpse. The deceased robber's Colt revolver, serial number 13,908, was the same one Case had on him when arrested back in 1895. (The gun had been returned to him upon his release from jail.) For further confirmation, the dead man's photo was sent to Roseburg, and indeed the Case was closed.

The evidence against Jim Poole was no stronger than it had been at his first trial, and Case clearly had been the leader of the Cow Creek Canyon train robbery. Once Case was dead, law officials decided to dismiss the indictment against Jim Poole.

Originally published in the August 2007 issue of Wild West.

Sacramento Daily Union, Volume 89, Number 116, 6 July 1895

OREGON TRAIN ROBBERS.

Three Men Under Arrest Suspected of Comitting the Deed.

OFFICERS CONFIDENT THEY HAVE THE RIGHT PARTIES.

James Poole, Albert Poole and John Case the Names of the Men in Custody, All of Whom Have Unsavory Records— Report That a Large Portion of the Robber's Plunder Has Been Found at Poole's House.

Canyonville Or., July 5. Yesterday afternoon, George Quino and one of the Pinkerton detectives arrested John Case on a charge of robbing the train at the mouth of Cow Creek Canyon on the night of July 1st. He was arrested about nine miles east of Canyonville and did not offer any resistance. He was taken to Riddle's Station. It appears that Albert Poole came to town and gave himself up to Deputy Sheriff Shambrook of this (Douglas) county. He did not surrender as a train robber, but in answer to an indictment against him for cattle stealing. This morning George Quine arrested James Poole nearly opposite the Pacific Postal Telegraph office. Quine called on him to stop. Poole answered that he did not have to, whereupon Quine pulled his gun on him and again called on him to stop or he would put a hole through him. At this juncture, Vernon Poole came up and said they were innocent and that they could prove it. There is some damaging evidence in the case that makes it pretty certain that they have the right men. Quine and the Pinkerton men worked like beavers on this case, and followed up the robbers from the scene of the robbery to, or near, the place of their domicile.

Case claims to be related to the Pooles and has a bad reputation. James Poole is a desperate character and has been in the penitentiary several times. He was convicted of cattle-stealing in Idaho and he murdered a man at Elk Creek, Douglas County, but could not be prosecuted owing to the death of witnesses. There was a warrant in the Sheriff's hands for Poole's arrest for cattle-stealing. It is believed that if Poole and Case are not directly concerned in the robbery, they can furnish information to the officers that will lead to a clue to the whereabouts of the culprits. They are in jail.

Mike Deane, a farmer living two miles east of the scene of the robbery, identifies the robbers as passing his house on the night of the hold-up. It is said Deane went where their horses were, and pointed out the very horse one of them rode and the saddle. George Quine exhibited a part of a seamless sack which had been found on the train, and which was torn in a zigzag manner that left an angular notch in a section of the sack. Quine secured from the person of Case a piece torn from a seamless grain bag. Now this section of the sack also had a notch in it that exactly fits the section of sack found at the holdup. Quine found where they tied their horses in the brush, and by examining the passages from the horses found whole grains of corn. This was a good clue for Quine and the Pinkertons, and for eighteen miles east of the robbery, they scrutinized the passages in the road closely. When very near the robbers' home they found the corn in the refuse again.

John Case, one of the robbers, is known to have bought a suit of clothes from Carl Munter of Canyonville after the robbery, while on the road home. At 3 o'clock this afternoon Quine and the two Pinkertons and Mr. Hodgson passed through Canyonville going to Poole's home, rumor has it, to arrest old man Poole. The quartet were well armed, and are nervy lellows, and some shooting may be expected if any show of resistance is offered by the Pooles. It will be remembered that there are four other Poole boys besides the ones under arrest.

It is reported this evening that a large wad of the boodle was found in Poole's house, in an old pair of overalls.

THE TWO SUSPECTS. Riddle (Or). July 5th. —Deputy Sheriff George K. Quine, who has been in pursuit of the looters of the Oregon express in Cow Creek Canyon, has arrived here and has in custody James Poole and John McDowell, on suspicion of being the men who held up the train. McDowell gave the name of Case, who was convicted two years ago for burglary, and has been away from the penitentiary for a few months. Poole, his companion, is a tough character. He was tried for the murder of William McNeil of Elk Creek and convicted of manslaughter. He served time until the Supreme Court reversed the decision, and in the new trial the important witnesses were dead and missing. Three members of the Poole family are under indictment for stealing cattle, and a brother of Poole's is in jail awaiting trial. Poole and Case were caught in the mountains about ten miles from Canyonville. They were surprised by the appearance of the Sheriff, but made no resistance. McDowell was easily recognized and admitted that his real name was Case. The detectives on the case, who have had a good look at McDowell, believe the passengers' descriptions tally with his.

Kent Jone's Notes

"Poole, his companion, is a tough character. He was tried for the murder of William McNeil of Elk Creek and convicted of manslaughter. He served time until the Supreme Court reversed the decision, and in the new trial the important witnesses were dead and missing."

Per Kent Jones, as told to him by Arlene Cox Poole, these men were also accused of killing the witnesses. Kent states they didn't, but that their Father, Napoleon Bonaparte Poole, was the one who killed them.

From Kent: (3rd Cousin)

My conversation a couple of years ago with my Aunt Arlene (Arlene Poole Cox), who spent 50 years working on the Poole genealogy, was something like this. I said "I imagine it was the brothers that got rid of the witnesses" and she said, "Oh no, that would have been the old man."

Kent Jones is the grandson of Vernon Napoleon Pode (Albert Poole's brother). Kent grew up around the Poole's in Days Creek Oregon.

James & Albert Poole & John Case

July 13, 1985 Train Robbery July 13, 1895

(Great Uncle and Great Grandfather)

Per Kent Jones: Did I tell you there were at least 4 train robberies? 2 up Cow Creek, one in "Shady" near Roseburg and another near Cottage Grove.

The Poole's lived on the "Woodrat" in Drew, Oregon, the mountain ranch that locals recognize today as Brad Thompson's old home. They robbed the train on Upper Cow Creek, later in Shady, and in Cottage Grove. They were the chief suspects in one near Klamath Falls. My grandfather Walt Poole told me over 50 years ago that Jim, Jule, Albert, and Vernon Poole had assisted Harry Tracy in his prison break from OSP.

When James Poole was arrested for murdering a man near Elk Creek (Drew), the article in the Sacramento paper says he had to be released due to the "deaths and disappearances" of the witnesses. When I read this, I called my Aunt Arlene Poole Cox and asked her if she thought the brothers were responsible. She said, "No, most likely the old man (Napoleon).

'Peck' was Delbert, Walter's brother. My grandmother Alice married Walt Poole, had my mother, divorced him a couple of years later, then married Delbert (Peck) Poole, about 5 years later.

True Detective magazine said Sheriff Moore had snuck up to the Poole's barn after the Cow Creek robbery, saw lathered horses, still breathing heavy. He then crawled to the side of the barn and was looking down at the house when Albert Poole (Jean Gay Thomas ' great-grandfather) shot him through the cheeks of his ass, then took him into Canyonville in the early hours of the morning and left him hogtied and naked on the main Street. Moore is a common name.

From Kent's Friend: I have wondered why there has never been a movie about Harry Tracy.

Kent: Richard Chasm especially about the jail break, he shot and killed 3 guards on the way out, then followed a six-month manhunt.

James Poole had been in OSP with Tracy on at least 2 occasions, and in an article about the prison break, the warden is quoted as saying "that someone with intimate knowledge of the penitentiary had smuggled guns into Tracy.

I'd gone to the Tri-City drive-in to see Butch Cassidy and the Sundance Kid, and I was telling my grandfather about it. He told me that the Poole Brothers had helped Tracy break out and that his father, Vernon Poole, had hidden Tracy in a wagon and taken him to Portland. James, Jule, and Albert Poole were all living in the Spokane area at the time and that's where Tracy finally got cornered and killed himself. I think (just speculating) he may have been there hiding out with the Poole's.

David Terry that's a mountain of info about the prison break on the net. Authorities never, to my knowledge anyway, knew who assisted Tracy. Read the article in the Sacramento newspaper about sending the Pinkertons to Oregon to arrest the Poole brothers. They talk about James having done numerous stretches there.

David Terry, there have been a couple of books about the Poole's, and True Detective did a story on the Cow Creek robbery when the Poole's greased down the tracks and spun out the train.

Case claimed to be a cousin of the Poole's. But I have never been able to confirm that, and I think it's more likely that he and James Poole met in prison.

There is an article, or used to be, in the Douglas County Museum with a front-page headline that reads "Outlaw Gang Rides Through Canyonville". The first line states, "The notorious Poole Brothers and the half-breed renegade Rondeau rode brazenly through town. Isn't Robert related to the Rondeaus?

Junction City Times Sat. July 13, 1895 (Oregon)

The examination of John Case alias McDowell for the robbery of the overland at Riddle recently took place this week. He was identified by brakeman Norman and T.P. Arrousay, a passenger, as the principal robber. The latter was very positive as to the identity, as he saw the face several times when the mask blew aside. M. Dean identifies Case as the man who passed his place on Monday, going toward the scene of the robbery. The case was bound over in the sum of $10,000. The examination of John Case, James Poole, and Albert Poole for robbing the United States Mail on July 1 was held on Wednesday before United States Commissioner Judge Loughary. The prosecution was represented by United States District Attorney Daniel R. Murphey of Portland, and the defense by W. W. Cardwell of Roseburg. Cardwell stated that himself and United States District Attorney Murphey had agreed to waive examination in the charges against John Case and James Poole and asked that the charge of complicity against Albert Poole dismissed, which was done. Their bonds were fixed at $5,000.

IN SELF DEFENSE

Julius Poole Shoots John Herron, a Half-Breed.

Kettle Falls, April 10.—At about 11:30 o'clock last evening John Herron, a thrifty half-breed Indian, was shot and killed by Julius Poole who was tending bar for E. J. Catlett.

Herron had been drinking very heavily all the afternoon and toward evening he bought a revolver and proceeded to intimidate everyone he met by flourishing it in their faces. He visited all the saloons and flourished the gun promiscuously returning several times to the Catlett saloon here he abused friends and strangers alike, demanding liquor at the point of a gun which was given him, in fact he was given the freedom of the house by demand with demonstrations to enforce it.

When the shooting occurred he had turned his attention to Mr. Poole and told him to drink a certain glass of beer which had been turned out for him (Herron). Poole refused when Herron drew his gun and with it cocked and held in both hands stuck the muzzle into Poole's face. By this time Poole had moved along the bar to where Mr. Catlett's gun lay, all the while protesting against Herron's recklessness and cautioning him to stop and go to bed, seizing the gun and with the muzzle of the other gun under his nose he fired point blank at Herron, the first shot penetrating the flesh by the side of and ranging along the temple and out the back of the head. The second shot struck his right arm and passed right out, while the third entered the body under the right arm below the point of the shoulder, passing through the liver and into or near the heart, causing death in a few minutes. Four shots were fired, three taking effect. The weapon was a 38 Smith & Wesson.

Mr. Poole immediately went to Dr. Parker's house and brought him over but the man was dead.

Prosecuting Attorney Kirkpatrick and Coroner Ballard were summoned and came at once.

The following were summoned as jurors: Geo. Kent, E. I. Shackleton, Thos. Anglin, I. W. Swan, Thos. Brant and Louis Brant. Attorney Crozier took charge of Mr. Poole's case and after about ten witnesses were heard the matter was left with the jury who brought in a verdict of justifiable homicide.

Herron's friends have been notified and will take charge of the remains at once.

**Statesman-Index
April 13, 1900**

More from Kent Jones

Google "James Poole, train robber" and read about the exploits of my great-grandfather and his brothers. They lived on the "Woodrat" in Drew, Oregon, the mountain ranch that locals recognize today as Brad Thompson's old home. They robbed the train on Upper Cow Creek, later in Shady, and in Cottage Grove. They were the chief suspects in one near Klamath Falls. My grandfather Walt Poole told me over 50 years ago that Jim, Jule, Albert, and Vernon Poole had assisted Harry Tracy in his prison break from OSP.

When James Poole was arrested for murdering a man near Elk Creek (Drew), the article in the Sacramento paper says he had to be released due to the "deaths and disappearances" of the witnesses. When I read this, I called my Aunt Arlene Poole Cox and asked her if she thought the brothers were responsible. She said, "No, most likely the old man (Napoleon).

PARTING COMMENTS

Although each family was from a line having a family crest and remnants of lineage to royalty, each in their own way was unsettled with their life in the British Isles, so much so that in some cases they indentured themselves, trading years of hard work for payment for their passage. What drove these people . . . poverty, religious beliefs, a chance to better their place in life, wanderlust, adventure, perhaps a mix of all.

I found much pain, loved ones buried at sea on the trip to America, probable death during childbirth, unrest with the native Americans and the French resulting in death, others whose religions were different, almost constant movement from one place to another, seeking better agricultural land for the most part-hoping to find it over the next hill, homesteading, always further west. Traveling in groups by wagon train, or prairie schooners as they were called, not strangers but friends and family members sharing a common dream and together for comfort and protection. There was a constant search for new places and new opportunities. Time and time again our ancestors set their hands to clearing land and turning over soil, along the way creating new towns on the edge of the wilderness.

One thing that is clear is that the American dream had a strong hold on them. They cherished hope, freedom and opportunity. Along the way they populated America from its very beginnings, families with a dozen children time and again. One thing they found was freedom, freedom over their own lives and the ability to make their own choices. A strong sense of grit and determination of necessity ruled their lives, of will fraught with struggles, walking, walking, walking 100s of miles following their own stars in the sky and with faith, faith in God, and faith in their own abilities and faith that their next move would land them in a better place.

A thought or two about this effort. These pages were written during the COVID pandemic during the winter of 2020-2021, with a second edition update in 2026. It is humbling to take on a task of this magnitude as the "facts" are elusive and sources unreliable, and energy and focus are limited. In reality, there is no beginning or end in such an effort, and no "proper" way to go about it. My perspective regardless of the many errors that no doubt exist, was to provide a taste of our family's place in the history of this country. There, **SAMUEL HEADLEY**, is much more that can be done, and this effort may open the doors for those sharing this interest to take it to another level.

ABOUT THE AUTHOR

This effort was prepared by James ("Jay") E. Hadley with technical support from his wife Beth A. Taylor. Jay is the son of Howard and Mary Hadley born in 1946 in Ellensburg, WA and raised primarily in Auburn, WA.

Jay received an Economics Degree from the University of Washington in 1968 and a Juris Doctorate Degree from the University of Virginia in 1974. In 1968 he was drafted, attended Officer Candidate School at Fort Belvoir, Virginia serving in Viet Nam as a First Lieutenant where he received a Bronze Star Medal.

He has always loved being a father to his children Bryson and Madelyn, and a grandfather to Julia and Thomas.

In addition to practicing law for more than 40 years with two prominent firms in Seattle, Washington, he has followed his passion for antiquities, travel, restoring and racing vintage sports cars and architecture.

Jay and his wife Beth are enjoying retirement spending a substantial part of their time in Italy (in the Val d' Orica UNESCO Heritage area), where they restored a 9th century village house and then a 13th century mill. Ever busy they are learning Italian, working in their olive grove and slowly developing their small valley into a private park.